Web Developm with Blazor

with Blazor

A hands-on guide for .NET developers to build
interactive UIs with C#

Jimmy Engström

BIRMINGHAM—MUMBAI

Web Development with Blazor

Copyright © 2021 Packt Publishing

Group Product Manager: Ashwin Nair
Publishing Product Manager: Ashwin Nair
Senior Editor: Hayden Edwards
Content Development Editor: Abhishek Jadhav
Technical Editor: Saurabh Kadave
Copy Editor: Safis Editing
Language Support Editor: Safis Editing
Project Coordinator: Manthan Patel
Proofreader: Safis Editing
Indexer: Rekha Nair
Production Designer: Roshan Kawale

First published: June 2021

Production reference: 1180621

Published by Packt Publishing Ltd.
Livery Place
35 Livery Street
Birmingham
B3 2PB, UK.

ISBN 978-1-80020-872-8

www.packt.com

I dedicate this book to my mom and dad, who got me my first computer, which got me started with programming.

To my brother, who took the time to teach me how to code, and to my sister, who helped me with my English homework growing up.

This would never have been possible without you all!

I would also like to dedicate the book to my wife, Jessica, who has helped me along the way by both reviewing the book and picking up my slack.

Love you!

A huge thanks to the reviewers, who have done a tremendous job reviewing the book.

– Jimmy Engström

Foreword

It's been about 6 years since I first met Jimmy at an event in Stockholm, where I quickly noticed his passion for technology, user experience, and pop culture. We spent the better part of an hour debating Marvel versus DC comic characters and storylines, and I knew this was a person who studied for both his craft and his hobbies. His presentations regarding Blazor, HoloLens, and delivering better applications for our users are always cutting edge and always lead the audience to the best practices for each technology.

The author has been a Microsoft MVP and community leader for almost a decade. The Swedish developer community has grown under his leadership and benefitted from his insights to build better applications and services. The Blazm components library that he wrote and made available is a prime example of helping other developers in his local community and across the world.

This book has been written for the practical Blazor developer. Clear definitions of why you need to consider each feature of the framework are followed by examples and clear solutions that will make you immediately successful. You'll learn by following along with the very relatable example project of a blog engine. From user interface topics through API design and security considerations, the blog engine you will build with Blazor and ASP.NET Core in this book will run in production and can easily serve your blog. The final chapter of this book is an awesome reference for new and seasoned developers, with answers to the typical problems that will surface during the lifetime of your application, and it should be kept as a desktop reference for years to come.

Jeff Fritz

Principal Program Manager at Microsoft and Leader in Live Video Technical Community Engagement

Contributors

About the author

Jimmy Engström has been developing ever since he was 7 years old and got his first computer. He loves to be on the cutting edge of technology, trying new things. When he got wind of Blazor, he immediately realized the potential and adopted it already when it was in beta. He has been running Blazor in production since it was launched by Microsoft.

His passion for the .NET industry and community has taken him around the world, speaking about development. Microsoft has recognized this passion by awarding him the Microsoft Most Valuable Professional award 8 years in a row.

About the reviewers

Jessica Engström is a CEO, teacher, and international speaker who has traveled the world sharing knowledge about her passions.

She is a Microsoft MVP and has been part of the developer community for many years. She organizes conferences, events, and hackathons, and runs multiple user groups. Adapting technology to humans is something that she thinks is important and that is why UX and presentation skills are her main focus.

Jessica is the co-host of Coding After Work, a podcast and a stream on Twitch.

Bozhi Qian has been a developer and architect for more than 20 years, focusing on .NET application development, security, and hosting across a variety of Microsoft platforms, including ASP.NET and Azure.

He is passionate about cloud technologies and holds some Microsoft certifications, including MCSD and Azure Architecture Specialist.

He lives in Melbourne, Australia, with his wife and children.

Jürgen Gutsch is a .NET-addicted web developer. He has worked with .NET and ASP.NET since the early versions in 2002. Before that, he wrote server-side web applications using classic ASP. He is also an active part of the .NET developer community. Jürgen writes for the dotnetpro magazine, one of the most popular German-speaking developer magazines. He also publishes articles in English on his blog *ASP.NET Hacker* and contributes to several open source projects. Jürgen has been a Microsoft MVP since 2015.

The best way to contact him is using Twitter.

He works as a developer, consultant, and trainer for the digital agency YOO Inc., located in Basel, Switzerland. YOO Inc. serves national as well as international clients and specializes in creating custom digital solutions for distinct business needs.

Table of Contents

Section 2: Building an Application with Blazor

3

Introducing Entity Framework Core

4

Understanding Basic Blazor Components

5

Creating Advanced Blazor Components

6

Building Forms with Validation

7

Creating an API

8

Authentication and Authorization

Section 3: Debug, Test, and Deploy

12
Debugging

13
Testing

14
Deploy to Production

15

Where to Go from Here

Preface

Until now, creating interactive web pages meant using JavaScript. But with Blazor, Microsoft's new way to create .NET web applications, developers can easily build interactive and rich web applications using C#. This book will guide you through the most commonly encountered scenarios when starting your journey with Blazor.

Firstly, you'll discover how to leverage the power of Blazor and learn what you can do with both the server side and WebAssembly. By showing you how all the elements work together practically, the book will help you solve some of the common roadblocks that developers face. As you advance, you'll learn how to create server-side Blazor and Blazor WebAssembly projects, how Razor syntax works, and how to validate forms and create your own components. The book then introduces you to the key concepts involved in web development with Blazor, which you will be able to put into practice straight away.

By the end of this Blazor book, you'll have gained the confidence to create and deploy production-ready Blazor applications.

Who this book is for

The book is for web developers and software developers who want to explore Blazor to learn how to build dynamic web UIs. This book assumes familiarity with C# programming and web development concepts.

What this book covers

Chapter 1, Hello Blazor, will teach you about the difference between server-side and client-side Blazor. You will get an overview of how the technology works and a brief history of where Blazor comes from. Knowing the structure and differences between the hosting models is essential for understanding the technology.

Chapter 2, Creating Your First Blazor App, helps you understand how to install and set up your development environment. You will create your first Blazor app (both server-side and client-side) and learn about the structure of the project template.

Chapter 3, Introducing Entity Framework Core, teaches you how to create your database where you will store your data (blog posts, categories, and tags). You will be using the dotnet tool to create a new project to get a feel for the tool.

Chapter 4, Understanding Basic Blazor Components, digs deeper into components, life cycle events, adding parameters, and sharing parameters between components. You will also create reusable components in this chapter.

Chapter 5, Creating Advanced Blazor Components, digs even deeper into components, adding functionality such as child components, cascading parameters, and values, and covering how to use actions and callbacks.

Chapter 6, Building Forms with Validation, takes a look at forms, how to validate forms, and how to build your own validation mechanism. This chapter will cover the most common use cases when it comes to handling forms, such as file upload, text, numbers, and triggering code when checking a checkbox.

Chapter 7, Creating an API, looks at creating an API. When using Blazor WebAssembly, we need an API to get data.

Chapter 8, Authentication and Authorization, looks at adding authentication and authorization to Blazor and making sure navigation such as redirecting to a login page works as expected.

Chapter 9, Sharing Code and Resources, teaches you how it is possible to share code between client-side and server-side Blazor projects by adding all the things you need into a shared library. In this chapter, you will build a shared library that can be packaged as a NuGet package and shared with others.

Chapter 10, JavaScript Interop, explores how you can leverage JavaScript libraries when using Blazor and make calls from C# to JavaScript. You will also take a look at how JavaScript is able to call C# functions in our Blazor app.

Chapter 11, Managing State, looks into the different ways of managing state (persisting data), such as using LocalStorage or just keeping data in memory by using dependency injection. You will not only cover persisting data in a database, but you will also cover how dependency injection works on the different project types.

Chapter 12, Debugging, teaches you how to debug your applications and add extended logging to figure out what's wrong in your application. You will not only look at traditional debugging but also at debugging C# code directly from within the web browser.

Chapter 13, Testing, looks at automated testing so that you can make sure your components work as they should (and continue to do so). There is no built-in method to test Blazor applications but there is a really good community project called bUnit.

Chapter 14, Deploying to Production, will take you through the different things you need to think about when it comes to running Blazor in production.

Chapter 15, Where to Go from Here, is a short chapter with a call to action, some resources you can use, and a finale.

To get the most out of this book

I recommend that you read the first few chapters to make sure that you are up to speed with the basic concepts of Blazor in general. The project we are creating is adapted for real-world use but some parts are left out, such as proper error handing. You should, however, get a good grasp of the building blocks of Blazor.

The book focuses on using Visual Studio 2019; that said, though, feel free to use whatever version you are comfortable with that supports Blazor.

Software/hardware covered in the book	OS requirements
Visual Studio 2019 ,Visual Studio for Mac, or Visual Studio Code	Windows 10 or later, macOS, or Linux

If you are using the digital version of this book, we advise you to type the code yourself or access the code via the GitHub repository (link available in the next section). Doing so will help you avoid any potential errors related to the copying and pasting of code.

I would love for you to share your progress while reading this book or in Blazor development in general. Tweet me `@EngstromJimmy`.

I hope you have as much fun reading this book as I had writing it.

Download the example code files

You can download the example code files for this book from GitHub at `https://github.com/PacktPublishing/Web-Development-with-Blazor`. In case there's an update to the code, it will be updated on the existing GitHub repository.

We also have other code bundles from our rich catalog of books and videos available at `https://github.com/PacktPublishing/`. Check them out!

Download the color images

We also provide a PDF file that has color images of the screenshots/diagrams used in this book. You can download it here: `https://static.packt-cdn.com/downloads/9781800208728_ColorImages.pdf`.

Conventions used

There are a number of text conventions used throughout this book.

`Code in text`: Indicates code words in text, database table names, folder names, filenames, file extensions, pathnames, dummy URLs, user input, and Twitter handles. Here is an example: "In this case, when the page gets downloaded, it will trigger a download of the `blazor.webassembly.js` file."

A block of code is set as follows:

```
public void ConfigureServices(IServiceCollection services)
{
    services.AddRazorPages();
    services.AddServerSideBlazor();
    services.AddSingleton<WeatherForecastService>();
}
```

When we wish to draw your attention to a particular part of a code block, the relevant lines or items are set in bold:

```
<div class="top-row pl-4 navbar navbar-dark">
    <a class="navbar-brand" href="">MyBlogServerSide</a>
    <button class="navbar-toggler"
        @onclick="ToggleNavMenu">
```

Any command-line input or output is written as follows:

```
dotnet new blazorserver -o BlazorServerSideApp
cd MyBlog.Data
```

Bold: Indicates a new term, an important word, or words that you see onscreen. For example, words in menus or dialog boxes appear in the text like this. Here is an example: "Select **System info** from the **Administration** panel."

> **Tips or important notes**
> Appear like this.

Get in touch

Feedback from our readers is always welcome.

General feedback: If you have questions about any aspect of this book, mention the book title in the subject of your message and email us at customercare@packtpub.com.

Errata: Although we have taken every care to ensure the accuracy of our content, mistakes do happen. If you have found a mistake in this book, we would be grateful if you would report this to us. Please visit www.packtpub.com/support/errata, selecting your book, clicking on the Errata Submission Form link, and entering the details.

Piracy: If you come across any illegal copies of our works in any form on the Internet, we would be grateful if you would provide us with the location address or website name. Please contact us at copyright@packt.com with a link to the material.

If you are interested in becoming an author: If there is a topic that you have expertise in and you are interested in either writing or contributing to a book, please visit authors.packtpub.com.

Share Your Thoughts

Once you've read *Web Development with Blazor*, we'd love to hear your thoughts! Scan the QR code below to go straight to the Amazon review page for this book and share your feedback.

https://www.amazon.in/review/create-review/
error?asin=1-800-20872-3&

Your review is important to us and the tech community and will help us make sure we're delivering excellent quality content.

Section 1: The Basics

The goal of this section is for you to understand the project structure, learn the differences between different hosting models, and get a brief history of where Blazor comes from. Also, you will learn how to set up your development environment and create your first app.

This section includes the following chapters:

- *Chapter 1, Hello, Blazor*
- *Chapter 2, Creating Your First Blazor App*

1
Hello Blazor

Thank you for picking up your copy of *Web Development with Blazor*. This book intends to get you started as quickly and pain-free as possible, chapter by chapter, without you having to read this book from cover to cover before getting your Blazor on.

This book will start by guiding you through the most common scenarios you'll come across when you start your journey with Blazor, and will also dive into a few more advanced scenarios. The goal of this book is to show you what Blazor is – both Blazor Server and Blazor WebAssembly – how it all works practically, and to help you avoid any traps along the way.

A common belief is that Blazor is WebAssembly, but WebAssembly is just one way of running Blazor. Many books, workshops, and blog posts on Blazor focus heavily on WebAssembly. This book will cover both WebAssembly and server side. There are a few differences between Blazor Server and Blazor WebAssembly, and I will point those out as we go along.

This first chapter will explore where Blazor came from, what technologies made Blazor possible, and the different ways of running Blazor. We will also touch on which type is best for you.

In this chapter, we will cover the following topics:

- Preceding Blazor
- Introducing WebAssembly
- Introducing .NET 5
- Introducing Blazor

Technical requirements

It is recommended that you have some knowledge of .NET before you start as this book is aimed at .NET developers who wants to utilize their skills to make interactive web applications. However, it's more than possible that you will pick up a few .NET tricks along the way if you are new to the world of .NET.

Preceding Blazor

You probably didn't get this book to read about **JavaScript**, but it helps to remember that we are coming from a pre-Blazor time. I recall that time – the dark times. Many of the concepts used in Blazor are not that far from the concepts used in many JavaScript frameworks, so I will start with a brief overview of the challenges we faced.

As developers, we have many different platforms we can develop for, including desktop, mobile, games, the cloud (or server side), AI, and even IoT. All these platforms have a lot of different languages to choose from but there is, of course, one more platform: the apps that run inside the browser.

I have been a web developer for a long time, and I've seen code move from the server so that it can run within the browser. It has changed the way we develop our apps. Frameworks such as Angular, React, Aurelia, and Vue have changed the web from having to reload the whole page to updating just small parts of the page on the fly. This *new* on-the-fly update method has enabled pages to load quicker, as the perceived load time has been lowered (not necessarily the whole page load).

But for many developers, this is an entirely new skill set to learn; that is, switching between a server (most likely C#, if you are reading this book) to a frontend that's been developed in JavaScript. Data objects are written in C# in the backend and then serialized into JSON, sent via an API, and then deserialized into another object written in JavaScript in the frontend.

JavaScript used to work differently in different browsers, which jQuery tried to solve by having a common API that was translated into something the web browser could understand. Now, the differences between different web browsers are much smaller, which has rendered jQuery obsolete in many cases.

JavaScript differs a bit from other languages, since it is not object-oriented or typed, for example. In 2010, Anders Hejlsberg (known for being the original language designer of C#, Delphi, and Turbo Pascal) started to work on **TypeScript**, an object-oriented language that can be compiled/transpiled into JavaScript.

You can use Typescript with Angular, React, Aurelia, and Vue, but in the end, it is JavaScript that will run the actual code. Simply put, to create interactive web applications today using JavaScript/TypeScript, you need to switch between languages, and also choose and keep up with different frameworks.

In this book, we will look at this in another way. Even though we will talk about JavaScript, our main focus will be on developing interactive web applications using mostly C#.

Now, we know a bit of history about JavaScript. JavaScript is no longer the only language that can run within a browser, thanks to WebAssembly, which we will cover in the next section.

Introducing WebAssembly

In this section, we will look at how **WebAssembly** works. One way of running Blazor is by using WebAssembly, but for now, let's focus on what WebAssembly is.

WebAssembly a binary instruction format that is compiled and therefore smaller. It is designed for native speeds, which means that when it comes to speed, it is closer to C++ than it is to JavaScript. When loading JavaScript, the JS files (or inline) are downloaded, parsed, optimized, and JIT-compiled; most of those steps are not needed when it comes to WebAssembly.

WebAssembly has a very strict security model that protects users from buggy or malicious code. It runs within a sandbox and cannot escape that sandbox without going through the appropriate APIs. If you want to communicate outside of WebAssembly, for example, by changing the **Document Object Model** (**DOM**) or downloading a file from the web, you will need to do that with JavaScript interop (more on that later, and don't worry – Blazor will solve this for us).

To get a bit more familiar with WebAssembly, let's look at some code.

In this section, we will create an app that sums two numbers and returns the result, written in C (to be honest, this is about the level of C I'm comfortable with).

We can compile C into WebAssembly in a few easy steps:

1. Navigate to `https://wasdk.github.io/WasmFiddle/`.

2. Add the following code:

    ```
    int main() {
        return 1+2;
    }
    ```

3. Press **Build** and then **Run**.

You will see the number 3 being displayed in the output window toward the bottom of the page, as shown in the following screenshot:

Figure 1.1 – WasmFiddle

WebAssembly is a stack machine language, which means that it uses a stack to perform its operations.

Consider this code:

```
1+2
```

Most compilers (including the one we just used) are going to optimize the code and simply return 3.

But let's assume that all the instructions should be executed. This is the way WebAssembly would do things:

1. It will start by pushing 1 onto the stack (`instruction: i32.const 1`), followed by pushing 2 onto the stack (`instruction: i32.const 2`). At this point, the stack contains 1 and 2.

2. Then, we must execute the add-instruction (`i32.add`), which will pop (`get`) the two top values (1 and 2) from the stack, add them up, and push the new value onto the stack (3).

This demo shows that we can build WebAssembly from C code. Now, we have C code that's been compiled into WebAssembly running in our browser.

> **Other languages**
>
> Generally, it is only low-level languages that can be compiled into WebAssembly (such as C or Rust). However, there are a plethora of languages that can run on top of WebAssembly. Here is a great collection of some of these languages: `https://github.com/appcypher/awesome-wasm-langs`.

WebAssembly is super performant (near-native speeds) – so performant that game engines have already adapted this technology for that very reason. Unity, as well as Unreal Engine, can be compiled into WebAssembly.

Here are a couple of examples of games running on top of WebAssembly:

- **Angry Bots (Unity)**: `https://beta.unity3d.com/jonas/AngryBots/`
- **Doom**: `https://wasm.continuation-labs.com/d3demo/`

This is an amazing list of different WebAssembly projects: `https://github.com/mbasso/awesome-wasm`.

This section touched the surface of how WebAssembly works and in most cases, you won't need to know much more than that. We will dive into how Blazor uses this technology later in this chapter.

To write Blazor apps, we must leverage the power of .NET 5, which we'll look at next.

Introducing .NET 5

To build Blazor apps, we must use **.NET 5**. The .NET team has been working hard on tightening everything up for us developers for years. They have been making everything simpler, smaller, cross-platform, and open source – not to mention easier to utilize your existing knowledge of .NET development.

.NET core was a step of the journey toward a more unified .NET. It allowed Microsoft to reenvision the whole .NET platform and build it in a completely new way.

There are three different types of .NET runtimes:

- .NET Framework (full .NET)
- .NET Core
- Mono/Xamarin

Different runtimes had different capabilities and performances. This also meant that creating a .NET core app (for example) had different tooling and frameworks that needed to be installed.

.NET 5 is the start of our journey toward one single .NET. With this unified toolchain, the experience to create, run, and so on will be the same across all the different project types. .NET 5 is still modular in a similar way that we are used to, so we do not have to worry that merging all the different .NET versions is going to result in a bloated .NET.

Thanks to the .NET platform, you will be able to reach all the platforms we talked about at the beginning of this chapter (web, desktop, mobile, games, the cloud (or server side), AI, and even IoT) using only C# and with the same tooling.

Now that you know about some of the surrounding technologies, in the next section, it's time to introduce the main character of this book: Blazor.

Introducing Blazor

Blazor is an open source web UI SPA framework. That's a lot of buzzwords in the same sentence, but simply put, it means that you can create interactive SPA web applications using HTML, CSS, and C# with full support for bindings, events, forms and validation, dependency injection, debugging, and much more. We will take a look at these this book.

In 2017, Steve Sanderson (well-known for creating the Knockout JavaScript framework, and who works for the ASP.NET team at Microsoft) was about to do a session called *Web Apps can't really do *that*, can they?* at the developer conference NDC Oslo.

But Steve wanted to show a cool demo, so he thought to himself, *would it be possible to run C# in WebAssembly?* He found an old inactive project on GitHub called *Dot Net Anywhere*, which was written in C and used tools (similar to what we just did) to compile the C code into WebAssembly.

He got a simple console app running inside the browser. For most people, this would have been an amazing demo, but Steve wanted to take it one step further. He thought, *is it possible to create a simple web framework on top of this?*, and went on to see if he could get the tooling working as well.

When it was time for his session, he had a working sample where he could create a new project, create a todo-list with great tooling support, and then run the project inside the browser.

Damian Edwards (the .NET team) and David Fowler (the .NET team) were at the NDC conferences as well. Steve showed them what he was about to demo, and they described the event as their heads exploded and their jaws dropped.

And that's how the prototype of Blazor came into existence.

The name Blazor comes from a combination of Browser and Razor (which is the technology used to combine code and HTML). Adding an *L* made the name sound better, but other than that, it has no real meaning or acronym.

There are a couple of different flavors of Blazor Server, including Blazor WebAssembly, WebWindow, and Mobile Bindings. There are some pros and cons of the different versions, all of which I will cover in the upcoming sections and chapters.

Blazor Server

Blazor Server uses SignalR to communicate between the client and the server, as shown in the following diagram:

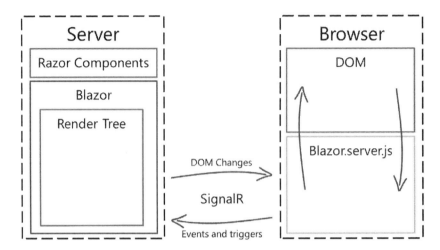

Figure 1.2 – Overview of Blazor Server

SignalR is an open source, real-time communication library that will create a connection between the client and the server. SignalR can use many different means of transporting data and automatically select the best transport protocol for you, based on your server and client capabilities. SignalR will always try to use WebSockets, which is a transport protocol built into HTML5. If WebSockets is not enabled for any reason, it will gracefully fall back to another protocol.

Blazor is built with reusable UI elements called **components** (more on components in *Chapter 3, Introducing Entity Framework Core*). Each component contains C# code, markup, and can even include another component. You can use Razor syntax to mix markup and C# code or even do everything in C# if you wish to. The components can be updated by user interaction (pressing a button) or by triggers (such as a timer).

The components get rendered into a **render tree**, a binary representation of the DOM that contains object states and any properties or values. The render tree will keep track of any changes compared to the previous render tree, and then send only the things that changed over SignalR using a binary format to update the DOM.

On the client side, JavaScript will receive the changes and update the page accordingly. If we compare this to traditional ASP.NET, we only render the component itself, not the entire page, and we only send over the actual changes to the DOM, not the entire page.

There are, of course, some disadvantages to Blazor Server:

- You need to always be connected to the server since the rendering is done on the server. If you have a bad internet connection, the site might not work. The big difference compared to a non-Blazor Server site is that a non-Blazor Server site can deliver a page and then disconnect until it requests another page. With Blazor, that connection (SignalR) must always be connected (minor disconnections are ok).

- There is no offline/PWA mode since it needs to be connected.

- Every click or page update must do a round trip to the server, which might result in higher latency. It is important to remember that Blazor Server will only send the data that was changed. I have not experienced any slow response times.

- Since we have to have a connection to the server, the load on that server increases and makes scaling difficult. To solve this problem, you can use the Azure SignalR hub, which will handle the constant connections and let your server concentrate on delivering content.

- To be able to run it, you have to host it on an ASP.NET Core-enabled server.

However, there are advantages to Blazor Server as well:

- It contains just enough code to establish that the connection is downloaded to the client so that the site has a small footprint.

- Since we are running on the server, the app can take full advantage of the server's capabilities.

- The site will work on older web browsers that don't support WebAssembly.

- The code runs on the server and stays on the server; there is no way to decompile the code.

- Since the code is executed on your server (or in the cloud), you can make direct calls to services and databases within your organization.

At my workplace, we already had a large site in place, so we decided to use Blazor Server for our projects. We had a customer portal and an internal CRM tool. Our approach was to take one component at a time and convert it into a Blazor component.

We quickly realized that, in most cases, it was faster to remake the component in Blazor rather than continuing to use ASP.NET MVC and add functionality on top of that. The **User Experience (UX)** for the end user became even better as we converted.

The pages loaded faster, we could reload parts of the page as we needed instead of the whole page, and so on.

We did find that Blazor introduced a new problem, though: the pages became *too* fast. Our users didn't understand if data had been saved because *nothing happened*; things *did* happen, but too fast for the users to notice. Suddenly, we had to think more about UX and how to inform the user that something had changed. This is, of course, a very positive side effect from Blazor in my opinion.

Blazor Server is not the only way to run Blazor – you can also run it on the client (in the web browser) using WebAssembly.

Blazor WebAssembly

There is another option: instead of running Blazor on a server, you can run it inside your web browser using WebAssembly.

As we mentioned previously, there is currently no way to compile C# into WebAssembly. Instead, Microsoft has taken the mono runtime (which is written in C) and compiled that into WebAssembly.

The WebAssembly version of Blazor works very similar to the server version, as shown in the following diagram. We have moved everything off the server and it is now running within our web browser:

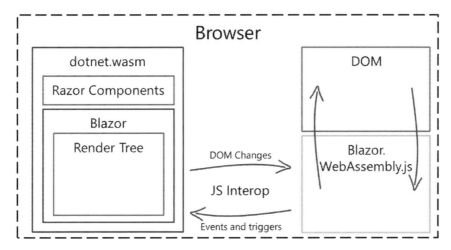

Figure 1.3 – Overview of Blazor Web Assembly

A render tree is still created and instead of running the Razor pages on the server, they are now running inside our web browser. Instead of SignalR, since WebAssembly doesn't have direct DOM access, Blazor updates the DOM with direct JavaScript interop.

The mono runtime that's compiled into WebAssembly is called **dotnet.wasm**. The page contains a small piece of JavaScript that will make sure to load `dotnet.wasm`. Then, it will download `blazor.boot.json`, which is a JSON file containing all the files the application needs to be able to run, as well as the entry point of the application.

If we look at the default sample site that is created when we start a new Blazor project in Visual Studio, the `Blazor.boot.json` file contains 63 dependencies that need to be downloaded. All the dependencies get downloaded and the app boots up.

As we mentioned previously, `dotnet.wasm` is the mono runtime that's compiled into WebAssembly. It runs .NET DLLs – the ones you have written, as well as the ones from .NET Framework (which is needed to run your app) – inside your browser.

When I first heard of this, I got a bit of a bad taste in my mouth. It's running the whole .NET runtime inside my browser?! But then, after a while, I realized how amazing that is. You can use any .NET Standard DLLs and run them in your web browser.

In the next chapter, we will look at exactly what happens and in what order code gets executed when a WebAssembly app boots up.

The big concern is the download size of the site. The simple **file new** sample app is about 1.3 MB in size, which is quite large if you are putting a lot of effort into download size. What you should remember, though, is that this is more like a **Single-Page Application (SPA)** – it is the whole site that has been downloaded to the client. I compared the size to some well-known sites on the internet; I then only included the JS files for these sites but also included all the DLLs and JavaScript files for Blazor.

The following is a diagram of my findings:

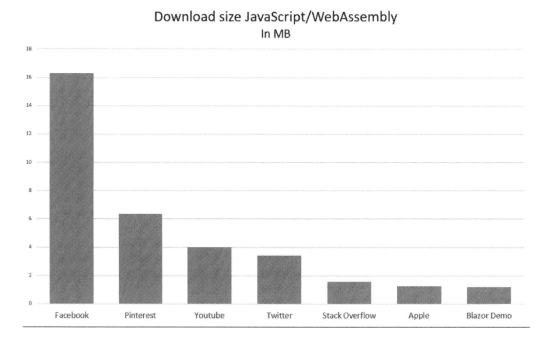

Figure 1.4 – JavaScript download size for popular sites

Even though the other sites are larger than the sample Blazor site, you should remember that the Blazor DLLs are compiled and should take up less space than a JavaScript file. WebAssembly is also faster than JavaScript is.

There are some disadvantages to Blazor WebAssembly:

- Even if we compare it to other large sites, the footprint of a Blazor WebAssembly is large and there are a large number of files to download.

- To access any on-site resources, you will need to create a Web API to access them. You cannot access the database directly.

- The code is running in the browser, which means that it can be decompiled. This is something all app developers are used to, but for web developers, it is perhaps not as common.

There are, of course, some advantages of Blazor WebAssembly as well:

- Since the code is running in the browser, it is easy to create a **Progressive Web App** (**PWA**).
- Since we're not running anything on the server, we can use any kind of backend server or even a file share (no need for a .NET-compatible server in the backend).
- No round trips mean that you will be able to update the screen faster (that is why there are game engines that use WebAssembly).

I wanted to put that last advantage to the test! When I was 7 years old, I got my first computer, a Sinclair ZX Spectrum. I remember that I sat down and wrote the following:

```
10 PRINT "Jimmy"
20 GOTO 10
```

That was *my* code; I made the computer write my name on the screen over and over!

That was the moment I decided that I wanted to become a developer, so that I could make computers do stuff.

After becoming a developer, I wanted to revisit my childhood and decided I wanted to and to build a ZX Spectrum emulator. In many ways, the emulator has become my test project, instead of a simple *Hello World*, when I encounter new technology. I've had it running on a Gadgeteer, Xbox One, and even on a HoloLens (to name a few).

But is it possible to run my emulator in Blazor?

It took me only a couple of hours to get the emulator working with Blazor WebAssembly by leveraging my already built .NET Standard DLL; I only had to write the code that was specific to this implementation, such as the keyboard and graphics. This is one of the reasons Blazor (both Server and WebAssembly) is so powerful: it can run libraries that have already been made. Not only can you leverage your knowledge of C#, but you can also take advantage of the large ecosystem and .NET community.

You can find the emulator here: https://zxspectrum.azurewebsites.net/. This is one of my favorite projects to work on, as I keep finding ways to optimize and improve the emulator.

Building this type of web application used to only be possible with JavaScript. Now, we know can use Blazor WebAssembly and Blazor Server, but which one of these new options is the best?

Blazor WebAssembly versus Blazor Server

Which one should we choose? The answer is, as always, it depends. You have seen the advantages and disadvantages of both.

If you have a current site that you want to port over to Blazor, I would go for server side; once you have ported it, you can make a new decision as to whether you want to go for WebAssembly as well.

If your site runs on a mobile browser or another unreliable internet connection, you might want to consider going for an offline-capable (PWA) scenario with Blazor WebAssembly since Blazor Server needs a constant connection.

The startup time for WebAssembly is a bit slow, but there are ways of combining the two hosting models so that you can have the best of two worlds. We will cover this in *Chapter 9, Sharing Code and Resources*.

There is no silver bullet when it comes to this question, but read up on the advantages and disadvantages and see how those affect your project and use cases.

We can run Blazor server side and on the client, but what about desktop and mobile apps? There are solutions for that as well, by using WebWindow and Mobile Blazor Bindings.

WebWindow

There is an experimental technology called **WebWindow**, which is an open source project from Steve Sanderson. It enables us to create Windows applications using Blazor.

WebWindow is outside the scope of this book, but I still want to mention it because it shows how powerful the technology really is and that there is no end to the possibilities with Blazor.

You can find out and read more about this project here: `https://github.com/SteveSandersonMS/WebWindow`.

Blazor Mobile Bindings

Another example of a project that is outside the scope of this book but is still worth mentioning is **Blazor Mobile Bindings**. It's a project that makes it possible to create mobile applications for iOS and Android by leveraging Blazor.

Blazor Mobile Bindings uses Razor syntax just like Blazor does; however, the components are completely different.

Although Microsoft is behind both Blazor and Blazor Mobile Bindings, we can't actually share the code between the different web versions (WebAssembly, Server, or WebWindow).

You can find out and read more about this project here: `https://docs.microsoft.com/en-us/mobile-blazor-bindings/`.

As you can see, there are a lot of things you can do with Blazor, and this is just the beginning.

Summary

In this chapter, you were provided with an overview of the different technologies you can use with Blazor, such as server side, client side (WebAssembly), desktop, and mobile. This overview should have helped you make an informed decision about what technology to choose for your next project.

We then talked about how Blazor was created and its underlying technologies, such as SignalR and WebAssembly. You also learned about the render tree and how the DOM gets updated to give you an understanding of how Blazor works under the hood.

In the upcoming chapters, I will walk you through various scenarios to equip you with the knowledge to handle everything from upgrading an old/existing site, creating a new server-side site, to creating a new WebAssembly site.

In the next chapter, we'll get our hands dirty by configuring our development environment and creating and examining our first Blazor App.

Further reading

As a .NET developer, you might be interested in the Uno Platform (`https://platform.uno/`), which makes it possible to create a UI in XAML and deploy it to many different platforms, including WebAssembly.

If you want to see how the ZX Spectrum emulator is built, you can download the source code here: `https://github.com/EngstromJimmy/ZXSpectrum`.

2
Creating Your First Blazor App

In this chapter, we will set up our development environment so that we can start developing Blazor apps. We will create our first Blazor app and go through the project structure, highlighting the differences between Blazor Server and Blazor WebAssembly projects.

By the end of this chapter, you will have a working development environment and have created both a Blazor Server app as well as a Blazor WebAssembly app.

In this chapter, we will cover the following:

- Setting up your development environment
- Creating our first Blazor application
- Using the command line
- Figuring out the project structure

Technical requirements

We will create a new project (a blog engine) and will continue working on that project throughout the book.

You can find the source code for this chapter's end result at `https://github.com/PacktPublishing/Web-Development-with-Blazor/tree/master/Chapter02`.

Setting up your development environment

In this book, the focus will be on Windows development and any screenshots are going to be from Visual Studio (unless stated otherwise). But since .NET 5 is cross-platform, we will go through how to set up your development environment on Windows, macOS, and Linux.

The go-to link for all the platforms can be found at `https://visualstudio.microsoft.com/`.

From the web page, we can download Visual Studio, Visual Studio Code, or Visual Studio for Mac.

Windows

On Windows, we have many different options for developing Blazor applications. Visual Studio 2019 is the most powerful tool we can use.

There are three different editions, which are as follows:

- Community 2019
- Professional 2019
- Enterprise 2019

In short, the Community Edition is free while the others cost money. The Community Edition does have some limitations and we can compare the different editions here: `https://visualstudio.microsoft.com/vs/compare/`.

For this book, we can use any of these versions. Take the following steps:

1. Download Visual Studio 2019 from `https://visualstudio.microsoft.com/vs/`. Choose the version that is right for you.

2. Install Visual Studio and during the installation, make sure to select **ASP.NET and web development**, as shown in *Figure 2.1*:

Figure 2.1 – Visual Studio 2019 installation on Windows

We can also use Visual Studio Code to develop Blazor on Windows, but we won't talk about the installation process for Windows.

macOS

On macOS, we also have some options. Visual Studio for Mac is the most powerful IDE we can use.

Download Visual Studio for Mac from `https://visualstudio.microsoft.com/vs/mac/` as follows:

1. Click on the **Download Visual Studio for Mac** button.

2. Open the file that was downloaded.

3.   Make sure to select **.NET Core**, as shown in *Figure 2.2*:

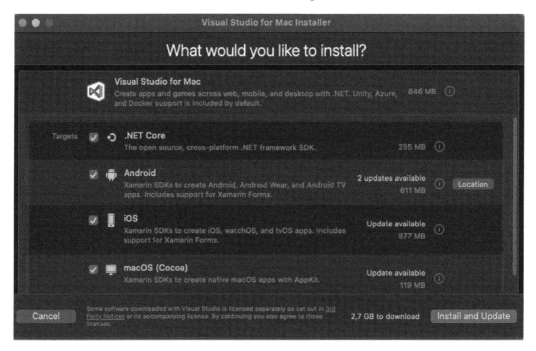

Figure 2.2 – Visual Studio for Mac installation screen

Since Visual Studio Code is a cross-platform software, we can use it here as well.

Linux (or macOS or Windows)

Visual Studio Code is cross-platform, which means we can use it on Linux, macOS, or Windows.

The different versions are available at `https://code.visualstudio.com/Download`.

Once installed, we also need to add two extensions:

1.   Open Visual Studio Code and press *Ctrl + Shift + X*.

2.   Search for `C# for Visual Studio Code (powered by OmniSharp)` and click **Install**.

3.   Search for `JavaScript Debugger (Nightly)` and click **Install**.

To create a project, we can use the .NET CLI, which we will come back to throughout this book, but we won't do a deep dive into the .NET CLI.

Now that we have everything all set up, let's create our first app.

Creating our first Blazor application

Throughout the book, we will create a blog engine. There won't be a lot of business logic that you'll have to learn; the app is simple to understand but will touch base on many of the technologies and areas you will be faced with when building a Blazor app.

The project will allow visitors to read blog posts and search for them. It will also have an admin site where you can write a blog post, which will be password-protected.

We will make the same app for both Blazor Server and Blazor WebAssembly, and I will show you the steps you need to do differently for each platform.

> **Important note**
> This guide will use Visual Studio 2019 from now on but other platforms have similar ways of creating projects.

Creating a Blazor Server application

To start, we will create a Blazor Server application and play around with it:

1. Start Visual Studio 2019 and you will see the following screen:

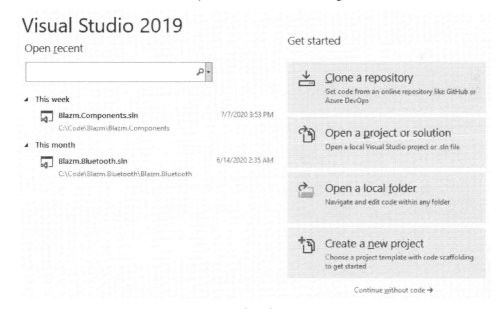

Figure 2.3 – Visual Studio startup screen

2. Press **Create a new project**, and in the search bar, type blazor.

3. Select **Blazor App** from the search results and press **Next**:

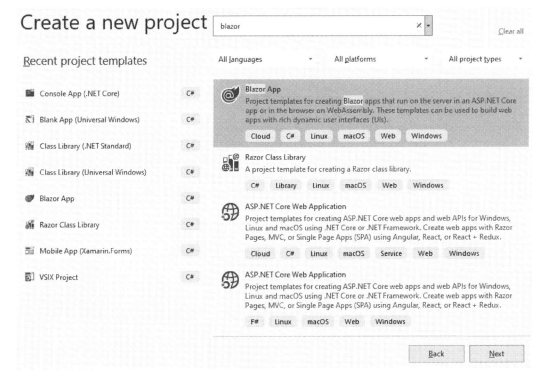

Figure 2.4 – The Visual Studio Create a new project screen

4. Now name the project (this is the hardest part of any project but fear not, I have done that already!). Name the application MyBlogServerSide, change the solution name to MyBlog, and press **Create**:

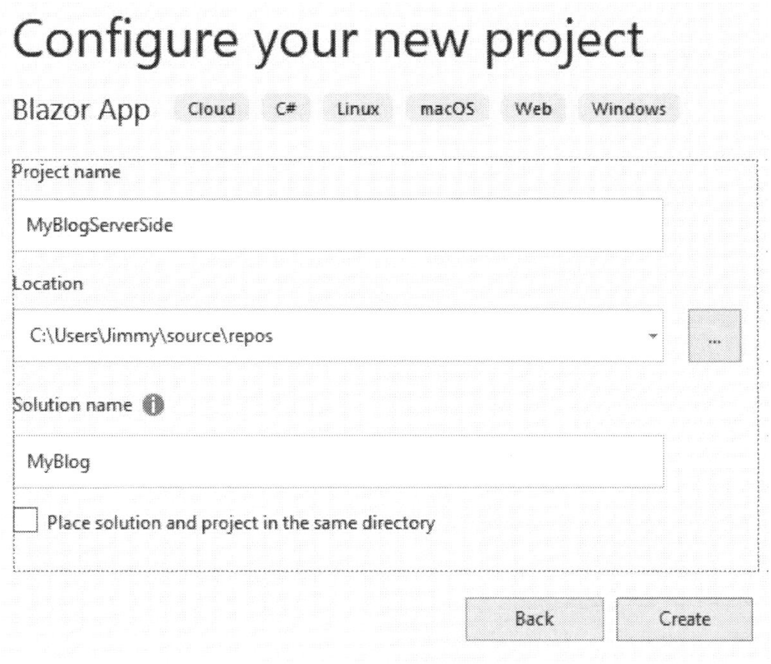

Configure your new project

Blazor App   Cloud   C#   Linux   macOS   Web   Windows

Project name

MyBlogServerSide

Location

C:\Users\Jimmy\source\repos

Solution name ⓘ

MyBlog

☐ Place solution and project in the same directory

Back   Create

Figure 2.5 – The Visual Studio Configure your new project screen

5.   Next, choose what kind of Blazor app we should create. Select **.NET 5.0 (Current)** from the drop-down menu and press **Create**:

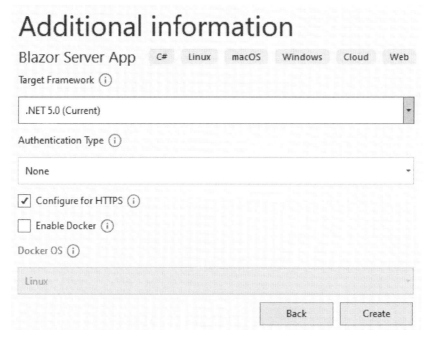

Figure 2.6 – Visual Studio screen for creating a new Blazor app

6.   Now run the app by pressing *Ctrl + F5* (we can also find it under the **Debug | Start without debugging**).

Congratulations! You have just created your first Blazor Server application. The site should look something like in *Figure 2.7*:

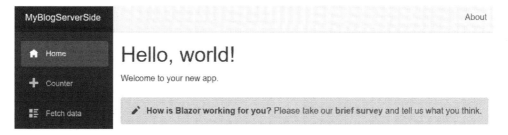

Figure 2.7 – A new Blazor Server server-side application

Explore the site a bit, navigate to **Counter** and **Fetch data** to get a feeling for the load times, and see what the sample application does.

The sample application has some sample data ready for us to test.

This is a Blazor Server project, which means that for every trigger (for example, a button press), a command will be sent via SignalR over to the server. The server will rerender the component and send the changes back over to the client and update the UI.

Press *F12* in your browser (to access the developer tools), switch to the **Network** tab, and then reload the page (*F5*). You'll see all the files that get downloaded to the browser.

In *Figure 2.8*, you can see some of the files that get downloaded:

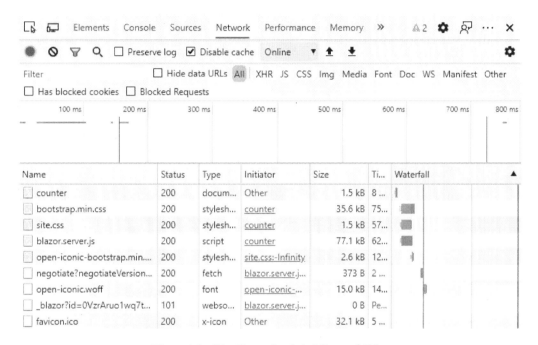

Figure 2.8 – The Network tab in Microsoft Edge

The browser downloads the page, some CSS, and then `blazor.server.js`, which is responsible for setting up the SignalR connection back to the server. It then calls the `negotiate` endpoint (to set up the connections).

The call to `_blazor?id=` (followed by a bunch of letters) is a **WebSocket** call, which is the open connection that the client and the server communicate through.

If you navigate to the **Counter** page and press the **Click me** button, you will notice that the page won't be reloaded. The trigger (click event) is sent over SignalR to the server and the page is rerendered on the server and gets compared to the render tree, and only the actual change is pushed back over the WebSocket.

For a button click, three calls are being made:

1. The page triggers the event (for example, a button click).
2. The server responds with the changes.
3. The page then sends back a response to acknowledge that the **Document Object Model** (**DOM**) has been updated.

In total, there are 490 bytes sent back and forth for a button click.

Now we have created a solution and a Blazor Server project and tried it out. Next up, we will add a Blazor WebAssembly app to that solution.

Creating a WebAssembly application

Now it is time to take a look at a WebAssembly app. We will create a new Blazor WebAssembly app and add it to the same solution as the Blazor Server app we just created:

1. Right-click on the **MyBlog** solution and select **Add | New Project**.
2. Search for `Blazor`, select **Blazor WebAssembly App** in the search results, and press **Next**:

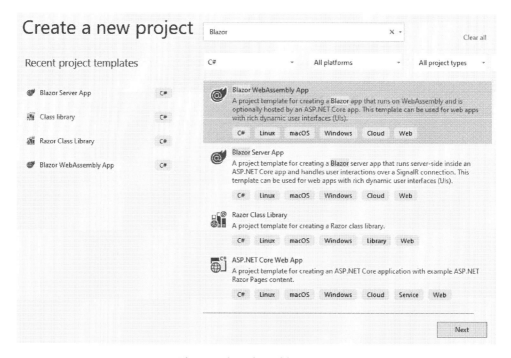

Figure 2.9 – The Visual Studio Add a new project screen

3. Name the app `MyBlogWebAssembly`. Leave the location as is (Visual Studio will put it in the right folder by default) and press **Create**:

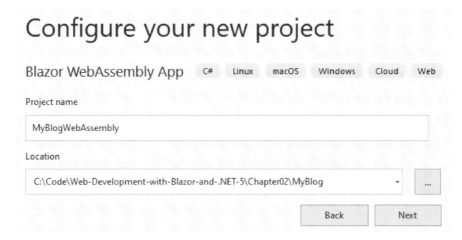

Figure 2.10 – The Visual Studio Configure your new project screen

4. On the next screen, select **.NET 5.0 (Current)** from the dropdown.

5. In this dialog box, two new choices appear that were not available in the Blazor Server template. The first option is **ASP.NET Core hosted**, which will create an ASP. NET backend project and will host the WebAssembly app, which is good if you want to host web APIs for your app to access; you should check this box.

The second option is **Progressive Web Application**, which will create a `manifest.json` file and a `service-worker.js` file that will make your app available as a **Progressive Web Application** (**PWA**). For this project, leave it unchecked and then press **Create**:

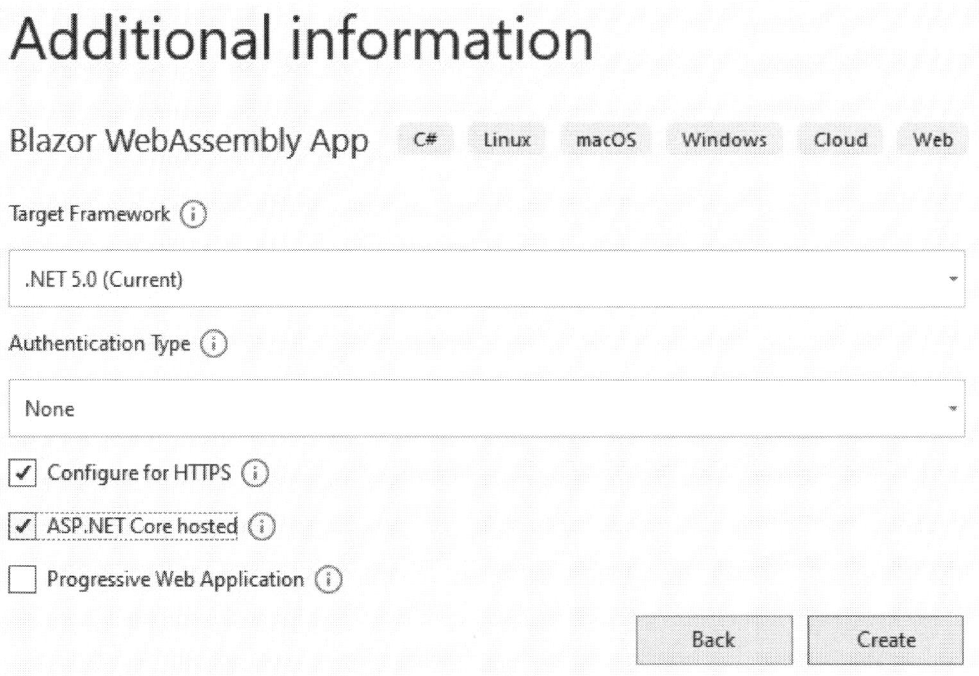

Additional information

Blazor WebAssembly App   C#   Linux   macOS   Windows   Cloud   Web

Target Framework (i)

.NET 5.0 (Current)   ▾

Authentication Type (i)

None   ▾

☑ Configure for HTTPS (i)

☑ ASP.NET Core hosted (i)

☐ Progressive Web Application (i)

                                                                    Back   Create

Figure 2.11 – Visual Studio screen for creating a new Blazor app

6. Right-click on the **MyBlogWebAssembly.Server** project and select **Set as Startup Project**.

> **Note:**
> It can be confusing that this project also has **Server** in the name.
>
> Since we chose **ASP.NET Core hosted** when we created the project, we are hosting the backend for our client side (WebAssembly) in **MyBlogWebAssembly.Server** and it is not related to Blazor Server.
>
> Just remember that if you want to run the WebAssembly app, you should run the **MyBlogWebAssembly.Server** project; that way we know the backend ASP.NET Core project will run as well.

7. Run the app by pressing *Ctrl + F5* (start without debugging).

Congratulations! You have just created your first Blazor WebAssembly application, as shown in *Figure 2.12*:

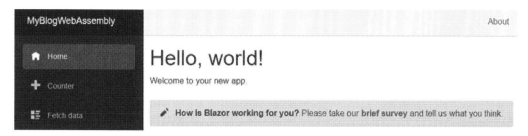

Figure 2.12 – A new Blazor WebAssembly app

Explore the site by clicking the **Counter** and **Fetch data** links. The app should behave in the same way as the Blazor Server version.

Press *F12* in your browser (to access the developer tools), switch to the **Network** tab, and reload the page (*F5*); you'll see all the files that get downloaded to the browser.

In *Figure 2.13*, you can see some of the files that got downloaded:

Name	Status	Type	Initiator	Size	Time	Waterfall
localhost	200	document	Other	688 B	5 ms	
blazor.webassembly.js	304	script	(index)	95 B	5 ms	
open-iconic-bootstrap.min.css	200	stylesheet	app.css	(memory ca...	0 ms	
open-iconic.woff	200	font	open-iconic-bootstrap...	(memory ca...	0 ms	
blazor.boot.json	200	fetch	blazor.webassembly.js:1	90 B	4 ms	
favicon.ico	200	x-icon	Other	32.2 kB	172 ms	
dotnet.3.2.0.js	200	script	blazor.webassembly.js:1	78 B	36 ms	
MyBlogWebAssembly.Client.dll	200	fetch	blazor.webassembly.js:1	78 B	24 ms	
System.Net.Http.Json.dll	200	fetch	blazor.webassembly.js:1	78 B	24 ms	
System.Buffers.dll	200	fetch	blazor.webassembly.js:1	77 B	96 ms	
mscorlib.dll	200	fetch	blazor.webassembly.js:1	78 B	575 ms	
System.Threading.Tasks.Extensions.dll	200	fetch	blazor.webassembly.js:1	78 B	25 ms	
System.Memory.dll	200	fetch	blazor.webassembly.js:1	78 B	24 ms	

Figure 2.13 – The Network tab in Microsoft Edge

In this case, when the page gets downloaded, it will trigger a download of the `blazor.webassembly.js` file. Then, `blazor.boot.json` gets downloaded. *Figure 2.14* shows an example of part of `blazor.boot.json`:

```
▼{cacheBootResources: true, config: [], debugBuild: true, entryAssembly: "MyBlogWebAssembly.Client",…}
    cacheBootResources: true
    config: []
    debugBuild: true
    entryAssembly: "MyBlogWebAssembly.Client"
    icuDataMode: 0
    linkerEnabled: false
  ▼resources: {,…}
    ▼assembly: {Microsoft.AspNetCore.Authorization.dll: "sha256-GgCkcCalx/3h2tzZqbfi/H5H4zwf+gA7wOIJWVGaW3Y=",…}
        Microsoft.AspNetCore.Authorization.dll: "sha256-GgCkcCalx/3h2tzZqbfi/H5H4zwf+gA7wOIJWVGaW3Y="
        Microsoft.AspNetCore.Components.Forms.dll: "sha256-zrn/FnIALTHMExILtqdkxOH1pM1etFsHZKdup5iX8tU="
        Microsoft.AspNetCore.Components.Web.dll: "sha256-grRzaeXO/Dfsteh5jEm/m7g4YCXi8+fFZ2v1BNIMeQA="
        Microsoft.AspNetCore.Components.WebAssembly.dll: "sha256-grJppr5rXiGmkAtdiCR04Z7NXclvICBPwE6aHeOvMEQ="
        Microsoft.AspNetCore.Components.dll: "sha256-tjgurODETDIWCTj+df3XjjWnMRi72XZXE78H5YaTpDc="
        Microsoft.AspNetCore.Metadata.dll: "sha256-ggV83y6tiNFycAgetcOWTss/XnO8cK2ya4q+tOda4q4="
        Microsoft.CSharp.dll: "sha256-8nKI+prFZGoXjtLAykW9nDisJwjBUBue3+jqE7+OY3M="
        Microsoft.Extensions.Configuration.Abstractions.dll: "sha256-NYecKM0ZpUvzj4spvgi6xUu80rkx8PX7fiRok/BNaHw="
```

Figure 2.14 – Part of the blazor.boot.json file

The most important thing `blazor.boot.json` contains is the entry assembly, which is the name of the DLL the browser should start executing. It also contains all the framework DLLs the app needs to run. Now our app knows what it needs to start up.

The JavaScript will then download `dotnet.5.0.*.js`, which will download all the resources mentioned in `blazor.boot.json`: this is a mix of your code compiled to a .NET Standard DLL, Microsoft .NET Framework code, and any community or third-party DLLs you might use. The JavaScript then downloads `dotnet.wasm`, the Mono runtime compiled to WebAssembly, which will now start booting up your app.

If you watch closely, you might see some text when you reload your page saying **Loading**. Between **Loading** showing up and the page finishing loading, JSON files, JavaScript, WebAssembly, and DLLs are downloaded and everything is booting up. According to Microsoft Edge, it takes 1.8 seconds to do that running in debug mode and with unoptimized code.

Now we have the base for our project, including a Blazor WebAssembly version and a Blazor Server version. Throughout this book, we will use Visual Studio but there are other ways to run your Blazor site, such as using the command line. The command line is a super powerful tool and in the next section, we will run our Blazor app using the command line.

Using the command line

With .NET 5, you get a super powerful tool called `dotnet.exe`. Developers that have used .NET Core before will already be familiar with the tool, but with .NET 5, it is no longer exclusively for .NET Core developers.

It can do a lot of the things Visual Studio can do, for example, creating projects, adding and creating NuGet packages, and much more. In the next example, we will create a Blazor Server project.

Creating a Blazor Server project using the command line

The following steps are just for demonstrating the power of using the command line. We will not use this project later in the book, so if you don't want to try it, go ahead and skip this section. To create a new Blazor Server project, you can use this command:

```
dotnet new blazorserver -o BlazorServerSideApp
```

Here, `dotnet` is the command, and to create a new project, you use the `new` parameter.

`blazorserver` is the name of the template and `-o` is the output folder (in this case, the project will be created in a subfolder called `BlazorServerSideApp`).

You can run your Blazor apps using the `Dotnet` command. Start PowerShell and navigate to the `MyBlogServerSide` folder, then type the following command:

```
Dotnet run
```

It will compile the code and start a web server running your app:

```
info: Microsoft.Hosting.Lifetime[0]
      Now listening on: https://localhost:5001
info: Microsoft.Hosting.Lifetime[0]
      Now listening on: http://localhost:5000
info: Microsoft.Hosting.Lifetime[0]
      Application started. Press Ctrl+C to shut down.
info: Microsoft.Hosting.Lifetime[0]
      Hosting environment: Development
info: Microsoft.Hosting.Lifetime[0]
      Content root path:
        D:\Source\B16009\Ch2\MyBlog\MyBlogServerSide
```

If you then launch a web browser and navigate to `http://localhost:5000`, you will see your site.

> **Note: the .NET CLI**
>
> The idea is that you should be able to do everything from the command line. If you prefer working with the command line, you should check out the .NET CLI; you can read more about the .NET CLI here: `https://docs.microsoft.com/en-us/dotnet/core/tools/`.

Let's go back to the Blazor template, which has added a lot of files for us. In the next section, we will take a look at what Visual Studio has generated for us.

Figuring out the project structure

Now it's time to take a look at the different files and how they may differ in different projects. Take a look at the code in the two projects we just created (in the *Creating our first Blazor app* section) while we go through them.

Program.cs

`Program.cs` is the first class that gets called. It also differs between Blazor Server and Blazor WebAssembly.

WebAssembly Program.cs

In the `MyBlogWebAssembly.Client` project, there is a file called `Program.cs` and it looks like this:

```
public class Program
{
    public static async Task Main(string[] args)
    {
        var builder = WebAssemblyHostBuilder.CreateDefault
            (args);
        builder.RootComponents.Add<App>("#app");
        builder.Services.AddScoped(sp => new HttpClient {
            BaseAddress = new Uri
                (builder.HostEnvironment.BaseAddress) });
```

```
    await builder.Build().RunAsync();
   }
}
```

The `Main` method is the first method that gets called; it will add `app` as the root component, and the whole single-page application site will be rendered inside of the `App` component (we will get back to that component later in the chapter).

It adds `HttpClient` as a scoped dependency. In *Chapter 3*, *Introducing Entity Framework Core*, we will dig deeper into dependency injection, but for now, it is a way to abstract the creation of objects and types by injecting objects (dependencies) so you don't create objects inside a page. The objects get passed into the page/classes instead, which will make testing easier, and the classes don't have any dependencies we don't know about.

The WebAssembly version is running in the browser so the only way it can get data is by making external calls (to a server, for example); therefore, we need to be able to access `HttpClient`. WebAssembly is not allowed to make any direct calls to download data, therefore `HttpClient` is a special implementation for WebAssembly that will make JavaScript interop calls to download data.

As I mentioned before, WebAssembly is running in a sandbox, and to be able to communicate outside of this sandbox, it needs to go through appropriate JavaScript/browser APIs.

Blazor Server Program.cs

Blazor Server projects look a bit different (but do pretty much the same thing). In the `MyBlogServerSide` project, the `Program.cs` file looks like this:

```
public class Program
{
    public static void Main(string[] args)
    {
        CreateHostBuilder(args).Build().Run();
    }
    public static IHostBuilder CreateHostBuilder(string[]
        args) =>
        Host.CreateDefaultBuilder(args)
            .ConfigureWebHostDefaults(webBuilder =>
            {
```

```
                        webBuilder.UseStartup<Startup>();
            });
}
```

Just as with WebAssembly, the `Main` method is the first thing that gets called. It will call the `CreateDefaultBuilder` method, which will hand off everything to the `Startup` class. You will notice that we are not registering any services here; it is instead done in the `Startup` class.

Startup

The startup file is responsible for hooking up all the services and configuring the app; it is only available in Blazor Server projects (not in Blazor WebAssembly). In the startup file, there are a couple of methods, which we will go through one by one.

In the `MyBlogServerSide` project, we have the `Startup.cs` file:

```
public Startup(IConfiguration configuration)
{
    Configuration = configuration;
}
public IConfiguration Configuration { get; }
```

The `Startup` method is a constructor that takes an `IConfiguration` object. Using the `Configuration` property, we can access any settings we may need.

The next method is `ConfigureServices`:

```
public void ConfigureServices(IServiceCollection services)
{
    services.AddRazorPages();
    services.AddServerSideBlazor();
    services.AddSingleton<WeatherForecastService>();
}
```

The `ConfigureServices` method is where we add all the dependencies we need in our application. In this case, we add `RazorPages`, which is the pages that run Blazor (these are the `.cshtml` files). Then we add `ServerSideBlazor`, which will give us access to all the objects we need to run Blazor Server. Then we add `WeatherForcastService`, which is used when you navigate to the **Forecast** page.

Next up we have the `Configure` method, which configures everything we need:

```
public void Configure(IApplicationBuilder app,
IWebHostEnvironment env)
{
    if (env.IsDevelopment())
    {
        app.UseDeveloperExceptionPage();
    }
    else
    {
        app.UseExceptionHandler("/Error");
        app.UseHsts();
    }
    app.UseHttpsRedirection();
    app.UseStaticFiles();
    app.UseRouting();
    app.UseEndpoints(endpoints =>
    {
        endpoints.MapBlazorHub();
        endpoints.MapFallbackToPage("/_Host");
    });
}
```

`UseDeveloperExceptionPage` will make sure that while we are running in a development environment, our application will show a developer exception page with greater detail, which makes it easier to debug the application. If we are not running in development, it will redirect to an exception handler and show a friendlier error message.

It also configures **HTTP Strict Transport Security (HSTS)**, forcing your application to use HTTPS, and will make sure that your users don't use any untrusted resources or certificates. We also make sure that the site redirects to HTTPS to make the site secure.

`UseStaticFiles` enables downloading static files such as CSS or images.

The different `Use*` methods add request delegates to the request pipeline or middleware pipeline. Each request delegate (`DeveloperException`, `httpRedirection`, `StaticFiles`, and so on) is called consecutively from the top to the bottom and back again.

This is why the exception handler is the first one to be added.

If there is an exception in any of the request delegates that follow, the exception handler will still be able to handle it (since the request travels back through the pipeline), as shown in *Figure 2.15*:

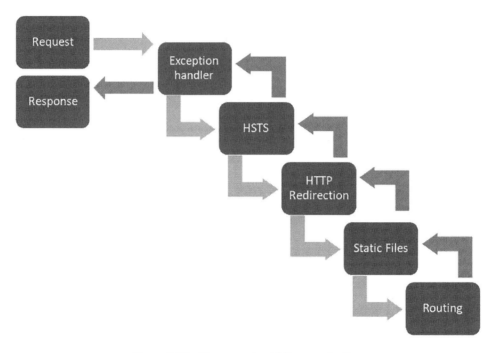

Figure 2.15 – The request middleware pipeline

If any of these request delegates handle the request in the case of a static file, for example, there is no need to involve routing and the remaining request delegates will not get called. There is no need to involve routing if the request was for a static file. In some cases, it is important to add the request delegated in the right order.

> **Note:**
> There is more information about this here if you want to dig even further:
> `https://docs.microsoft.com/en-us/aspnet/core/`
> `fundamentals/middleware/?view=aspnetcore-5.0.`

At the end of the `Configure` method, we hook up routing and add endpoints. We create an endpoint for the Blazor SignalR hub and if we don't find anything to return, we make sure that we will call the _host file that will handle routing for the app. When _host has triggered, the first page of the app will get loaded.

Index/_host

The next thing that happens is that the Index or _host file runs. It contains the information to load the necessary JavaScript.

_Host (Blazor Server)

The Blazor Server project has a _Host.cshtml file that is located in the pages folder. It is a Razor page, which is not the same thing as a Razor component:

- A **Razor page** is a way to create views or pages. It can use Razor syntax but cannot be used as a component (a component can be used as part of a page and inside of another component).

- A **Razor component** is a way to build reusable views (called **components**) that you can use throughout your app. You can build a Grid component (for example, a component that renders a table) and use it in your app, or package it as a library for others to use. However, a component can be used as a page by adding an @ page directive to your component and it can be called a page (more on that later).

For most Blazor applications, you should only have one .cshtml page; the rest should be Razor components.

At the top of the page, you will find some @ directives (such as page, namespace, using, and addTagHelper):

```
@page "/"
@namespace BlazorTestServerSide.Pages
@using MyBlogServerSide
@addTagHelper *, Microsoft.AspNetCore.Mvc.TagHelpers
@{
    Layout = null;
}
```

There are a couple of aspects of this file that are worth noting. The @ directives make sure to set the URL for the page, add a namespace, add a tag helper, and that we are not using a Layout page. We will cover directives in *Chapter 4, Understanding Basic Blazor Components.*

The reason we do not want a layout for this page is that the layout will be loaded in the app component.

Then we have some standard HTML doctypes, metatags, titles, and styles. The only thing that is Blazor-specific is the base tag:

```
<base href="~/" />
```

It makes sure that your pages will find the Blazor SignalR hub. If you do not have the base tag, as soon as you navigate to a page within a folder, your site will break because the relative URL no longer finds the Blazor SignalR hub.

Next, we have the body tag, and it contains the app component:

```
<component type="typeof(App)" render-mode="ServerPrerendered"
/>
```

This is where the entire application will be rendered. The App component handles that. This is also the way you would add a Blazor component into your existing non-Blazor app using the component tag helper.

It will render a component called App. There are five different render modes:

- The first one is the default ServerPrerendered mode, which will render all the content on the server and deliver it as part of the content when the page gets downloaded for the first time. Then it will hook up the Blazor SignalR hub and make sure your changes will be pushed to and from the server; however, the server will make another render and push those changes over SignalR. Normally, you won't notice anything, but if you are using certain events on the server, they may get triggered twice and make unnecessary database calls, for example.

- The second option is Server, which will send over the whole page and add placeholders for the components. It then hooks up SignalR and lets the server send over the changes when it is done (when it has retrieved data from the database, for example).

- The third option is Static, which will render the component and then disconnect, which means that it will not listen to events and it won't update the component any longer. This can be a good option for static data.

- The fourth option is WebAssembly, which will render a marker for the WebAssembly application but not output anything from the component.

- The fifth option is WebAssemblyPrerendered, which will render the component into static HTML and then bootstrap the WebAssembly app into that space.

It will make the app feel like it loads faster.

> **Note:**
>
> To dig deeper into options 3 to 5, follow this link: `https://docs.`
> `microsoft.com/en-us/aspnet/core/blazor/components/`
> `prerendering-and-integration.`

We will not go deeper into those different options.

`ServerPrerendered` is technically the fastest way to get your page up on the screen; if you have a page that loads quickly, then this is a good option. If you want your page to have a perceived fast loading time that shows you content fast and then loads the data when the server is done getting the data from a database, then `Server` is a better option.

I prefer the `Server` option because the site should feel fast. Switching to `Server` is the first thing I change when creating a new Blazor site; I'd much rather have the data pop up a couple of milliseconds later because the page will feel like it loads faster.

In the `_host` file, there is a small part of the UI that will show if there are any error messages:

```
<div id="blazor-error-ui">
    <environment include="Staging,Production">
        An error has occurred. This application may no
        longer respond until reloaded.
    </environment>
    <environment include="Development">
        An unhandled exception has occurred. See browser
        dev tools for details.
    </environment>
    <a href="" class="reload">Reload</a>
    <a class="dismiss">X</a>
</div>
```

I would recommend keeping this error UI (or a variation of it) because JavaScript is involved in updating the UI. In some cases, your page may break, the JavaScript will stop running, and the SignalR connection will fail. If that happens, you will get a nice error message in the JavaScript console. But by having the error UI pop up, you'll know that you need to check the console.

The last thing we will cover on the _host page is also where all the magic happens, the JavaScript responsible for hooking everything up:

```
<script src="_framework/blazor.server.js"></script>
```

The script will create a SignalR connection to the server and is responsible for updating the DOM from the server and sending triggers back to the server.

Index (WebAssembly)

The WebAssembly project looks pretty much the same.

In the MyBlogWebAssembly.Client project, open the wwwroot/index.html file. This file is HTML only, so there are no directives at the top like in the Blazor Server version.

Just like the Blazor Server version, you will find a base tag:

```
<base href="/" />
```

Instead a component tag (as with Blazor Server) you'll find a div tag here instead, there was a line in Program.cs that connects the App component to the div tag (see the previous *Program.cs* section):

```
<div id="app">Loading...</div>
```

You can replace Loading... with something else if you want to – this is the content that will be shown while the app is starting.

The error UI looks a bit different as well. There is no difference between development or production as we have in Blazor Server. Here you only have one way of displaying errors:

```
<div id="blazor-error-UI">
    An unhandled error has occurred.
    <a href="" class="reload">Reload</a>
    <a class="dismiss">X</a>
</div>
```

Lastly, we have a `script` tag that loads JavaScript. This makes sure to load all the code needed for the WebAssembly code to run:

```
<script src="_framework/blazor.webassembly.js"></script>
```

Just like how the script for Blazor Server communicates with the backend server and the DOM, the WebAssembly script communicates between the WebAssembly .NET runtime and the DOM.

At this point, the app is starting up and the differences between Blazor Server and Blazor WebAssembly are not there anymore; it is all Razor components from now on. The first component that will be loaded is the App component.

App

The App component is the same for both Blazor WebAssembly and Blazor Server. It contains a `Router` component:

```
<Router AppAssembly="@typeof(Program).Assembly">
    <Found Context="routeData">
        <RouteView RouteData="@routeData"
         DefaultLayout="@typeof(MainLayout)" />
    </Found>
    <NotFound>
        <LayoutView Layout="@typeof(MainLayout)">
            <p>Sorry, there's nothing at this address.</p>
        </LayoutView>
    </NotFound>
</Router>
```

This file handles the routing, finding the right component to show (based on the @page directive). It shows an error message if the route can't be found. In *Chapter 8, Authentication and Authorization*, we will make changes to this file when we implement authentication.

The App component also includes a default layout. The layout can be overridden per component but usually, you'll have one layout page for your site. In this case, the default layout is called `MainLayout`.

MainLayout

MainLayout contains the default layout for all components when viewed as a page. The main layout contains a couple of div tags, one for the sidebar and one for the main content:

```
@inherits LayoutComponentBase
<div class="page">
    <div class="sidebar">
        <NavMenu />
    </div>
    <div class="main">
        <div class="top-row px-4">
            <a href="http://blazor.net" target="_blank"
                class="ml-md-auto">About</a>
        </div>
        <div class="content px-4">
            @Body
        </div>
    </div>
</div>
```

The only things you need in this document are @inherits LayoutComponentBase and @Body; the rest is just Bootstrap. The @inherits directive inherits from LayoutComponentBase, which contains all the code to use a layout. @Body is where the component will be rendered (when viewed as a page).

Bootstrap

Bootstrap is one of the most popular CSS frameworks for developing responsive and mobile-first websites.

We can find a reference to Bootstrap in the wwwroot\index.html file.

It was created by and for Twitter. You can read more about Bootstrap here: https://getbootstrap.com/.

Toward the top of the layout, you can see <NavMenu>, which is a Razor component. It is located in the Shared folder and looks like this:

```
<div class="top-row pl-4 navbar navbar-dark">
    <a class="navbar-brand" href="">MyBlogServerSide</a>
    <button class="navbar-toggler"
        @onclick="ToggleNavMenu">
        <span class="navbar-toggler-icon"></span>
    </button>
</div>
<div class="@NavMenuCssClass" @onclick="ToggleNavMenu">
    <ul class="nav flex-column">
        <li class="nav-item px-3">
            <NavLink class="nav-link" href=""
                Match="NavLinkMatch.All">
                <span class="oi oi-home"
                    aria-hidden="true"></span> Home
            </NavLink>
        </li>
        <li class="nav-item px-3">
            <NavLink class="nav-link" href="counter">
                <span class="oi oi-plus"
                    aria-hidden="true"></span> Counter
            </NavLink>
        </li>
        <li class="nav-item px-3">
            <NavLink class="nav-link" href="fetchdata">
                <span class="oi oi-list-rich"
                    aria-hidden="true"></span> Fetch data
            </NavLink>
        </li>
    </ul>
</div>
@code {
    private bool collapseNavMenu = true;
```

```
    private string NavMenuCssClass =>
        collapseNavMenu ? "collapse" : null;
    private void ToggleNavMenu()
    {
        collapseNavMenu = !collapseNavMenu;
    }
}
```

It contains the left-side menu and is a standard Bootstrap menu. It also has three menu items and logic for a hamburger menu (if viewed on a phone). This type of nav menu is usually done with JavaScript but this one is done with CSS and C# solely.

You will find another component, `NavLink`, which is built into the framework. It will render an anchor tag but will also check the current route. If you are currently on the same route/URL as the nav link, it will automatically add a CSS class called `active` to the tag.

We will run into a couple more built-in components that will help us along the way. There are also some pages in the template, but we will leave them for now and go through them in the next chapter when we go into components.

Summary

In this chapter, we got the development environment up and running, and we created our first Blazor app for both Blazor WebAssembly and Blazor Server. You learned in what order classes, components, and layouts are called, which will make it easier to follow the code. We also covered some of the differences between a Blazor Server project versus a Blazor WebAssembly project.

In the next chapter, we will take a break from Blazor to take a look at Entity Framework Core 5 and set up our database. If you already know about Entity Framework, you can skip to *Chapter 4*, *Understanding Basic Blazor Components*, where we will go through components, dig deeper into the components in the template, and then create our first component.

Section 2: Building an Application with Blazor

In this section, you will learn about Razor syntax, validate forms, build and share components, understand dependency injection, and call JavaScript and C# from JavaScript.

This section includes the following chapters:

3
Introducing Entity Framework Core

In this chapter, we will go through Entity Framework and create a database where we can store our blog posts. Since most applications use data in one form or another, the goal of this chapter is to be able to use data from our database in our Blazor application. We will also create an API to access the data.

By the end of this chapter, we will have learned how to use the .NET CLI to create a new project, add new NuGet packages, and create migrations.

In this chapter, we will cover the following:

- Creating a data project
- Adding `DbContext` to Blazor

Technical requirements

Make sure you have followed the previous chapters, or use the `Ch2` folder as the starting point.

In this chapter, we will create a database project using Entity Framework Core 5. If you have no interest in using Entity Framework Core, you can skip this chapter and download the Ch3 folder from the GitHub repo to get back on track. We are not going to go into depth when it comes to Entity Framework, but we will cover some of the new features of Entity Framework Core 5.

You can find the source code for this chapter's end result at `https://github.com/PacktPublishing/Web-Development-with-Blazor/tree/master/Chapter03`.

Creating a data project

To save our blog posts, we will use Entity Framework, which is Microsoft's **Object Relational Mapping** (or **ORM**). It enables developers to work with data using domain-specific classes and not worry about the underlying database (as tables, columns, and relations are generated from the classes).

Entity Framework maps classes to the tables in the database. There are two ways to use Entity Framework:

- **The database-first approach**: This is when we already have an existing database and generate classes based on that database.

- **The code-first approach**: This is when we first write the classes, which will then generate the database.

For this project, we will use the code-first approach.

Let's create a new data project, using the command line to get a feel for what the `dotnet` command can do.

Creating a new project

There are many ways to store the data; for simplicity, we will use an SQLite database while building the blog. The data will be accessible from both our Blazor WebAssembly project and the Blazor Server project, so we want to create a new project (not just put the code in one of the projects we created previously).

We can create a project from within Visual Studio as well (to be honest, that's how I would do it) but to get to know the .NET CLI, let's do it from command line instead.

To create a new project, follow these steps:

1. Open a PowerShell prompt.

2. Navigate to the `MyBlog` folder.

3. Create a class library (`classlib`) by typing the following command:

```
dotnet new classlib -o MyBlog.Data
```

The `dotnet` tool should now have created a folder called `MyBlog.Data`.

4. Add the new project to our solution by running the following command:

```
dotnet sln add MyBlog.Data
```

It will look for any solution in the current folder. If for any reason we already have a solution, we need to specify that as well.

The next step is to add the NuGet packages that we need for the project.

Adding NuGet packages

To be able to use Entity Framework Core, we need to add a couple of NuGet packages to our project:

1. Open PowerShell and navigate to the `MyBlog.Data` folder:

```
cd MyBlog.Data
```

2. Add the `Microsoft.EntityFrameworkCore.Tools` package to the project using the following command:

```
dotnet add package Microsoft.EntityFrameworkCore.Tools
```

3. Add the `Microsoft.EntityFrameworkCore.Sqlite` package to the project with the following command:

```
dotnet add package Microsoft.EntityFrameworkCore.Sqlite
```

In this project, I decided to use SQLite so we don't have to install an Microsoft SQL Server or another database engine. We can, of course, change this package to the database of our choice; the rest of the tutorial should be the same regardless of the underlying database.

It is worth mentioning that we can use SQL Server Express LocalDB, which is built into Visual Studio.

The Blazor templates that include authentication will use SQLite if we create a project using the command line (to be cross-platform), and will use LocalDB if we use Visual Studio to create our project.

In this case, we want our project to be cross-platform and use SQLite.

The next step is to create the data classes.

Creating data classes

Now we have all the packages we need, we need to create a class for our blog post. To do that we will go back to Visual Studio:

1. Open the **MyBlog** solution in Visual Studio (if it is not already open).

   We should now have a new project called **MyBlog.Data** in our solution. We might get a popup asking if we want to reload the solution; click **Reload** if so.

2. Right-click on the **MyBlog.Data** project and select **Add | New Folder**. Name the folder Interfaces.

3. Next, we need to create an interface, just so that we don't have to repeat the code later on. Right-click in the Interfaces folder and select **Add | Class**. In the list of different templates, select **Interface** and name it IMyBlogItem.cs.

4. Open IMyBlogItem.cs and replace its content with the following code:

   ```
   namespace MyBlog.Data.Interfaces
   {
       interface IMyBlogItem
       {
           public int Id { get; set; }
       }
   }
   ```

   The interface only contains one property, which is Id. By having a common interface with the Id property, we can write generic functions for handling the saving of objects.

   We will add this interface to all the data classes we will create; this is just so that we won't need to duplicate a lot of code when we start with the API.

5. Now we need to create three data classes. Right-click on **MyBlog.Data** and select **Add | New Folder**. Name the folder Models.

6. Right-click on the Models folder and select **Add | Class**. Name the class BlogPost.cs and press **Add**:

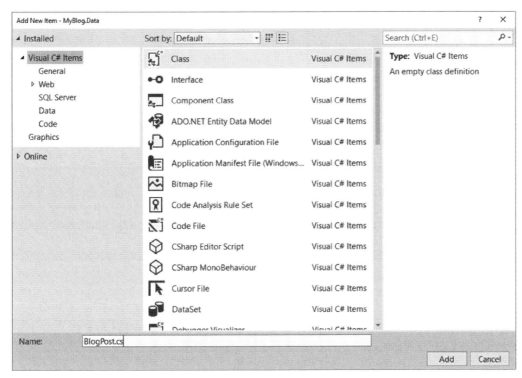

Figure 3.1 – Visual Studio's Add New Item dialog

7. Right-click on the Models folder and select **Add | Class**. Name the class Category.cs and press **Add**.

8. Right-click on the Models folder and select **Add | Class**. Name the class Tag.cs and press **Add**.

9. Open BlogPost.cs and replace the content with the following code:

```
using System;
using System.Collections.Generic;
using MyBlog.Data.Interfaces;

namespace MyBlog.Data.Models
{
    public class BlogPost : IMyBlogItem
    {
        public int Id { get; set; }
        public string Title { get; set; }
        public string Text { get; set; }
```

```
        public DateTime PublishDate { get; set; }
        public Category Category { get; set; }
        public ICollection<Tag> Tags { get; set; }
    }
}
```

In this class, we define the content of our blog post. We need an `Id` to identify the blog post, a title, some text (the article), and a publishing date. We also have a `category` property in the class, which is of the `Category` type. In this case, a blog post can only have one category. A blog post can also contain zero or more tags. We define the `Tag` property with `ICollection<Tag>`.

10. Open `Category.cs` and replace the content with the following code:

```
using System.Collections.Generic;
using MyBlog.Data.Interfaces;


namespace MyBlog.Data.Models
{
    public class Category : IMyBlogItem
    {
        public int Id { get; set; }
        public string Name { get; set; }
        public ICollection<BlogPost> BlogPosts { get;
          set; }
    }
}
```

The `Category` class contains `Id`, `Name`, and a collection of blog posts. We can have many blog posts that have the same category, so the category object can have many blog posts connected to it.

11. Open `Tag.cs` and replace the content with the following code:

```
using System;
using System.Collections.Generic;
using MyBlog.Data.Interfaces;


namespace MyBlog.Data.Models
{
```

```
        public class Tag : IMyBlogItem
        {
            public int Id {get; set; }
            public string Name { get; set; }
            public ICollection<BlogPost> BlogPosts { get;
                set; }
        }
    }
```

The Tag class contains an Id, Name, and a collection of blog posts. By adding a collection of blog posts in the Tag class and a collection of tags in the BlogPost class, Entity Framework will understand that there should be a many-to-many relationship and will automatically create a reference table that connects the two tables (BlogPosts and Tags).

This is one of the things that makes code-first such an excellent technology to use; we as developers can focus on the business objects and how they relate, and Entity Framework can create the database and the relations between the tables.

Now we have created a couple of classes that we will use. I have kept the complexity of these classes down to a minimum since we are here to learn about Blazor.

We also need to create a database context, which is a way to access each of these classes (or tables) in the database.

Creating the Database Context

The Database Context is the class from which we will access the database. This is how we create one:

1. Right-click on the **MyBlog.Data** project and select **Add | Class**. Name the class MyBlogDBContext.cs.

2. Open the new MyBlogDBContext.cs file and replace the content with the following code:

```
using Microsoft.EntityFrameworkCore;
using Microsoft.EntityFrameworkCore.Design;
using MyBlog.Data.Models;

namespace MyBlog.Data
{
```

```
public class MyBlogDbContext : DbContext
{
    public MyBlogDbContext(DbContextOptions
        <MyBlogDbContext> context) : base(context)
    {

    }

    public DbSet<BlogPost> BlogPosts { get; set; }
    public DbSet<Category> Categories { get; set; }
    public DbSet<Tag> Tags { get; set; }
}

public class MyBlogDbContextFactory :
    IDesignTimeDbContextFactory<MyBlogDbContext>
{
    public MyBlogDbContext CreateDbContext
        (string[] args)
    {
        var optionsBuilder = new
            DbContextOptionsBuilder<MyBlogDbContext>();
        optionsBuilder.UseSqlite("Data Source =
                                        test.db");

        return new MyBlogDbContext
            (optionsBuilder.Options);
    }
}
```

There are two classes in this file: MyBlogDbContext and
MyBlogDbContextFactory. MyBlogDbContext is DbContext for
our database, the class that lets us access the database. The second class
MyBlogDbContextFactory is for configuring our database while we are
creating the migrations (we'll get back to migrations in the next step), so it is just
code that will run when we run migrations, never in production.

> **Important note**
>
> Normally, I never have multiple classes in the same file, but in this case the `MyBlogDbContextFactory` class is only used when we create migrations and is the code for configuring our `MyBlogDbContext`.

In previous versions of Entity Framework Core, we had to manually specify many-to-many relationships (such as with `Tags`) in `DbContext`, or create classes that map the relationship between the object/tables. In Entity Framework Core 5, we don't even have to specify that relationship, it is all done for us.

Since `BlogPost` has a collection of `Tags` and `Tags` has a collection of `BlogPosts`, Entity Framework will automatically create the table containing the relationship.

Next, we have to create the migration.

Creating a migration

A **migration** is a piece of code for setting up the database, including creating the database and creating/updating tables. We can do this from within Visual Studio (or using the command line, which I think is easier):

1. Start PowerShell and navigate to our `MyBlog.Data` folder.

2. If this is the first time we start PowerShell, we might need to launch it as an administrator and run the following command:

```
Set-ExecutionPolicy -ExecutionPolicy Unrestricted -Scope
LocalMachine
```

   This will make sure we can run commands in PowerShell. Note that we can also use the VS 2019 Command Prompt instead of PowerShell.

3. To install the Entity Framework tools run the following command:

```
dotnet tool install --global dotnet-ef
```

4. Now it is time to create our migration. A migration contains the differences between the database now (which is an empty database in our case) and the changes we have done in our model classes and our `MyBlogDbContext`.

5. To create a migration run the following command:

```
dotnet ef migrations add InitialDatabaseMigration
```

We can also use the Package Manager Console inside Visual Studio to do run these commands. We can get to the Package Manager Console through **View | Other Windows | Package Manager Console**.

We are using the `dotnet` command together with the Entity Framework tool we installed in *step 2* to add a migration called `InitialDatabaseMigration`. If we go back to Visual Studio we will see that in the **MyBlog.Data** project there is now a `Migrations` folder containing two files – `MyBlogDbContextModelSnapshot.cs`, and one that starts with the date and ends with `_InitialDatabaseMigration.cs`. These two files contain generated code to create the database and tables for our models.

Now we have created our database model and our data models.

The next step is to create a simple API; even though we can access the database directly when we are running the Blazor Server project, we will make sure to have a small layer between the Blazor code and database access. This is so that we can reuse our code for both Blazor WebAssembly and the Blazor Server project.

Creating an interface

In this section, we will create an API. Since we are currently working with Blazor Server, we can access the database directly, so the API we create here will have a direct connection to the database:

1. Right-click in the `Interfaces` folder and select **Add | Class**.

2. In the list of different templates, select **Interface** and name it `IMyBlogApi.cs`.

3. Open `IMyBlogApi.cs` and replace its content with the following:

```
using System.Collections.Generic;
using System.Threading.Tasks;
using MyBlog.Data.Models;


namespace MyBlog.Data.Interfaces
{
    public interface IMyBlogApi
    {
        Task<int> GetBlogPostCountAsync();
        Task<List<BlogPost>> GetBlogPostsAsync(int
            numberofposts, int startindex);
```

```
        Task<List<Category>> GetCategoriesAsync();
        Task<List<Tag>> GetTagsAsync();


        Task<BlogPost> GetBlogPostAsync(int id);
        Task<Category> GetCategoryAsync(int id);
        Task<Tag> GetTagAsync(int id);


        Task<BlogPost> SaveBlogPostAsync(BlogPost item);
        Task<Category> SaveCategoryAsync(Category item);
        Task<Tag> SaveTagAsync(Tag item);


        Task DeleteBlogPostAsync(BlogPost item);
        Task DeleteCategoryAsync(Category item);
        Task DeleteTagAsync(Tag item);


    }

}
```

The interface contains all the methods we need to get, save, and delete blog posts, tags, and categories.

Now we have an interface for the API with the methods we need to list blog posts, tags, and categories, as well as saving (creating/updating), and deleting them. Next, let's implement the interface.

Implementing the interface

To implement the interface for the Blazor Server implementation, follow these steps:

1. First, we need to create a class. Right-click on the **MyBlog.Data** project, select **Add** | **Class**, and name the class `MyBlogApiServerSide.cs`.

2. Open `MyBlogApiServerSide.cs` and replace the code with the following:

```
using System.Collections.Generic;
using System.Linq;
using System.Threading.Tasks;
using Microsoft.EntityFrameworkCore;
using Microsoft.EntityFrameworkCore.Internal;
using MyBlog.Data.Interfaces;
```

```
using MyBlog.Data.Models;
namespace MyBlog.Data
{
    public class MyBlogApiServerSide : IMyBlogApi
    {


    }
}
```

We start by adding the namespaces we need and then create a class that implements the `ImyBlogApi` interface.

3. Add the following code to `MyBlogApiServerSide.cs` inside of the class.

```
IDbContextFactory<MyBlogDbContext> factory;
public MyBlogApiServerSide
   (IDbContextFactory<MyBlogDbContext> factory)
{
    this.factory = factory;
}
```

To access the data we will add our `DbContext`, but we won't add it directly. We will use a `DbContextFactory`; it is recommended for Blazor to use the data contexts in a unit of work, which means that we should create the data context and then dispose of it for every data access we do.

`DbContext` is not thread-safe (which means that if multiple threads access the same `DbContext`, we will experience problems such as exceptions when running more than one query at a time). Luckily the overhead of creating a new object is quite small and there is a class, `DbContextFactory`, that will help us with that.

We first create a private `IDbContextFactory` and use our data context as a generic parameter; this is the class that will help us quickly create the data context. In the constructor, we pass in an `IDbContextFactory`; this is where the dependency injection mechanism will deliver a factory to us.

We will talk more about dependency injection in *Chapter 4, Understanding Basic Blazor Components*.

4. Add the following code to our `MyBlogApiServerSide.cs` just under the code we just added in the class:

```
public async Task<BlogPost> GetBlogPostAsync(int id)
{
    using var context = factory.CreateDbContext();
    return await context.BlogPosts.Include
      (p=>p.Category).Include(p=>p.Tags).
        FirstOrDefaultAsync(p => p.Id == id);
}
public async Task<int> GetBlogPostCountAsync()
{
    using var context = factory.CreateDbContext();
    return await context.BlogPosts.CountAsync();
}
public async Task<List<BlogPost>> GetBlogPostsAsync(int
numberofposts, int startindex)
{
    using var context = factory.CreateDbContext();
    return await context.BlogPosts.OrderByDescending
      (p=>p.PublishDate).Skip(startindex).Take
        (numberofposts).ToListAsync();
}
```

Take a look at the `GetBlogPostAsync` method. It starts with `using var context = factory.CreateDbContext();`, which used the factory to create an instance of our data context. The `using` keyword at the beginning of the line makes sure to dispose of the factory as soon as the method is done.

We get one single blogpost from the database and use `.Include(p=>p.Category)` and `.Include(p=>p.Tags)` to retrieve the related data for those properties.

All the `get` methods we just implemented look pretty much the same (they return all items or a specific item by `Id`) except for `GetBlogPostsAsync`, which also has a start index and the number of posts we want to get, so that we can get a range of posts.

5. Add the following code under the code we just added:

```
public async Task<List<Category>> GetCategoriesAsync()
{
    using var context = factory.CreateDbContext();
    return await context.Categories.ToListAsync();
}
public async Task<Category> GetCategoryAsync(int id)
{
    using var context = factory.CreateDbContext();
    return await context.Categories.Include(p =>
        p.BlogPosts).FirstOrDefaultAsync(c=>c.Id==id);
}
```

This is the code to get categories, which works in the same way as getting the blog posts. In this case, we don't have a way to just get a few of them (as we have with blog posts) since they are probably very few in number.

6. Next, we do the same thing for tags. Add the following code just under the code we added in *step 5*:

```
public async Task<Tag> GetTagAsync(int id)
{
    using var context = factory.CreateDbContext();
    return await context.Tags.Include(p =>
        p.BlogPosts).FirstOrDefaultAsync(c => c.Id == id);
}
public async Task<List<Tag>> GetTagsAsync()
{
    using var context = factory.CreateDbContext();
    return await context.Tags.ToListAsync();
}
```

These *steps 4* to *6* are all the methods that get data from the API. Since all the methods we just added get one or more items from the database, I won't go through them all, but I will point out some important parts.

Now it's time to implement the `delete` methods.

7. Add the following code just under the code we just added in *step 6*:

```
private async Task DeleteItem(IMyBlogItem item)
{
    using var context = factory.CreateDbContext();
    context.Remove(item);
    await context.SaveChangesAsync();
}
```

To avoid repeating the delete code for all three data classes, we have added a helper method that will delete any object we pass to the method. Since all our data classes implement IMyBlogItem, we can have one delete method that handles all deletions.

8. We could have done the same in our API, just having one delete method, but there might be a moment where we want to handle deletions differently depending on the type. In the IMyBlogApi we have different delete methods for each type.

In MyBlogApiServerSide add the following code beneath the code we just added:

```
public async Task DeleteBlogPostAsync(BlogPost item)
{
    await DeleteItem(item);
}
public async Task DeleteCategoryAsync(Category item)
{
    await DeleteItem(item);
}
public async Task DeleteTagAsync(Tag item)
{
    await DeleteItem(item);
}
```

As we can see, the implementations of these methods all call the DeleteItem method.

9. Add the following code beneath the code we just added:

```
private async Task<IMyBlogItem> SaveItem(IMyBlogItem
item)
{
```

```csharp
        using var context = factory.CreateDbContext();
        if (item.Id == 0)
        {
            context.Add(item);
        }
        else
        {
            if (item is BlogPost)
            {
                var post = item as BlogPost;
                var currentpost = await
                  context.BlogPosts.Include
                    (p => p.Category).Include(p =>
                      p.Tags).FirstOrDefaultAsync
                        (p => p.Id == post.Id);
                currentpost.PublishDate = post.PublishDate;
                currentpost.Title = post.Title;
                currentpost.Text = post.Text;
                var ids = post.Tags.Select(t => t.Id);
                currentpost.Tags = context.Tags.Where(t =>
                  ids.Contains(t.Id)).ToList();
                currentpost.Category = await
                  context.Categories.FirstOrDefaultAsync
                    (c => c.Id == post.Category.Id);
                await context.SaveChangesAsync();
            }
            else
            {
                context.Entry(item).State =
                  EntityState.Modified;
            }
        }
        await context.SaveChangesAsync();
        return item;
}
public async Task<BlogPost> SaveBlogPostAsync(BlogPost
item)
{
```

```
        return (await SaveItem(item)) as BlogPost;
    }
    public async Task<Category> SaveCategoryAsync(Category
    item)
    {
        return (await SaveItem(item)) as Category;
    }
    public async Task<Tag> SaveTagAsync(Tag item)
    {
        return (await SaveItem(item)) as Tag;
    }
```

If the Id is 0, we add item to context, using the context.Add method to add the item to the database. If the Id is not 0, we assume that the item is already in the database and therefore should only be attached (connected) to the database.

Since BlogPost refers to other database objects, we need to load them as well. While writing this method it became apparent that this might not be the best solution for our scenario, but I wanted to show the possibility so I decided to keep it like this.

When an item has been saved, it will be returned (possibly with an updated Id if the item is created).

Our database and data models are done!

In the end, there will be five tables in the database. We know three of the tables, since they correspond to the classes we have created:

- BlogPost, containing our blog posts
- Categories, containing our categories
- Tags, containing our tag

The other two tables are as follows:

- BlogPostTag, containing the relation between Tags and BlogPost
- __EFMigrationsHistory, which contains and tracks the migrations

The `BlogPostTag` table is created for us since Entity Framework Core has identified a many-to-many relationship. Migrations use the `__EFMigrationsHistory` table to know what migrations have already been executed on the table.

The next step is to add and configure the Blazor project to use the database.

Adding the DbContext to Blazor

Using `DbContext`, we will be able to access the data from our database. We need to add `DbContext` to our Blazor project to be able to access the data from Blazor:

1. Beneath the `MyBlogServerSide` node in **Solution Explorer**, find **Dependencies**. Right-click on **Dependencies** and select **Add Project reference**.

2. In the list of projects, check the **MyBlog.Data** project and click **OK**:

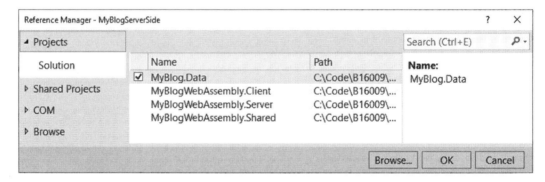

Figure 3.2 – Visual Studio Reference manager

Now we have all the external items in place, including the external NuGet packages and a reference to our **MyBlog.Data** project.

3. In the **MyBlogServerSide** project, open the `Startup.cs` file and add the following `using` statements:

```
using Microsoft.EntityFrameworkCore;
using MyBlog.Data;
using MyBlog.Data.Interfaces;
using MyBlogServerSide.Data;
```

4. Add following code to the `ConfigureServices` method:

```
services.AddDbContextFactory<MyBlogDbContext>(opt => opt.
UseSqlite($"Data Source=../MyBlog.db"));
services.AddScoped<IMyBlogApi, MyBlogApiServerSide>();
```

This is how we configure the database access. We add a `DbContextFactory` service and send in our `MyBlogDbContext` class, so when we ask for `IDbFactory<MyBlogDbContext>` it will return a `DbFactory` instance capable of instantiating a `MyBlogDbContext` class. In *Chapter 4, Understanding Basic Blazor Components*, we will explore dependency injection further and will explain what we just did in more depth.

We also add a configuration for our database, in this case, a SQLite database. Then we add `IMyBlogApi` as scoped, so whenever we ask the dependency injection for `IMyBlogApi`, it will return a `MyBlogApiServerSide` instance.

5. Finally, we need to make sure the database gets created and that the migration (the code that sets up the database) runs. In `Startup.cs`, edit the `Configure` method so it starts like this:

```
public void Configure(IApplicationBuilder
app, IWebHostEnvironment env,
IDbContextFactory<MyBlogDbContext> factory)
{
    factory.CreateDbContext().Database.Migrate();
```

The method has an `IDbContextFactory<MyBlogDbContext>` parameter that will trigger the dependency injection (that we configured in the previous step) and deliver `DbContextFactory<MyBlogDbContext>`. We then create an instance of our `DbContext` and execute the `Migrate` method; this will create the database (if it doesn't exist) and run the migration (in this case, creating all the tables and relations).

Now we can use our API to access the database in our Blazor Server project.

Summary

In this chapter, we learned about Entity Framework Core 5. We created a database using SQLite and used migrations to create the database. Most applications use some kind of data, so knowing how to use a database together with Blazor is very important.

We also created an API to access the database (which will become important when we take a look at sharing resources between projects in *Chapter 9, Sharing Code and Resources*).

In the next chapter, we will learn about components, particularly the built-in components in Blazor templates. We will also create our first component using the API and database we created in this chapter.

4

Understanding Basic Blazor Components

In this chapter, we will take a look at the components that come with the Blazor template, as well as starting to build our own components. Knowing the different techniques used for building Blazor websites will help us when we start building our components.

Blazor uses components for most things, so we will use the knowledge we get from this chapter throughout the book.

We will start this chapter with theory and end by creating a component to show some blog posts using the API we created in the previous chapter, *Chapter 3, Introducing Entity Framework Core.*

In this chapter, we will cover the following topics:

- Exploring components
- Learning Razor syntax
- Parameters
- Writing our first component

Technical requirements

In this chapter, we will start building our components, and for that, you'll need the code we created in the previous chapter, *Chapter 3, Introducing Entity Framework Core*. If you have followed the instructions in the previous chapters, then you are good to go; if not, then make sure you clone/download the repo. The starting point for this chapter can be found in the `ch3` folder and the finished code in `ch4`.

You can find the source code for this chapter's end result at `https://github.com/PacktPublishing/Web-Development-with-Blazor/tree/master/Chapter04`.

For this chapter, we will be working with the Blazor Server project so make sure to right-click on the **MyBlogServerSide** project and select **Set as Startup Project**.

Exploring components

In Blazor, a **component** is a `.razor` file that can contain a small, isolated functionality (code and markup) or can be used as a page itself. A component can host other components as well. This chapter will show us how components work and how to use them.

There are three different ways we can create a component:

- Using Razor syntax, with code and HTML sharing the same file
- Using a code-behind file together with a `.razor` file
- Using only a code-behind file

We will go through the different options. The templates we will go through next all use the first option, `.razor` files where we have a mix of code and HTML in the same file.

The components in the template are as follows:

- `counter`
- `FetchData`

counter

The counter page shows a button and a counter; if we press the button, the counter increases. We will now break the page apart so it is easier to understand.

At the top of the page is the @page directive, which makes it possible to route to the component directly, as we can see in this code:

```
@page "/counter"
```

If we start the MyBlogServerSide project and add /counter to the end of the URL, we see that we can directly access the component by using its route. We can make the route take parameters as well, but we will come back to that in a little while.

Next, let's explore the code. To add code to the page, we use the @code statement, and within that statement, we can add ordinary C# code, as shown:

```
@code {
    private int currentCount = 0;
    private void IncrementCount()
    {
        currentCount++;
    }
}
```

In the preceding code block, we have a private currentCount variable that is set to 0. Then we have a method called IncrementCount(), which increments the currentCount variable by 1.

We show the current value by using the @ sign. In Razor, the @ sign indicates that it is time for some code:

```
<p>Current count: @currentCount</p>
```

As we can see, Razor is very smart because it understands when the code stops and the markup continues, so there is no need to add something extra to transition from code to the markup (more on that in the next section).

As we can see in the preceding example, we are mixing HTML tags with @ currentCount and Razor understands the difference. Next, we have the button that is a trigger for changing the value:

```
<button class="btn btn-primary" @onclick="IncrementCount">Click me</button>
```

This is an HTML button with a Bootstrap class on it (to make it look a bit nicer). @ onclick is binding the button's onclick event to the IncrementCount() method. If we were to use onclick, without the @, it would refer to the JavaScript event and not work. So, when we press the button, it will call the IncrementCount() method (depicted by **1** in *Figure 4.1*), the method increments the variable (depicted by **2**), and by changing the variable, the UI will automatically be updated (depicted by **3**), as shown in *Figure 4.1*:

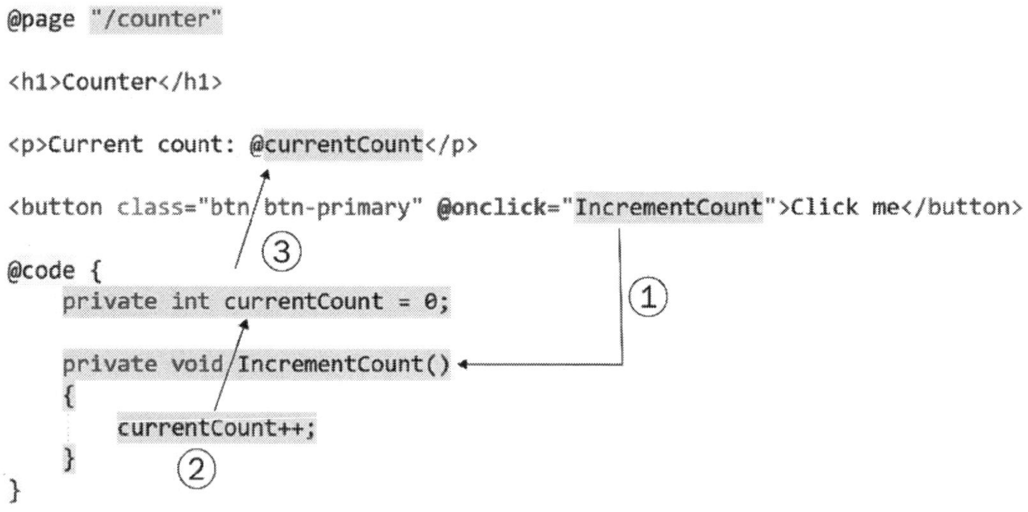

```
@page "/counter"

<h1>Counter</h1>

<p>Current count: @currentCount</p>

<button class="btn btn-primary" @onclick="IncrementCount">Click me</button>
                        ③                  ①
@code {
    private int currentCount = 0;

    private void IncrementCount()
    {
        currentCount++;
    }       ②
}
```

Figure 4.1 – The flow of the counter component

The counter component is implemented the same way for both Blazor WebAssembly and Blazor Server. The FetchData component has two different implementations, simply because the Blazor Server project can access the server data directly and Blazor WebAssembly needs to access it through a web API.

We use the same approach with our API so that we get a feel for how we can leverage **Dependency Injection** (**DI**) and also connect to a database directly when we use Blazor Server.

FetchData

The next component we will take a look at is the `FetchData` component. It's located in the `Pages/FetchData.razor` folder.

The main implementation of the `FetchData` component looks the same for both Blazor WebAssembly and Blazor Server. The top rows of the files, as well as the way it gets data, differ in the two versions. For Blazor Server, it looks like this:

```
@page "/fetchdata"
@using MyBlogServerSide.Data
@inject WeatherForecastService ForecastService
```

It defines a route, adds a namespace, and injects a service. We can find the service in the `Data` folder in the `MyBlogServerSide` project.

The service is a class that creates some random forecast data; the code looks like this:

```
public class WeatherForecastService
{
    private static readonly string[] Summaries = new[]
    {
        "Freezing", "Bracing", "Chilly", "Cool", "Mild",
        "Warm", "Balmy", "Hot", "Sweltering", "Scorching"
    };
    public Task<WeatherForecast[]> GetForecastAsync
        (DateTime startDate)
    {
        var rng = new Random();
        return Task.FromResult(Enumerable.Range(1,
            5).Select(index => new WeatherForecast
        {
            Date = startDate.AddDays(index),
            TemperatureC = rng.Next(-20, 55),
            Summary = Summaries[rng.Next(Summaries.Length)]
        }).ToArray());
    }
}
```

As we can see, it generates summaries and randomizes temperatures.

In the `code` section of the `FetchData` component, we will find the code that calls the service:

```
private WeatherForecast[] forecasts;
protected override async Task OnInitializedAsync()
{
    forecasts = await
      ForecastService.GetForecastAsync(DateTime.Now);
}
```

The code will get the data from the service and populate an array of `WeatherForecast` called `forecasts`.

In the `MyBlogWebAssembly.Client` project, things look a bit different. First of all, the top rows of the file look like this:

```
@page "/fetchdata"
@using MyBlogWebAssembly.Shared
@inject HttpClient Http
```

The code defines a route using a `page` directive, adds a namespace to our shared library, and injects `HttpClient` instead of the service. `HttpClient` is used to get the data from the server, which is a more realistic real-world scenario.

`HttpClient` is defined in the `Program.cs` file and has the same base address as the `MyBlogWebAssembly.Server` project since the server project is hosting the client project.

Getting the data looks like this:

```
private WeatherForecast[] forecasts;
protected override async Task OnInitializedAsync()
{
    forecasts = await Http.GetFromJsonAsync
      <WeatherForecast[]>("WeatherForecast");
}
```

The code will get the data and populate an array of `WeatherForecast` called `forecasts`. But instead of getting the data from the service, we are making a call to the `"WeatherForecast"` URL. We can find the web API in the `MyBlogWebAddembly.Server` project.

The controller (`Controllers/WeatherForcastController.cs`) looks like this (with a lot of similarities to the service):

```
[ApiController]
[Route("[controller]")]
public class WeatherForecastController : ControllerBase
{
    private static readonly string[] Summaries = new[]
    {
        "Freezing", "Bracing", "Chilly", "Cool", "Mild",
        "Warm", "Balmy", "Hot", "Sweltering", "Scorching"
    };
    private readonly ILogger<WeatherForecastController> logger;
    public WeatherForecastController
        (ILogger<WeatherForecastController> logger)
    {
        this.logger = logger;
    }
    [HttpGet]
    public IEnumerable<WeatherForecast> Get()
    {
        var rng = new Random();
        return Enumerable.Range(1, 5).Select(index => new
            WeatherForecast
        {
            Date = DateTime.Now.AddDays(index),
            TemperatureC = rng.Next(-20, 55),
            Summary = Summaries[rng.Next(Summaries.Length)]
        })
        .ToArray();
    }
}
```

It looks pretty much the same as the service does but is implemented as a web API instead. As the data looks the same in both versions, getting the data (in both cases) will populate an array with weather forecast data.

In `Pages/FetchData.razor`, the code for showing the weather data looks like this in both Blazor WebAssembly and Blazor Server:

```
<h1>Weather forecast</h1>
<p>This component demonstrates fetching data from a service.</p>
@if (forecasts == null)
{
    <p><em>Loading...</em></p>
}
else
{
    <table class="table">
        <thead>
            <tr>
                <th>Date</th>
                <th>Temp. (C)</th>
                <th>Temp. (F)</th>
                <th>Summary</th>
            </tr>
        </thead>
        <tbody>
            @foreach (var forecast in forecasts)
            {
                <tr>
                    <td>@forecast.Date.ToShortDateString()
                    </td>
                    <td>@forecast.TemperatureC</td>
                    <td>@forecast.TemperatureF</td>
                    <td>@forecast.Summary</td>
                </tr>
            }
        </tbody>
```

```
        </table>
    }
```

As we can see, by using the Razor syntax, we are seamlessly mixing code with HTML. The code checks whether there is any data – if yes, then it will render the table; if not, it will show a loading message. We have full control over the HTML, and Blazor will not add anything to the generated HTML.

There are component libraries that can make this process a bit simpler, which we will take a look at in the next chapter, *Chapter 5, Creating Advanced Blazor Components*.

Now that we know how the sample template is implemented, it is time to dive a little bit deeper into the Razor syntax itself.

Learning Razor syntax

One of the things I like about the Razor syntax is that it is easy to mix code and HTML tags. This section will be a lot of theory to help us get to know the Razor syntax.

To transition from HTML to code (C#), we use the @ symbol. There are a couple of ways we can add code to our file:

- Razor code blocks
- Implicit Razor expressions
- Explicit Razor expressions
- Expression encoding
- Directives

Razor code blocks

We have already seen some code blocks. A `code` block looks like this:

```
@code {
    //your code here
}
```

If we wish, we can skip the `code` keyword, like so:

```
@{
    //your code here
}
```

Inside those curly braces, we can mix HTML and code like this:

```
@{
    void RenderName(string name)
    {
        <p>Name: <strong>@name</strong></p>
    }
    RenderName("Steve Sandersson");
    RenderName("Daniel Roth");
}
```

Notice how the `RenderName()` method just transitions from code into the paragraph tags and back to code; this is an implicit transition.

If we want to output text without having an HTML tag, we can use the `text` tag instead of using the paragraph tags, as shown in the following example:

```
<text>Name: <strong>@name</strong></text>
```

This would render the same result as shown in the previous code but without the paragraph tags. The `text` tag won't be rendered.

Implicit Razor expressions

Implicit Razor expressions are when we add code inside HTML tags.

We have already seen this in the `FetchData` example:

```
<td>@forecast.Summary</td>
```

We start with a `<td>` tag, then use the @ symbol to switch to C#, and then back to HTML for the end tag. We can use the `await` keyword together with a method call, but other than that, implicit Razor expressions cannot contain any spaces.

We cannot call a generic method using implicit expressions since `<>` would be interpreted as HTML. Hence, to solve this issue, we can use explicit expressions.

Explicit Razor expressions

We can use explicit Razor expressions if we want to use spaces in the code. Simply write the code with the @ symbol followed by parentheses, ( ). So, it would look like this: @().

In this sample, we subtract 7 days from the current date:

```
<td>@(DateTime.Now - TimeSpan.FromDays(7))</td>
```

We can also use explicit Razor expressions to concatenate text; for example, we can concatenate text and code like this:

```
<td>Temp@(forecast.TemperatureC)</td>
```

The output would then be `<td>Temp42</td>`.

Using explicit expressions, we can easily call generic methods by using this syntax:

```
<td>@(MyGenericMethod<string>())</td>
```

The Razor engine knows whether we are using code or not. It also makes sure to encode strings to HTML when outputting it to the browser, which is called **expression encoding**.

Expression encoding

If we have HTML as a string, it will be escaped by default. Take this code, for example:

```
@("<span>Hello World</span>")
```

The rendered HTML would look like this:

```
&lt;span&gt;Hello World&lt;/span&gt;
```

To output the actual HTML from a string (something we want to do later on), you can use this syntax:

```
@((MarkupString)"<span>Hello World</span>")
```

By using `MarkupString`, the output will be HTML, which will show the HTML tag span. In some cases, one line of code isn't enough; then we can use code blocks.

Directives

There are a bunch of directives that change the way a component gets parsed or can enable functionality. These are reserved keywords that follow the @ symbol. We will go through the most common and useful ones.

We can use code-behind to write our code to get a bit more separation between the code and layout. I find that it is pretty nice to have the layout and the code inside of the same `.razor` file. Later in this chapter, we will look at how to use code-behind instead of using Razor syntax for everything.

In the following examples, we will look at how we would do the same thing using code-behind.

Adding an attribute

To add an attribute to our page, we can use the `attribute` directive:

```
@attribute [Authorize]
```

If we were using a code-behind file, we would use the following syntax instead:

```
[Authorize]
```

Adding an interface

To implement an interface (`IDisposable` in this case), we would use the following code:

```
@implements IDisposable
```

Then we would implement the methods the interface needs in a `@code{}` section.

To do the same in a code-behind scenario, we would add the interface after the class name, as shown in the following example:

```
public class SomeClass : IDisposable {}
```

Inheriting

To inherit another class, we should use the following code:

```
@inherits TypeNameOfClassToInheritFrom
```

To do the same in a code-behind scenario, we would add the class we want to inherit from after the class name:

```
public class SomeClass : TypeNameOfClassToInheritFrom {}
```

Generics

We can define our component as a generic component.

Generics make it possible for us to make components that let us define the data type, so the component works with any data type.

To define a component as a generic component, we add the `@typeparam` directive; then we can use the type in the code of the component like this:

```
@typeparam TItem
@code
{
    [Parameter]
    public List<TItem> Data { get; set; }
}
```

Generics are super powerful when creating reusable components and we will come back to generics in *Chapter 6, Building Forms with Validation.*

Changing the layout

If we want to have a specific layout for a page (not the default one specified in the app. razor file), we can use the `@layout` directive:

```
@layout AnotherLayoutFile
```

This way, our component will use the layout file specified (this only works for components that have the `@page` directive).

Setting a namespace

By default, the namespace of the component will be the name of the default namespace of our project, plus the folder structure. If we want our component to be in a specific namespace, we can use the following:

```
@namespace Another.NameSpace
```

Setting a route

We have already touched on the `@page` directive. If we want our component to be directly accessed using a URL, we can use the `@page` directive:

```
@page "/theurl"
```

The URL can contain parameters, subfolders, and much more, which we will come back to later in this chapter.

Adding a using statement

To add a namespace to our component, we can use the @using directive:

```
@using System.IO
```

If there are namespaces that we use in many of our components, then we can add them to the _Imports.razor file instead. This way, it will be available in all the components we create.

Now we know more about how Razor syntax works. Don't worry, we will have plenty of time to practice it. There is one more directive that I haven't covered in this section and that is inject. We have seen it a couple of times already but to cover all the bases, we first need to understand what DI is and how it works, which we will see in the next section.

Understanding dependency injection

DI is a software pattern and a technique to implement **Inversion of Control (IoC)**.

IoC is a generic term that means we can indicate that the class needs a class instance, instead of letting our classes instantiate an object. We can say that our class wants either a specific class or a specific interface. The creation of the class is somewhere else, and it is up to IoC what class it will create.

When it comes to DI, it is a form of IoC where an object (class instance) is passed through constructors, parameters, or service lookups.

In Blazor, we can configure DI by providing the way to instantiate an object. In Blazor, this is a key architecture pattern that we should use. We have seen a couple of references to it already, for example, in Startup.cs:

```
services.AddSingleton<WeatherForecastService>();
```

Here, we say that if any class wants WeatherForecastService, the application should instantiate an object of the WeatherForecastService type. In this case, we don't use an interface; instead, we could have created an interface and configured it like this:

```
services.AddSingleton<IWeatherForecastService
,WeatherForecastService>();
```

In this case, if a class asks for an instance of `IWeatherForecastService`, the app would instantiate a `WeatherForecastService` object and return it. We did this in the previous chapter, *Chapter 3, Introducing Entity Framework Core*. We created an `IMyBlogApi` interface that returned an instance of `MyBlogApiServerSide`; when we implement the WebAssembly version, the DI will return another class instead.

There are many advantages to using DI. Our dependencies are loosely coupled, which means that we don't instantiate another class in our class. Instead, we ask for an instance, which makes it easier to write tests, as well as changing implementations depending on platforms.

Any external dependencies will be a lot clearer since we need to pass them into the class. We also can set the way we should instantiate the object in a central place. We configure the DI in `Startup.cs` (for Blazor Server) and `Program.cs` (for WebAssembly).

We can configure the creation of objects in different ways, such as the following:

- Singleton
- Scoped
- Transient

Singleton

When we use singleton, the object will be the same for all users of our site. The object will only be created once.

To configure a singleton service, use the following:

```
services.AddSingleton<IWeatherForecastService
,WeatherForecastService>();
```

We should use singleton when we want to share our object with all the users of our site but beware the state is shared so do not store any data connected to one particular user or user preferences, because it will affect all the users.

Scoped

When we use scoped, a new object will be created, once for each connection, and since Blazor Server needs a connection to work, it will be the same object as long as the user has a connection. WebAssembly does not have the concept of scoped since there is no connection being made, so all the code is running inside of the user's web browser. If we use scoped, it will work the same way as a singleton for Blazor WebAssembly. The recommendation is still to use scoped if the idea is to scope the service to the current user.

To configure a scoped service, use the following:

```
services.AddScoped<IWeatherForecastService
,WeatherForecastService>();
```

We should use scoped if we have data that belongs to the user. We can keep the user's state by using scoped objects. More on that in *Chapter 11, Managing State.*

Transient

By using transient, a new object will be created every time we ask for it.

To configure a transient service, use the following:

```
services.AddTransient<IWeatherForecastService
,WeatherForecastService>();
```

We should use transient if we don't need to keep any state and we don't mind the object being created every time we ask for it.

Now that we know how to configure a service, we need to start using the service by injecting it.

Injecting the service

There are three ways to inject a service.

We have already seen the first method in the FetchData component code. We can use the @inject directive in the Razor file:

```
@inject WeatherForecastService ForecastService
```

This will make sure we have access to WeatherForecastService in our component.

The second way is to create a property by adding the Inject attribute if we are using code-behind:

```
[Inject]
public WeatherForecastService ForecastService { get; set; }
```

The third way is if we want to inject a service into another service, then we need to inject the services using the constructor:

```
public class MyService
{
```

```
    public MyService(WeatherForecastService
        weatherForecastService)
    {
    }
}
```

Now we know how DI works and why we should use it.

In this chapter, we have mentioned code-behind a couple of times. In the next section, we will take a look at how we can use code-behind together with Razor files, and even skip the Razor files altogether.

Figuring out where to put the code

We have seen examples of writing code directly in the Razor file. I prefer doing that unless the code gets too complicated.

There are four ways we can write our components:

- In the Razor file
- In a partial class
- Inheriting a class
- Only code

In the Razor file

If we are writing a file that is not that complex, it would be nice to not have to switch files when writing components. As we already covered in this chapter, we can use the @ code directive to add code directly to our Razor file. If we want to move the code to a code-behind file, then it is only the directives that we need to change. For the rest of the code, we can just move to the code-behind class. When I started with Blazor, it felt strange to write code and markup in the same file, but I would suggest that you try it out when you develop your web apps.

But many developers prefer code-behind, separating the code from the layout. For that, we can use a partial class.

In a partial class

We can create a partial class with the same filename as the Razor file and just add .cs.

If you have downloaded the source code (or we can check the code on GitHub) for *Chapter 3, Introducing Entity Framework Core*, you can take a look at FetchDataWithCodeBehind.razor.cs in the MyBlogServerSide project. I have moved all the code to the code-behind file; the result when compiling this will be the same as if we kept the code in the Razor file. It is just a matter of preference.

The code-behind looks like this:

```
public partial class FetchDataWithCodeBehind
{
    [Inject]
    public WeatherForecastService ForecastService { get; set; }
    private WeatherForecast[] forecasts;
    protected override async Task OnInitializedAsync()
    {
        forecasts = await ForecastService.GetForecastAsync
            (DateTime.Now);
    }
}
```

As we can see, instead of using @inject, we are using [Inject]. Other than that, I have just copied the code over from the Razor file.

This is not the only way to use a code-behind file; we can also inherit from a code-behind file.

Inheriting a class

We can also create a class called something completely different (the common thing is to call it the same thing as the Razor file and add Model at the end) and inherit it in our Razor file. For that to work, we need to inherit from ComponentBase. In the case of a partial class, the class already inherits from ComponentBase since the Razor file does that.

Any fields need to be protected or public (not private) for the page to be able to access them. My recommendation is to use the partial class if we don't need to inherit from our own base class.

This is a snippet of the code-behind class declaration:

```
public class FetchDataWithInheritsModel:ComponentBase
```

We'll need to inherit from `ComponentBase` or from a class that inherits from `ComponentBase`.

In the Razor file, we would use the `@inherits` directive:

```
@inherits FetchDataWithInheritsModel
```

The Razor file will now inherit from our code-behind class (this was the first available way to create code-behind classes).

Both the partial and inherit options are simple ways of moving the code to a code-behind file. But there is another option to completely skip the Razor file and use only code.

Only code

The Razor file will generate code at compile time. We can skip the Razor step if we want to and write our layout completely in code.

This file (`CounterWithoutRazor.cs`) is available on GitHub.

The counter sample would look like this:

```
using Microsoft.AspNetCore.Components;
using Microsoft.AspNetCore.Components.Rendering;
using Microsoft.AspNetCore.Components.Web;
namespace MyBlogServerSide.Pages
{
    [Route("/CounterWithoutRazor")]
    public class CounterWithoutRazor: ComponentBase
    {
        protected override void BuildRenderTree
            (RenderTreeBuilder builder)
        {
            builder.AddMarkupContent(0,
                "<h1>Counter</h1>\r\n\r\n");
            builder.OpenElement(1, "p");
            builder.AddContent(2, "Current count: ");
            builder.AddContent(3,currentCount);
```

```
            builder.CloseElement();
            builder.AddMarkupContent(4, "\r\n\r\n");
            builder.OpenElement(5, "button");
            builder.AddAttribute(6, "class",
               "btn btn-primary");
            builder.AddAttribute(7, "onclick",
               EventCallback.Factory.Create<MouseEventArgs>
                  (this,IncrementCount));
            builder.AddContent(8, "Click me");
            builder.CloseElement();
        }
    private int currentCount = 0;
    private void IncrementCount()
    {
        currentCount++;
    }
        }
}
```

The Razor file will first be converted to something that roughly looks the same as the previous code, and then the code is compiled. It adds the elements one by one, which, in the end, will render the HTML.

The numbers in the code are how Blazor keeps track of each element in the render tree. Some prefer to write the code as in the previous code block, rather than using the Razor syntax; there are even efforts in the community to simplify the process of writing the `BuildRenderTree()` function manually.

My recommendation is to never write this manually, but I've kept it in the book because it shows how Razor files get compiled. Now that we know how to use code-behind, let's take a look at the lifecycle events of Blazor and when they get executed.

Lifecycle events

There are a couple of lifecycle events we can use to run our code. In this section, we will go through them and see when we should use them. Most lifecycle events have two versions – synchronous and asynchronous.

OnInitialized and OnInitializedAsync

When the component is fully loaded, `OnInitialized()` is called and then `OnInitializedAsync()`. This is a great method to load any data as the UI has not been rendered yet at this point. If we are doing any long-running tasks (such as getting data from a database), we should put that code in the `OnInitializedAsync()` method.

These methods will not run again if a parameter changes (see `OnParameterSet()` and `OnParameterSetAsync()`).

OnParametersSet and OnParametersSetAsync

`OnParameterSet()` and `OnParameterSetAsync()` are called when the component is initialized (after `OnInitialized()` and `OnInitializedAsync()`), and whenever we change the value of a parameter.

If we, for example, load data in the `OnInitialized()` method but it does use a parameter, the data won't be reloaded if the parameter is changed since `OnInitialized()` will only run once. We need to trigger a reload of the data in `OnParameterSet()` or `OnParameterSetAsync()` or move the loading to that method, of course.

OnAfterRender and OnAfterRenderAsync

After the component is finished rendering, the `OnAfterRender()` and `OnAfterRenderAsync()` methods are called. When the methods are being called, all the elements are rendered, so if we want/need to call any JavaScript code, we have to do that from these methods (we will get an error if we try to make a JavaScript interop from any of the other lifecycle event methods). We also have access to a `firstRender` parameter so we can make sure to only run an initialization code once (only on the first render).

ShouldRender

`ShouldRender()` is called when our component is re-rendered, and if it returns `false`, then the component will not be rendered again. It will always render once; it is only when it is re-rendered that the method runs.

`ShouldRender()` does not have an asynchronous option.

Now we know when the different lifecycle events happen and in what order. A component can also have parameters, and in that way, we can reuse them but with different data.

Parameters

A **parameter** makes it possible to send a value to a component. To add a parameter to a component, we use the [Parameter] attribute on a public property:

```
@code {
    [Parameter]
    public string MyParameter { get; set; }
}
```

We can also do the same using a code-behind file. We can add a parameter using the @ page directive by specifying it in the route:

```
@page "/parameterdemo/{MyParameter}"
```

In this case, we have to have a parameter specified with the same name as the name inside of the curly braces. To set the parameter in the @page directive, we simply go to the URL: /parameterdemo/THEVALUE.

There are cases where we want to specify another type instead of a string (string is the default). We can add the data type after the parameter name like this:

```
@page "/parameterdemo/{MyParameter:int}"
```

This will match the route only if the data type is an integer. We can also pass parameters using cascading parameters.

Cascading parameters

If we want to pass a value to multiple components, we can use a cascading parameter.

Instead of using [Parameter], we can use [CascadingParameter] like this:

```
[CascadingParameter]
public int MyParameter { get; set; }
```

To pass a value to the component, we surround it with a CascadingValue component like this:

```
<CascadingValue Value="MyProperty">
    <ComponentWithCascadingParameter/>
</CascadingValue> @code {
    public string MyProperty { get; set; } = "Test Value";
}
```

CascadingValue is the value that we pass to the component and CascadingParameter is the property that receives the value.

As we can see, we don't pass any parameter values to the ComponentWithCascadingParameter component; the cascading value will match the parameter with the same data type. If we have multiple parameters of the same type, we can specify the name of the parameter in the component with the cascading parameter like this:

```
[CascadingParameter(Name = "MyCascadingParameter")]
```

We can also do so for the component that passes CascadingValue, like this:

```
<CascadingValue Value="MyProperty" Name="MyCascadingParameter">
    <ComponentWithCascadingParameter/>
</CascadingValue>
```

If we know that the value won't change, we can specify that by using the IsFixed property:

```
<CascadingValue Value="MyProperty" Name="MyCascadingParameter"
IsFixed="True">
    <ComponentWithCascadingParameter/>
</CascadingValue>
```

This way, Blazor won't look for changes. The cascading values/parameters cannot be updated upward but are updated only downward. This means that to update a cascading value, we need to implement it in another way; updating it from inside the component won't change any components that are higher in the hierarchy.

In *Chapter 5*, *Creating Advanced Blazor Components*, we will look at events that are one-way to solve the problem of updating a cascading value.

Phew! This has been an information-heavy chapter, but now we know the basics of Blazor components. Now it is time to build one!

Writing our first component

The first component we will build shows all the blog posts on a site. To be fair, we haven't written any blog posts yet but we will temporarily solve that so we can start doing something fun.

In *Chapter 3, Introducing Entity Framework Core*, we created a database and an API (or interface); now it is time to use them.

The first thing we want to see is a list of blog posts, so we want our route to be "/". The index page already has that route, so we are going to reuse that page.

To create our first component, follow these instructions:

1. In the MyBlogServerSide project, open Pages/Index.razor.

2. Replace the contents of that file with the following code:

```
@page "/"
@using MyBlog.Data.Interfaces
@using MyBlog.Data.Models
@inject IMyBlogApi api
@code{
    protected async Task AddSomePosts()
    {
        for (int i = 1; i <= 10; i++)
        {
            await api.SaveBlogPostAsync(new BlogPost()
            {
                PublishDate = DateTime.Now, Title =
                    $"Blog post {i}", Text = "Text"
            });
        }
    }
}
```

If we start from the top, we can see a page directive. It will make sure that the component will be shown when the route is "/". Then, we have three @using directives, bringing in the namespaces so that we can use them in the Razor file. Then we inject our API (using DI) and name the instance as api. In the code section, there is a method that adds 10 blog posts to our website. Next, we should list the blog posts.

3. Add a variable that holds all our posts. In the code section, add the following:

```
protected List<BlogPost> posts = new List<BlogPost>();
```

Now we need to load the data.

4. To load posts, add the following in the `code` section:

```
protected override async Task OnInitializedAsync()
{
    posts = await api.GetBlogPostsAsync(10, 0);
    await base.OnInitializedAsync();
}
```

Now, when the page loads, the posts will be loaded as well: 10 posts and page 0 (the first page).

5. Under the `@inject` row, add the following code:

```
<button @onclick="AddSomePosts">Add some fake posts</button>
<br />
<br />
<ul>
    @foreach (var p in posts)
    {
        <li>@p.Title</li>
    }
</ul>
```

We start by adding a button so that we can trigger the `AddSomePosts` function. Then we add an unordered list (`ul`) and inside that, we loop over `blogposts` and show the title.

6. Now we can run the application by pressing *Ctrl + F5* (**Debug | Start Without Debugging**).

7. The page that shows up should just show an **Add some fake posts** button. Click this button.

8. Since the page won't reload, `OnInitializedAsync()` won't run either. We need to reload our web browser for the data to show up. In a real-world application, we don't want our users to have to reload the browser, but since this step is just temporary, I didn't want to overcomplicate things.

Great job, we have created our first component!

Summary

In this chapter, we learned a lot about Razor syntax, something we will use throughout the book. We learned about DI, directives, and parameters, and, of course, created our first component. This knowledge will help us understand how to create components and how to reuse components.

In the next chapter, we will take a look at more advanced component scenarios.

5
Creating Advanced Blazor Components

In the last chapter, we learned all the basics of creating a component. In this chapter, we will learn how to take our components to the next level.

This chapter will focus on some of the features that will make our components reusable, which will enable us to save time, and also give us an understanding of how to use reusable components made by others.

We will also take a look at some of the built-in components that will help you by adding additional functionality (compared to using HTML tags) when you build your Blazor app.

In this chapter, we will cover the following topics:

- Exploring binding
- Adding `Actions` and `EventCallback`
- Using `RenderFragment`
- Exploring the new built-in component

Technical requirements

In this chapter, you will start building your components. For this, you'll need the code we developed in the previous *Chapter 4, Understanding Basic Blazor Components*. If you have followed the instructions in the previous chapters, then you are good to go. If not, then make sure you clone/download the repo. The starting point for this chapter can be found in the ch4 folder, and the finished chapter in ch5.

You can find the source code for this chapter's end result at `https://github. com/PacktPublishing/Web-Development-with-Blazor/tree/master/ Chapter05`.

Exploring binding

Using bindings, you can connect variables either within a component (so that it updates automatically) or by setting a component attribute.

In Blazor, we can bind values to components and there are two different ways to do this.

- One-way binding
- Two-way binding

By using binding, we can send information between components and make sure we can update a value when we want to.

One-way binding

One-way binding is something that we have already talked about in *Chapter 4, Creating Basic Blazor Components*. Let's take a look at the component again and continue to build on it in this section.

In this section, we will combine parameters and binding.

The `Counter.razor` example looks like this:

```
@page "/counter"
<h1>Counter</h1>
<p>Current count: @currentCount</p>
<button class="btn btn-primary" @onclick="IncrementCount">Click me</button>
@code {
    private int currentCount = 0;
    private void IncrementCount()
```

```
    {
        currentCount++;
    }
}
```

The component will show the current count and a button that will increment the current count. This is one-way binding and, even though the button can change, the value of currentcount only flows in one direction.

Since this part is designed to demonstrate the functionality and theory and it's not a part of the finished project we are building, you don't have to write or run this code. The source code for these components is available on GitHub.

We can add a parameter to the counter component. The code will then look like this:

```
@page "/counterwithparameter"
<h1>Counter</h1>
<p>Current count: @CurrentCount</p>
<button class="btn btn-primary" @onclick="IncrementCount">Click
me</button>
@code {
    [Parameter]
    public int IncrementAmount { get; set; } = 1;
    [Parameter]
    public int CurrentCount { get; set; } = 0;
    private void IncrementCount()
    {
        CurrentCount+=IncrementAmount;
    }
}
```

The code sample has two parameters, one for CurrentCount and one for IncrementAmount. By adding parameters to the components, we can change their behavior. This sample is, of course, a bit silly. The chances are that you won't have any use for a component like this, but it illustrates the idea very well.

We can now take the component and add it inside another component. This is the way we can create a reusable component and change its behavior by changing the value of the parameters.

We change its behavior like this:

```
@page "/parentcounter"
<CounterWithParameter IncrementAmount="@incrementamount"
CurrentCount="@currentcount"></CounterWithParameter>
The current count is: @currentcount
@code {
    int incrementamount = 10;
    int currentcount = 0;
}
```

In this sample, we have two variables, `incrementamount` and `currentcount`, that we pass into our `CounterWithParameter` component.

If we were to run this, we would see a `counter` component that counts in increments of `10`. However, the `currentcount` variable is not going to be updated since it is only a one-way binding (one direction).

To help us with that, we can implement two-way binding so that our parent component will be notified of any changes.

Two-way binding

Two-way binding binds values in both directions. Our `counter` component will be able to notify our parent component of any changes. In the next chapter, *Chapter 6, Building Forms with Validation*, we will talk even more about two-way binding.

To make our `CounterWithParameter` component bind in two directions, we need to add `EventCallback`. The name has to consist of the name of the parameter followed by `Changed`. This way, Blazor will make sure to update the value if it changes. In our case, we would need to name it `CurrentCountChanged`. The code would then look like this:

```
[Parameter]
public EventCallback<int> CurrentCountChanged { get; set; }
private void IncrementCount()
{
    CurrentCount += IncrementAmount;
    CurrentCountChanged.InvokeAsync(CurrentCount);
}
```

By merely using that naming convention, Blazor knows that `CurrentCountChanged` is the event that will get triggered when a change to `CurrentCount` occurs.

`EventCallback` cannot be null, so there is no reason to do a null check (more on that in the next section).

We also need to change how we listen for changes:

```
<CounterWithParameterAndEvent IncrementAmount="@
incrementamount" @bind-CurrentCount="currentcount"/>
```

We need to add `@bind-` before the `CurrentCount` binding. You can also use the following syntax to set the name of the event:

```
<CounterWithParameterAndEvent IncrementAmount="@
incrementamount" @bind-CurrentCount="currentcount" @bind-Curren
tCount:event="CurrentCountChanged"/>
```

By using `:event`, we can tell Blazor exactly what event we want to use, in this case, the `CurrentCountChanged` event.

In the next chapter, *Chapter 6, Building Forms with Validation*, we will continue to look at bindings with input/form components.

We can, of course, create events as well using `EventCallback`.

Adding Actions and EventCallback

To communicate changes, we can use `EventCallback`, as shown in the *Two-way binding* section. `EventCallback<T>` differs a bit from what we might be used to in .NET. `EventCallback<T>` is a class that is specially made for Blazor to be able to have the event callback exposed as a parameter for the component.

In .NET in general, you can add multiple listeners to an event (multi-cast), but with `EventCallback<T>`, you will only be able to add one listener (single-cast).

It is worth mentioning that you can, of course, use events the way you are used to from .NET in Blazor as well. However, you probably want to use `EventCallback<T>` because there are many upsides to using `EventCallback` over traditional .NET events.

.NET events use classes and `EventCallback` uses structs. This means that in Blazor, we don't have to perform a null check before calling `EventCallback` because a struct cannot be null.

EventCallback is asynchronous and can be awaited. When EventCallback has been called, Blazor will automatically execute StateHasChanged on the consuming component to make sure the component updates (if it needs to be updated).

So, if you require multiple listeners, you can use Action<T>, otherwise, you should use EventCallback<T>.

Some event types have event arguments that we can access. They are optional, so in most cases, you don't need to add them. You can add them by specifying them in a method or you can use a lambda expression, like this:

```
<button @onclick="@((e)=>message=$"x:{e.ClientX} y:{e.
ClientY}")">Click me</button>
```

button will set a variable called message to a string containing the mouse coordinates. The lambda has one parameter, e, which is of the MouseArgs type. You don't have to specify the type, however. The compiler understands what type the parameter is.

Now that we have added actions and used EventCallback to communicate changes, we will see how we can execute RenderFragment in the next section.

Using RenderFragment

To make our components even more reusable, we can supply them with a piece of Razor syntax. In Blazor, you can specify RenderFragment, which is a fragment of Razor syntax that you can execute and show.

Now that we have added actions and used EventCallback to communicate changes, we will see how we can execute RenderFragment in the next section.

There are two types of render elements, RenderFragment and RenderFragment <T>. RenderFragment is simply a Razor fragment without any input parameters, and RenderFragment <T> has an input parameter that you can use inside the Razor fragment code by using the context keyword. We won't go into depth about how to use this now, but later in this chapter, we will talk about a component (Virtualize) that uses RenderFragment<T> and, in the next chapter, *Chapter 6, Building Forms with Validation*, we will implement a component using RenderFragments<T>.

We can make RenderFragment the default content inside of the component tags as well as give it a default value. We will explore this next and build a component using these features.

> **Grid component**
>
> If you want to dig deeper into render fragments, please check out Blazm Components, which have a grid component that uses `RenderFragments<T>` heavily. Where I currently work, we use this component, and it has been developed using real-world scenarios.
>
> You can find it on GitHub here: `https://github.com/EngstromJimmy/Blazm.Components`.

ChildContent

By naming the render fragment `ChildContent`, Blazor will automatically use whatever is between the alert tags as content. This only works, however, if you are using a single render fragment; if you are using more than one, you will have to specify the `ChildComponent` tag as well.

Default value

We can supply `RenderFragment` with a default value or set it in code by using an @ symbol:

```
@<b>This is a default value</b>;
```

Building an alert component

To better understand how to use render fragments, let's build an alert component. The built-in templates are using Bootstrap, and so we will do the same for this component. Bootstrap has a lot of components that are easy to port to Blazor. When working on big projects with multiple developers, building components is an easy way to make sure that everyone in the team is writing code in the same way.

Let's build a simple alert component, based on Bootstrap:

1. Create a folder by right-clicking on **MyBlogServerSide project** | **Add** | **New folder** and name the folder `Components`.

2. Create a new Razor file by right-clicking on **Components** | **Add** | **Razor component** and name the component `Alert.razor`.

3. Replace the content with the following code in the `Alert.razor` file:

```
<div class="alert alert-primary" role="alert">
    A simple primary alert—check it out!
</div>
```

The code is taken from Bootstrap's web page, `http://getbootstrap.com`, and it shows an alert that looks like this:

A simple primary alert—check it out!

Figure 5.1 – The default look of a Bootstrap alert component

There are two ways in which we could customize this `alert` component. We could just add a `string` parameter for the message. However, since this is a section on render fragments, we are just going to explore the second option, yes, you guessed it, render fragments.

4. Add a code section with a `RenderFragment` property called `ChildContent` and replace the alert text with the new property:

```
<div class="alert alert-primary" role="alert">
    @ChildContent
</div>
@code{
    [Parameter]
    public RenderFragment ChildContent { get; set; }
        =@<b>This is a default value</b>;
}
```

Now we have `RenderFragment` with a default value and we are displaying the fragment between the `div` tags. We also want to add `enum` for the different ways in which you can style the alert box.

5. In the `code` section, add `enum` containing the different styles available:

```
public enum AlertStyle
{
    Primary,
    Secondary,
    Success,
    Danger,
    Warning,
    Info,
    Light,
    Dark
}
```

6. Add a parameter/property for the enum style:

```
[Parameter]
public AlertStyle Style { get; set; }
```

7. The final step is to update the class attribute for div. The complete file looks like this. Change the class attribute on the first line:

```
<div class="@($"alert alert-{Style.ToString().
ToLower()}")" role="alert">
    @ChildContent
</div>
@code{
    [Parameter]
    public RenderFragment ChildContent { get; set; }
      =@<b>This is a default value</b>;
    [Parameter]
    public AlertStyle Style { get; set; }
    public enum AlertStyle
    {
        Primary,
        Secondary,
        Success,
        Danger,
        Warning,
        Info,
        Light,
        Dark
    }
}
```

8. Right-click on the Pages folder, select **Add | Razor component**, and name it AlertTest.razor.

   Replace the code with the following snippet:

```
@page "/alerttest"
@using MyBlogServerSide.Components
<Alert Style="Alert.AlertStyle.Danger">
    This is a test
```

```
</Alert>
<Alert Style="Alert.AlertStyle.Success">
    <ChildContent>
        This is another test
    </ChildContent>
</Alert>
<Alert Style="Alert.AlertStyle.Success"/>
```

The page is showing three alert components:

The first one has the `Danger` style, and we are not specifying what property to set for the `This is a test` text, but by convention, it is going to use the property called `ChildContent`.

In the second one, we have specified the `ChildContent` property. If you are using more render fragments in your component, you will have to set them like this, with full names.

In the last one, we didn't specify anything, which will give the property the default render fragment that we specified in the component.

9. Run the project and navigate to `/AlertTest` to see the test page:

Figure 5.2 – Screenshot of the test page

We have finished our first reusable component!

Creating reusable components is the way in which I prefer to create my Blazor sites because I don't have to write the same code twice. This becomes even more apparent if you are working in a larger team. It makes it easier for all developers to produce the same code and end result, and with that get a higher code quality and require fewer tests.

With .NET 5 came a couple of new components that we didn't have before. In the next section, we will dig deeper into what they are and how to use them.

Exploring the new built-in component

When Blazor first came out, there were a couple of things that were hard to do and in some cases, we needed to involve JavaScript to solve the challenge. In this section, we will take a look at some of the new components that we got in .NET 5.

We will take a look at the following new components or functions:

- Setting the focus of the UI
- Influencing HTML head
- Component virtualization

Setting the focus of the UI

One of my first Blazor blog posts was about how to set the focus on a UI element, but now this is built into the framework. The previous solution involved JavaScript calls to change the focus on a UI element.

By using `ElementReference`, you can now set the focus on the element.

Let's build a component to test the behavior of this new feature:

1. Right-click on the `Pages` folder, select **New | Razor component**, and name it `SetFocus.Razor`.

2. Open `SetFocus.Razor` and add a `page` directive:

    ```
    @page "/setfocus"
    ```

3. Add an element reference:

    ```
    @code {
        ElementReference textInput;
    }
    ```

    This is exactly what it sounds like, a reference to an element. In this case, it is an input textbox.

4. Add the textbox and a button:

```
<input @ref="textInput" />
<button @onclick="() => textInput.FocusAsync()">Set
focus</button>
```

By using @ref, you specify a reference to an object that you can use to access the input box. The button onclick method will execute the FocusAsync() method and set the focus on the textbox.

5. Press *F5* to run the project and then navigate to /setfocus.

6. Press the **Set focus** button and notice how the textbox gets its focus.

It could seem like a silly example to bring up since this only sets the focus, but it is a really useful feature and the autofocus HTML attribute won't work for Blazor.

In my blog post, I had another approach. My goal was to set the focus of an element without having to use code. In the upcoming chapter, *Chapter 6, Building Forms with Validation*, we will implement the autofocus feature from my blog post, but using the new .NET features instead.

The new release of .NET 5 solves a lot of things that we previously had to write with JavaScript; setting the focus is one example, and influencing HTML head is another.

Influencing HTML head

Sometimes, we want to set the title of our page or change the meta tags for social networks. The head tag is located in index.html (for WebAssembly) or _host.cshtml (for server-side), and that part of the page isn't reloaded/rerendered (only the components within the app component are rerendered). In previous versions of Blazor, you would have to write code for that yourself using JavaScript.

But .NET has a couple of new components we can use to solve that:

- Title
- Link
- Meta

You only have to add these components to your component to change the title, link, or meta tag.

This feature never got into the final release of .NET 5. It is still in preview, but it was a very big deal, so I wanted to keep it in the book.

To use these components, we will create a page to view one of our blog posts. And we will use many of the techniques we have learned:

1. First we need to add a reference to the **Microsoft.AspNetCore.Components. Web.Extensions** NuGet package. In the solutions explorer beneath the **MyBlogServerSide** node, right-click on **Dependencies** and select **Manage Nuget Packages**.

2. Search for **Microsoft.AspNetCore.Components.Web.Extensions**, select it, and click **Install**. This package is only available in preview, so make sure to check the **Include prerelease** option.

3. Open `Pages/Index.razor`.

4. Change the `foreach` loop to look like this:

```
<li><a href="/Post/@p.Id">@p.Title</a></li>
```

We added a link to the title, so we can look at one blog post. Notice how we can use the @ symbol inside the `href` attribute to get the ID of the post.

5. Right-click on the `Pages` folder, select **Add | Razor component**, and name the component `Post.razor`.

6. In the `code` section, add a parameter that will hold the ID of the post:

```
[Parameter]
public int BlogPostId { get; set; }
```

This will hold the ID of the blogpost that comes from the URL.

7. Add a `page` directive to get the set, the URL, and the ID:

```
@page "/post/{BlogPostId:int}"
```

The `page` directive will set the URL for our blog post to `/post/`, followed by the ID of the post. We are also specifying that the type of `BlogPostId` is an integer. If the URL contains something that is not an integer, then Blazor will not find the page in question.

8. We don't have to add a `using` statement to all our components. Instead, open `_imports.razor` and add the following namespaces:

```
@using MyBlog.Data.Models;
@using MyBlog.Data.Interfaces;
@using Microsoft.AspNetCore.Components.Web.Extensions.
Head
```

This will make sure that all the components we build will have these namespaces by default.

9. Open Post.razor again and, just beneath the page directive, inject the API (the namespace is now supplied from _imports.razor):

```
@inject IMyBlogApi api
@inject NavigationManager navman
```

Our API will now be injected into the component and we can retrieve our blog post. We also have access to a navigation manager.

10. In the code section, add a property for our blog post:

```
public BlogPost BlogPost { get; set; }
```

This is going to contain the blog post we want to show on the page.

11. To load the blog post, add the following code:

```
protected async override Task OnParametersSetAsync()
{
    BlogPost=await api.GetBlogPostAsync(BlogPostId);
    await base.OnParametersSetAsync();
}
```

In this case, we are using the OnParameterSet() method. This is just to make sure that the parameter is set when we get data from the database, as well as to make sure that the content updates when the parameter changes.

12. We also need to show the post and add the necessary meta tags. To do that, add the following code just above the code section:

```
@if (BlogPost != null)
{
    <Title Value="@BlogPost.Title"></Title>
    <Meta property="og:title"
      content="@BlogPost.Title" />
    <Meta property="og:description" content="@(new
      string(BlogPost.Text.Take(100).ToArray()))" />
    <Meta property="og:image" content=
      "@($"{navman.BaseUri}/pathtoanimage.png")" />
    <Meta property="og:url" content="@navman.Uri" />
    <Meta name="twitter:card" content="@(new
```

```
        string(BlogPost.Text.Take(100).ToArray()))" />
    <h3>@BlogPost.Title</h3>
    @((MarkupString)BlogPost.Text)
}
```

When the page is first loaded, the `BlogPost` parameter can be null, so we first need to check whether we should show the content at all.

By adding the `Title` component, Blazor will set the title of our site to, in this instance, the title of our blog post.

According to the information gathered by me on **Search Engine Optimization (SEO)**, the meta tags we have added are the bare minimum for Facebook and Twitter. We don't have an image for each blog post, but we can have one that is site-wide (for all blogposts) if we would like. Just change `Pathtoanimage.png` to the name of the image and put the image in the `wwwroot` folder.

If the blog post is loaded, then show an `H3` tag with the title and the text beneath that. You might remember `MarkupString` from *Chapter 4, Understanding Basic Blazor Components*. This will output the string from our blog post without changing the HTML (not escaping the HTML).

13. Run the project by pressing *F5* and navigate to a blog post to see the title change:

Figure 5.3 – Blog post screenshot

Our blog is starting to take form. We have a list of blog posts and we can view a single blog post; we are, of course, far from done, but well on our way.

Component virtualization

`Virtualize` is a new component in Blazor that will make sure that it only renders the components or rows that are currently visible. If you have a large list of items, showing all of them will have a big impact on memory. Many third-party component vendors offer grid components that have the same kind of virtualization function. This component is, in my opinion, the most exciting thing in the .NET 5 release.

The `Virtualize` component will calculate how many items can fit on the screen (based on the size of the window and the height of an item). If you scroll the page, Blazor will add a `div` tag before and after the content list, making sure that the scrollbar is showing the right position (even though there are no items rendered).

The `Virtualize` component works just like a `foreach` loop.

The following is the code we currently have in our `index.razor` file:

```
<ul>
    @foreach (var p in posts)
    {
        <li><a href="/Post/@p.Id">@p.Title</a></li>
    }
</ul>
```

Right now, it will show all the blog posts we have in our database in a long list. Granted, we don't have that many right now, but one day we might have a lot of posts.

We can change the code (don't change the code just yet) to use the new `Virtualize` component by changing it to the following:

```
<Virtualize Items="posts" Context="p">
        <li><a href="/Post/@p.Id">@p.Title</a></li>
</Virtualize>
```

Instead of the `foreach` loop, we use the `Virtualize` component and add a render fragment that shows how each item should be rendered. The `Virtualize` component uses `RenderFragment<T>` which, by default, will send in an item of type `T` to the render fragment. In the case of the `Virtualize` component, the object is going to be one blog post (since items are `List<T>` of blog posts). We access each post with the variable named `context`. However, we can use the `Context` property on the `Virtualize` component to specify another name, so instead of `context`, we are now using p.

The `Virtualize` component is even more powerful than this, as we will see in the next feature that we implement:

1. Open `Pages/Index.razor`.

2. Delete the `OnInitializedAsync` method and `protected List<BlogPost> posts = new List<BlogPost>();`; we don't need this.

3. Change the loading of the post to `Virtualize`:

```
<ul>
    <Virtualize ItemsProvider="LoadPosts" Context="p">
        <li><a href="/Post/@p.Id">@p.Title</a></li>
    </Virtualize>
</ul>
```

In this case, we are using the `ItemsProvider` delegate that will take care of getting posts from our API.

We pass in a method called `LoadPosts`, which we also need to add to the file.

4. Now, let's add the `LoadPosts` method by adding the following code:

```
public int totalBlogposts { get; set; }
private async ValueTask<ItemsProviderResult<BlogPost>>
LoadPosts(ItemsProviderRequest request)
{
    if (totalBlogposts == 0)
    {
        totalBlogposts = await
            api.GetBlogPostCountAsync();
    }
    var numblogposts = Math.Min(request.Count,
        totalBlogposts - request.StartIndex);
    var employees = await
        api.GetBlogPostsAsync(numblogposts,
            request.StartIndex);
    return new
        ItemsProviderResult<BlogPost>(employees,
            totalBlogposts);
}
```

We add a `totalBlogposts` property where we store how many posts we currently have in our database. The `LoadPost` method returns `ValueTask` with `ItemsProviderResult<Blogpost>`. The method has `ItemsProviderRequest` as a parameter, which contains the number of posts the `Virtualize` component wants and how many it wants to skip.

If we don't already know how many posts in total we have, we need to retrieve that information from our API by calling the `GetBlogPostCountAsync` method. Then, we need to figure out how many posts we should get; either we get as many posts as we need, or we get all the posts that are remaining (whatever value is the smallest).

Then, we make a call to our API to get the actual posts by calling `GetBlogPostsAsync` and return `ItemsProviderResult`.

Now we have implemented a `Virtualize` component that will load and render only the number of blog posts needed to fill the screen.

Summary

In this chapter, we looked at more advanced scenarios for building components. Building components is what Blazor is all about. Components also make it easy to make changes along the way because there is only one point where you have to implement the change. We also implemented our first reusable component, which will help us to maintain the same standard across the entire team and reduce duplicated code.

We also used some of the new features in .NET 5 for Blazor to load and display data.

In the next chapter, we will take a look at forms and validation to start building the administration part of our blog.

6
Building Forms with Validation

In this chapter, we will learn about creating forms and validating them, which is a great opportunity to build our admin interface where we can manage our blog posts. We are also going to build multiple reusable components and learn about some of the new functionalities in .NET 5 for Blazor.

This is going to be a super fun chapter and we will use a lot of the things we learned up until now.

In this chapter, we will cover the following topics:

- Exploring form elements
- Adding validation
- Custom validation class attributes
- Building an admin interface

Technical requirements

Make sure you have followed the previous chapters or use the Ch5 folder as a starting point.

You can find the source code for this chapter's end result at `https://github.com/PacktPublishing/Web-Development-with-Blazor/tree/master/Chapter06`.

Exploring form elements

There are many form elements in HTML, and we can use them all in Blazor. In the end, what Blazor will output is HTML.

Blazor does have components that will add to the functionality, so we can and should try to use those components instead of HTML elements. This will give us great functionality for free; we will come back to this later in this chapter.

Blazor offers the following components:

- `EditForm`
- `InputBase<>`
- `InputCheckbox`
- `InputDate<TValue>`
- `InputNumber<TValue>`
- `InputSelect<TValue>`
- `InputText`
- `InputTextArea`
- `InputRadio`
- `InputRadioGroup`
- `ValidationMessage`
- `ValidationSummary`

Let's go through them all.

EditForm

EditForm renders as a form tag but it has a lot more functionalities.

First, we are not going to have an action or method like with traditional form tags; Blazor will handle all of that.

EditForm will create an EditContext instance as a cascading value so that all the components you put inside of EditForm will access the same EditContext. EditContext will track the metadata when it comes to the editing process, such as what fields have been edited, and keep track of any validation messages.

You need to assign either a model (a class that you wish to edit) or an EditContext instance.

For most use cases, assigning a model is the way to go, but for more advanced scenarios you might want to be able to trigger EditContext.Validate(), for example, to validate all the controls connected to EditContext.

EditForm has the following events that you can use to handle form submissions:

- OnValidSubmit gets triggered when the data in the form validates correctly (we will come back to validation in just a bit).

- OnInvalidSubmit gets triggered if the form does not validate correctly.

- OnSubmit gets triggered when the form is submitted, regardless of whether the form validates correctly or not. Use OnSubmit if you want to control the validation yourself.

Let's take a look at an example.

Consider a class that holds a person; the class has a name and an age for that person and looks like this:

```
public class Person
{
    public string Name { get; set; }
    public int Age { get; set; }
}
```

EditForm for this class would look like this (without any other elements for now):

```
<EditForm Model="personmodel" OnValidSubmit="validSubmit">
    ...
    <button type="submit">Submit</button>
</EditForm>

@code {
    Person personmodel = new Person();

    private Task validSubmit()
    {
        //Do database stuff
        return Task.CompletedTask;
    }
}
```

EditForm specifies a model (in this case personmodel), and we are listening to the OnValidSubmit event.

The **Submit** button is a regular HTML button that is not a specific Blazor component.

InputBase<>

All the Blazor input classes derive from the InputBase class. It has a bunch of things that we can use for all the input components; we will go through the most important ones.

InputBase handles AdditionalAttributes, which means that if we add any other attributes to the tag, they will automatically get transferred to the output. This means that the components that derive from this class can leverage any HTML attributes, since they will be part of the output.

InputBase has properties for Value, which we can bind to, and an event callback for when the value changes called ValueChanged.

We can also change DisplayName so that the automated validation messages will reflect the correct name and not the name of the property, which is the default behavior.

The DisplayName property is not supported by all controls. Some properties are only used inside of the component, and we will come back to those in a bit.

InputCheckbox

The `InputCheckbox` component will render as `<input type="checkbox">`.

InputDate<TValue>

The `InputDate` component will render as `<input type="date">`. We can use `DateTime` and `DateTimeOffset` as values for the `InputDate` component.

There is no way to format the date; it will use the web browser's current setting. This behavior is by design and is part of the HTML5 spec.

InputNumber<TValue>

The `InputNumber` component will render as `<input type="number">`. We can use `Int32`, `Int64`, `Single`, `Double`, and `Decimal` as values for the `InputNumber` component.

InputSelect<TValue>

The `InputSelect` component will render as `<select>`. We will create `InputSelect` later in this chapter so I won't go into further detail here.

InputText

The `InputText` component will render as `<input type="text">`.

InputTextArea

The `InputSelect` component will render as `<textarea>`. In this chapter, we will build our own version of this control.

InputRadio

The `InputRadio` component will render as `<input type="radio">`.

InputRadioGroup

The `InputRadioGroup` component will render as `<Input type="radio">`.

As we can see there is a Blazor component for almost all the HTML form controls with some added functionality such as validation which we will see in the next section.

Adding validation

We have already touched on the subject of validation; there are some built-in functionalities in the input components as well as EditForm to handle validation.

One way to add validation to our form is to use DataAnnotations. By using data annotations, we don't have to write any custom logic to make sure the data in the form is correct; we can instead add attributes to the data model and let DataAnnotationsValidator take care of the rest.

There are a bunch of DataAnnotations instances in .NET already that we can use; we can also build our own annotations.

Some of the built-in data annotations are as follows:

- Required: Makes the field required
- Email: Will check that the entered value is an email address
- MaxLength: Will check that the number of characters is not exceeded
- Range: Will check that the value is within a certain range

There are many more annotations that can help us validate our data. To test this out, let's add data annotations to our data classes:

1. In the MyBlog.Data project, open Models/BlogPost.cs.
2. At the top of the file, add a reference to System.ComponentModel.DataAnnotations:

    ```
    using System.ComponentModel.DataAnnotations;
    ```

3. Add the Required and MinLength attributes to the Title property:

    ```
    [Required]
    [MinLength(5)]
    public string Title { get; set; }
    ```

    The Required attribute will make sure we can't leave the title empty, and MinLength will make sure it has at least 5 characters:

4. Add the Required attribute to the Text property:

    ```
    [Required]
    public string Text { get; set; }
    ```

The `Required` attribute will make sure the `Text` property cannot be empty, which makes sense – why would we create an empty blog post?

5. Open `Models/Category.cs`, and at the top of the file, add a reference to `System.ComponentModel.DataAnnotations`.

6. Add the `Required` attribute to the `Name` property:

```
[Required]
public string Name { get; set; }
```

The `Required` attribute will make sure we can't leave the name empty.

7. Open `Models/Tag.cs`, and at the top of the file, add a reference to `System.ComponentModel.DataAnnotations`.

8. Add the `Required` attribute to the `Name` property:

```
[Required]
public string Name { get; set; }
```

The `Required` attribute will make sure we can't leave the name empty.

Great, now our data models have validation built into them. We need to give our users feedback on what went wrong with the validation.

We can do that by using the `ValidationMessage` or `ValidationSummary` components.

ValidationMessage

The `ValidationMessage` component can show us individual error messages for a specific property. We want to use this component to show validation errors under a form element.

To add a `ValidationMessage` component, we have to specify the `For` property with the name of the property we want to show the validation errors for:

```
<ValidationMessage For="@(() => model.Name)"/>
```

ValidationSummary

The `ValidationSummary` component will show all the validation errors as a list for the entire `EditContext`.

I prefer to show the error close to the problem so it's clear to the user where the issue is. But we also have the option to show the validation errors as a list using `ValidationSummary`.

To make sure our input controls match the Bootstrap theme (or whatever theme we might be using), we can create our own Custom validation class.

Custom validation class attributes

By simply using the edit form, input components, and `DataAnnotationValidator`, the framework will automatically add classes to the components when it's valid and when it's not valid.

By default, these classes are `.valid` and `.invalid`. In .NET 5, we are given a way to customize these class names ourselves.

When using Bootstrap, the default class names are `.is-valid` and `.is-invalid` and the class names must also have `.form-control` to get the right styles.

The component we are building next will help us to get the right Bootstrap styling on all of our form components.

We will create our own `FieldCssClassProvider` to customize what classes Blazor will use:

1. In the `MyBlogServerSide` project, right-click in the `Components` folder and select **Add class**, and name the class `BootstrapFieldCssClassProvider`.

2. Open the new class and add the following code:

```
using Microsoft.AspNetCore.Components.Forms;
using System.Linq;

namespace MyBlogServerSide.Components
{
    public class BootstrapFieldCssClassProvider :
        FieldCssClassProvider
    {
        public override string GetFieldCssClass
            (EditContext editContext, in FieldIdentifier
                fieldIdentifier)
        {
```

```
                var isValid =
                    !editContext.GetValidationMessages
                    (fieldIdentifier).Any();
                var isModified =
                    editContext.IsModified(fieldIdentifier);
                return (isModified, isValid) switch
                {
                    (true, true) => "form-control modified
                        is-valid",
                    (true, false) => "form-control
                        modified is-invalid",
                    (false, true) => "form-control",
                    (false, false) => "form-control"
                };
            }
        }
    }
```

BootstrapFieldCssClassProvider needs an EditContext instance
to work.

The code will check whether the form (or EditContext to be specific) is
valid and whether or not it has been modified. Based on that, it returns the
correct CSS classes.

It returns the form control for all elements; that way, we don't have to add it to every
element in the form. We could validate an untouched form as valid or invalid, but
we don't want it to show that the form is OK just because it hasn't been changed yet.

3. We need to get the EditContext instance from our EditForm and then set
   FieldCssClassProvider on EditContext as follows:

```
CurrentEditContext.SetFieldCssClassProvider(provider);
```

Next, we are going to do that in a more elegant way (in my humble opinion) with
the CustomCssClassProvider we will create next.

Earlier in this chapter, I mentioned that EditForm is exposing its EditContext
as CascadingValue.

That means we will build a component that we can just put inside of our `EditForm` and access `EditContext` that way:

1. In the `MyBlogServerSide` project, right-click on the `Components` folder and select **Add class**, and name the class `CustomCssClassProvider`.

2. Open the new file and add the following code:

```csharp
using Microsoft.AspNetCore.Components;
using Microsoft.AspNetCore.Components.Forms;
using System;


namespace MyBlogServerSide.Components
{
    public class CustomCssClassProvider<ProviderType>:
        ComponentBase where ProviderType:
            FieldCssClassProvider, new()
    {
        [CascadingParameter]
        EditContext? CurrentEditContext { get; set; }
        public ProviderType Provider { get; set; } =
            new ProviderType();
        protected override void OnInitialized()
        {
            if (CurrentEditContext == null)
            {
                throw new InvalidOperationException
                    ($"{nameof(DataAnnotationsValidator)}
                    requires a cascading " +
                    $"parameter of type
                    {nameof(EditContext)}.
                        For example, you can use
                        {nameof(DataAnnotationsValidator)}" +
                    $"inside an EditForm.");
            }
            CurrentEditContext.SetFieldCssClassProvider
                (Provider);
        }
    }
}
```

This is a generic component that takes a `type` value, in this case, the type of `Provider`.

We specified that `type` must inherit from `FieldCssClassProvider` and must have a constructor without parameters.

The component is inheriting from `ComponentBase`, which makes it possible to place the component inside of a Blazor component.

We have a `Cascading` parameter that will be populated from `EditForm`. We throw an exception if `EditContext` is missing for some reason (for example, if we place the component outside of `EditForm`).

Finally, we set `FieldCssClassProvider` on `EditContext`.

To use the component, we just have to add the following code inside of our `EditForm` (don't worry, we will create an `EditForm` soon):

```
<CustomCssClassProvider
 ProviderType="BootstrapFieldCssClassProvider"/>
```

We simply provide our `CustomCssClassProvider` component with the right `ProviderType BootstrapFieldCssClassProvider`.

Now, we have a component that will make our form controls look like Bootstrap controls. Next, it's time to put that into practice and create a couple of forms by building our admin interface.

Building an admin interface

Now it's time to build a simple admin interface for our blog.

We need to be able to do the following:

- List categories
- Edit categories
- List tags
- Edit tags
- List blog posts
- Edit blog posts

If we look at the preceding list, we might notice that some of the things seem similar – perhaps we can build components for those. Categories and tags are very similar; they have names, and the name is the only thing we should be able to edit.

Let's make a component for that. The component is going to be responsible for listing, adding, deleting, and updating the object.

Since the object we are working with is either `Category` or `Tag`, we need to be able to call different APIs depending on the object, so our component needs to be generic:

1. In the `MyBlogServerSide` project, right-click on the `Components` folder and select **Add | Razor component**, then name the component `ItemList.razor`.

2. Open the newly created file and in the `code` section, add the following lines of code:

```
[Parameter]
public List<ItemType> Items { get; set; } = new
List<ItemType>();
[Parameter]
public RenderFragment<ItemType> ItemTemplate { get; set;
}
```

We need two parameters: a list where we can add all the items and an `ItemTemplate` instance that we can use to change how we want the item to be shown.

In this case, we are using `RenderFragment<T>`, which will give us access to the item inside of the template (things will become clearer as soon as we implement it).

3. We also need a couple of events; add the following code to the `code` section:

```
[Parameter]
public EventCallback<ItemType> DeleteEvent { get; set; }
[Parameter]
public EventCallback<ItemType> SelectEvent { get; set; }
```

We added two events; the first is when we delete a tag or a category. We will send an event to the parent component where we can add the code needed to delete the item.

The second one is when we select an item so that we can edit the item.

4. Now it's time to add the UI; replace <h3>ItemList<h3> with the following code at the top of the file:

```
@typeparam ItemType
@using System.Collections.Generic
<h3>List</h3>
<table>
    <Virtualize Items="@Items" Context="item">
        <tr>
            <td><button class="btn btn-primary"
                @onclick="@(() =>
                    {SelectEvent.InvokeAsync(item); })">
                    Select</button>
            </td>
            <td>@ItemTemplate(item)</td>
            <td><button class="btn btn-danger"
                @onclick="@(() =>
                    {DeleteEvent.InvokeAsync(item);})">
                    Delete</button>
            </td>
        </tr>
    </Virtualize>
</table>
```

The first line with @typeparam is to make the component generic, and the variable holding the generic type is called ItemType.

If we look back to *Step 2*, we'll notice that we used the variable for the lists and RenderFragment.

Then, we use the new Virtualize component to list our items; to be fair, we might not have that many categories or tags, but why not use it when we can? We set the Items property to "Items" (which is the name of our list) and the Context parameter to "item".

We can give it whatever name we want; we're only going to use it inside of the Virtualize render template.

We added two buttons that simply invoke the EventCallback instance we added in *Step 3*. Between those buttons, we added @ItemTemplate(item); we want Blazor to render the template, but we also send the current item in the loop.

That means that we have access to the value of the item inside of our template.

Listing and editing categories

With our new component it's now time to create a component for listing and editing our categories.

1. In the `MyBlogServerSide` project, right-click on the `Pages` folder, select **Add | New folder**, and name the folder `Admin`.

2. Right-click on the `Pages/Admin` folder and select **Add | Razor component**, then name the component `CategoryList.razor`.

3. At the top of the component, replace `<h3>CategoryList</h3>` with the following code:

```
@page "/admin/categories"
@using MyBlogServerSide.Components
@inject IMyBlogApi api
<h3>Categories</h3>
```

We started with the `@page` directive, telling Blazor that if we navigate to the URL `"admin/categories"`, we will get to the `CategoryList.Razor` component.

We will add a `using` statement and then inject our API.

4. The next step is to add a form where we can edit the categories. Add the following code under the code from the previous step:

```
<EditForm OnValidSubmit="Save" Model="Item">
    <DataAnnotationsValidator />
    <CustomCssClassProvider
        ProviderType="BootstrapFieldCssClassProvider" />
    <InputText @bind-Value="@Item.Name" />
    <ValidationMessage For="@(()=>Item.Name)" />
    <button class="btn btn-success"
        type="submit">Save</button>
</EditForm>
```

We added `EditForm`, which will execute the `Save` method if the form validates OK. For validation, we added `DataAnnotationsValidator`, which will validate the supplied data against the annotations we added to the `Tag` and `Category` classes.

Since we are using Bootstrap, we want our form controls to look the same, so we added `CustomCssClassProvider` that we created earlier in this chapter.

We added `InputText` and connected it to a `Category` object called `Item` (which we will add in a just a second).

Below that, we added `ValidationMessage`, which will show any errors for the name property, and then a **Submit** button.

5. Now it's time to add our `ItemList` component; under the code we added in the previous step, add this code:

```
<ItemList Items="Items" DeleteEvent="@Delete"
SelectEvent="@Select" ItemType="Category">
    <ItemTemplate>
        @{
            var item = context as Category;
            if (item != null)
            {
                @item.Name;
            }
        }
    </ItemTemplate>
</ItemList>
```

We added our component, and we bind the `Items` property to a list of items (we will create that list in the next step).

We bind the `Select` and `Delete` events to methods and we specify the type of the list in the `ItemType` property. Then, we have `ItemTemplate`. Since we are using `RenderFragment<T>`, we now have access to a variable called `context`.

We convert that variable to a category and print out the name of the category. This is the template for each item that will be shown on the list.

6. Finally, we add the following code to the `code` section:

```
@code {
    private List<Category> Items { get; set; } = new
        List<Category>();
    public Category Item { get; set; } = new Category();
    protected async override Task OnInitializedAsync()
    {
        Items = await api.GetCategoriesAsync();
        await base.OnInitializedAsync();
```

```
        }
        private async Task Delete(Category category)
        {
            try
            {
                await api.DeleteCategoryAsync(category);
                Items.Remove(category);
            }
            catch { }
        }
        private async Task Save()
        {
            try
            {
                if (Item.Id == 0)
                {
                    Items.Add(Item);
                }
                await api.SaveCategoryAsync(Item);
                Item = new Category();
            }
            catch { }
        }
        private Task Select(Category category)
        {
            try
            {
                Item = category;
            }
            catch { }
            return Task.CompletedTask;
        }
    }
}
```

We added a list to hold all our categories and a variable that holds one item (the item currently being edited). We use OnInitializedAsync to load all the categories from the API.

The `Delete` and `Save` methods simply call the API's corresponding method, and the `Select` method takes the provided item and puts it into the item variable (ready to be edited).

7. Run the project and navigate to `/admin/categories`.

8. Try to add, edit, and delete a category as shown in *Figure 6.1*:

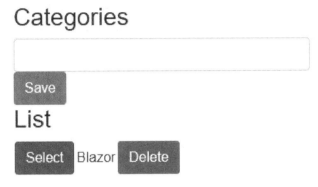

Figure 6.1 – The edit category view

Now we need a component for listing and editing tags as well – it is pretty much the same thing, but we need to use `Tag` instead of `Category`.

Listing and editing tags

We just created a component for listing and editing **Categories**, now we need to create a component to list and edit **Tags**.

1. Right-click on the `Pages/Admin` folder and select **Add | Razor component**, then name the component `TagList.razor`.

2. At the top of the component, replace `<h3>TagList</h3>` with the following code:

```
@page "/admin/tags"
@using MyBlogServerSide.Components
@inject IMyBlogApi api
<h3>Tags</h3>
```

We started with the `@page` directive telling Blazor that if we navigate to the URL `"admin/tags"`, we will get to the `TagList.Razor` component.

We add a `using` statement and then inject our API.

3.   The next step is to add a form where we can edit the tags. Add the following code under the code from the previous step:

```
<EditForm OnValidSubmit="Save" Model="Item">
    <DataAnnotationsValidator />
    <CustomCssClassProvider
      ProviderType="BootstrapFieldCssClassProvider" />
    <InputText @bind-Value="@Item.Name" />
    <ValidationMessage For="@(()=>Item.Name)" />
    <button class="btn btn-success"
      type="submit">Save</button>
</EditForm>
```

We added EditForm, which will execute the Save method if the form validates OK. For validation, we added DataAnnotationsValidator, which will validate the supplied data against the annotations we added to the Tag and Category classes.

Since we are using Bootstrap, we want our form controls to look the same, so we added CustomCssClassProvider, which we created earlier in this chapter.

We added InputText and connected it to a Tag object called Item (which we will add in a moment).

Below that, we add a ValidationMessage instance that will show any errors for the name property and then a **Submit** button.

4.   Now it's time to add our ItemList component. Under the code we added in the previous step, add this code:

```
<ItemList Items="Items" DeleteEvent="@Delete"
  SelectEvent="@Select" ItemType="Tag">
    <ItemTemplate>
        @{
            var item = context as Tag;
            if(item!=null)
            {
            @item.Name;
            }
        }
    </ItemTemplate>
</ItemList>
```

We added our component, and we bind the `Items` property to a list of items (we will create that list in the next step). We bind the `Select` and `Delete` events to methods and we specify the type of `List` in the `ItemType` property.

Then we have `ItemTemplate`; since we are using `RenderFragment<T>`, we now have access to a variable called `context`. We convert that variable to a tag and print out the name of the tag.

This is the template for each item that will be shown in the list.

5. Finally, we add the following code under the `code` section:

```
@code {
    private List<Tag> Items { get; set; } = new
        List<Tag>();
    public Tag Item { get; set; } = new Tag();
    protected async override Task OnInitializedAsync()
    {
        Items = await api.GetTagsAsync();
        await base.OnInitializedAsync();
    }
    private async Task Delete(Tag tag)
    {
        try
        {
            await api.DeleteTagAsync(tag);
            Items.Remove(tag);
        }
        catch { }
    }
    private async Task Save()
    {
        try
        {
            if (Item.Id == 0)
            {
                Items.Add(Item);
            }
            await api.SaveTagAsync(Item);
```

```
                Item = new Tag();
        }
    catch { }
}
private Task Select(Tag tag)
{
    try
    {
        Item = tag;
    }
    catch { }
    return Task.CompletedTask;
}
}
```

We added a list to hold all our tags and a variable that holds one item (the item currently being edited). We use OnInitializedAsync to load all the tags from the API.

The Delete and Save methods simply call the API's corresponding method and the Select method takes the provided item and puts it into the Item variable (ready to be edited).

6. Run the project and navigate to /admin/tags.

7. Try to add, edit, and delete a tag as shown in *Figure 6.2*:

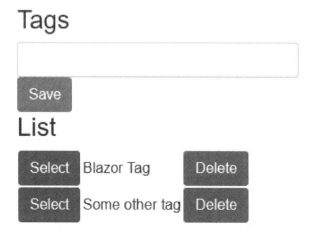

Figure 6.2 – The edit tag view

Now we only have two things left: we need ways to list and edit blog posts.

Listing and editing blog posts

Let's start with listing and editing blog posts:

1. Right-click on the Pages/Admin folder, select **Add | Razor component**, and name the component BlogPostList.razor.

2. At the top of the BlogPostList.razor file, replace <h3>BlogPostList</h3> with the following code:

```
@page "/admin/blogposts"
@inject IMyBlogApi api
<a href="/admin/blogposts/new">New blog post</a>
<ul>
    <Virtualize ItemsProvider="LoadPosts" Context="p">
        <li>@p.PublishDate
            <a href="/admin/blogposts/@p.Id">@p.Title</a>
        </li>
    </Virtualize>
</ul>
```

We added a page directive, injected our API, and listed the blog posts using the Virtualize component.

We also linked the posts to a URL with the Id instance of the blog post.

3. Replace the code section with the following code:

```
@code{
    public int TotalBlogposts { get; set; }
    private async ValueTask<ItemsProviderResult<BlogPost>>
        LoadPosts(ItemsProviderRequest request)
    {
        if (TotalBlogposts == 0)
        {
            TotalBlogposts = await
                api.GetBlogPostCountAsync();
        }
        var numblogposts = Math.Min(request.Count,
            TotalBlogposts - request.StartIndex);
```

```
        var posts = await
            api.GetBlogPostsAsync(numblogposts,
        request.StartIndex);
    return new ItemsProviderResult<BlogPost>(posts,
        TotalBlogposts);
    }
}
```

We added a method that can load posts from the database. This code is identical to the code we have on our **Index** page. Now there is only one thing left in the chapter: adding the page where we can edit the blog post.

A very popular way of writing blog posts is using Markdown; our blog engine will support that. Since Blazor supports any .NET Standard DLLs, we will add an existing library called `Markdig`.

This is the same engine that Microsoft uses for their docs site.

We can extend `Markdig` with different extensions (as Microsoft has done), but let's keep this simple and only add support for Markdown without all the fancy extensions:

1. Under the `MyBlogServerSide` project, right-click on the **Dependencies** node in the Solution Explorer and select **Manage NuGet Packages**.

2. Search for `Markdig` and click **Install** as shown in *Figure 6.3*:

Figure 6.3 – Add NuGet dialog

3. Right-click on the `components` folder and select **Add | Class**, then name the component `InputTextAreaOnInput.cs`.

4. Open the new file and add the following code:

```
using System.Diagnostics.CodeAnalysis;
using Microsoft.AspNetCore.Components.Rendering;
namespace Microsoft.AspNetCore.Components.Forms
{
```

```csharp
public class InputTextAreaOnInput :
InputBase<string?>
{
    protected override void
       BuildRenderTree(RenderTreeBuilder builder)
    {
        builder.OpenElement(0, "textarea");
        builder.AddMultipleAttributes(1,
           AdditionalAttributes);
        builder.AddAttribute(2, "class",
           CssClass);
        builder.AddAttribute(3, "value",
           BindConverter.FormatValue(CurrentValue));
        builder.AddAttribute(4, "oninput",
           EventCallback.Factory.CreateBinder
             <string?>(this, __value =>
               CurrentValueAsString = __value,
                 CurrentValueAsString));
        builder.CloseElement();
    }
    protected override bool
       TryParseValueFromString(string? value,
          out string? result, [NotNullWhen(false)]
             out string? validationErrorMessage)
    {
        result = value;
        validationErrorMessage = null;
        return true;
    }
}
```

The preceding code is taken from Microsoft's GitHub repository; it is how they implement the InputTextArea component.

In their build system, they can't handle .razor files, so that's why they implement the code this way. There is only one change made in this file and that is oninput, which is used to say OnChange.

For most cases, OnChange is going to be just fine, which means when I leave the textbox, the value will be updated (and trigger validations). But in our case, we want the preview of the HTML to be updated in real time, which is why we had to implement our own.

One option could have been to not use the InputTextArea component and instead use the TextArea tag, but then we would lose the validation highlighting. If we ever need to customize the behavior on an input control, this is the way to go.

I recommend using .razor files over .cs files if you are going to make a lot of changes to the implementation.

5. Right-click on the Pages/Admin folder, select **Add | Razor component**, and name the component BlogPostEdit.razor.

6. At the top of the BlogPostEdit.razor file, replace <h3>BlogPostEdit</h3> with the following code:

```
@page "/admin/blogposts/new"
@page "/admin/blogposts/{Id:int}"
@inject IMyBlogApi api
@inject NavigationManager manager
@using MyBlogServerSide.Components
@using Markdig;
```

We add two different page directives because we want to be able to create a new blog post as well as supply an ID to edit an already existing one. If we do not supply an ID, the Id parameter will be null (or the default).

We inject our API and NavigationManager as well as adding using statements.

7. Now we need to add the form; add the following code:

```
<EditForm Model="Post" OnValidSubmit="SavePost">
    <DataAnnotationsValidator />
    <CustomCssClassProvider
      ProviderType="BootstrapFieldCssClassProvider" />
    <InputText @bind-Value="Post.Title"></InputText>
    <InputDate @bind-Value="Post.PublishDate">
      </InputDate>
    <InputSelect @bind-Value="selectedCategory">
        <option value="0" disabled>None selected
          </option>
```

```
        @foreach (var category in Categories)
    {
    <option value="@category.Id">@category.Name </option>
}

    </InputSelect>
    <ul>
        @foreach (var tag in Tags)
        {
        <li>
            @tag.Name
            @if (Post.Tags.Any(t => t.Id == tag.Id))
            {
                <button type="button" @onclick="@(() => {
                    Post.Tags.Remove(Post.Tags.Single
                    (t=>t.Id==tag.Id)); })">Remove
                </button>
            }
            else
            {
                <button type="button" @onclick="@(()
                    => { Post.Tags.Add(tag); })">Add
                </button>
            }
        </li>
        }
    </ul>
        <InputTextAreaOnInput @bind-Value="Post.Text"
         @onkeyup="UpdateHTML">
        </InputTextAreaOnInput>
        <button type="submit" class="btn btn-success">
                Save</button>
    </EditForm>
```

We add `EditForm`, and when we submit the form (if it is valid), we execute the `SavePost` method. We add `DataAnnotationValidator`, which will validate our model against the data annotations in the class.

We add `customCssClassProvider` so that we get the correct Bootstrap class names. Then, we add boxes for the title, publish date, category, tags, and, last but not least, the text (the content of the blog post).

Finally, we add the text using the component we created in *Step 4* (the component that updates for each keystroke).

We also hook up the `@onkeyup` event so that we can update the preview for each keystroke.

8. We also need to add our `SavePost` method. Add the following code somewhere in the `code` section:

```
public async Task SavePost()
{
    if (selectedCategory != 0 && Categories != null)
    {
        var category = Categories.FirstOrDefault(c =>
            c.Id == selectedCategory);
        if (category != null)
        {
            Post.Category = category;
        }
    }
    await api.SaveBlogPostAsync(Post);
    manager.NavigateTo("/admin/blogposts");
}
```

9. Now it's time to show the preview. Add the following code just below `EditForm`:

```
@((MarkupString)markDownAsHTML)
```

We use `MarkupString` to make sure Blazor outputs the HTML code without escaping the characters. You might remember that from *Chapter 4, Understanding Basic Blazor Components*.

10. We also need some variables. Add the following code in the code section:

```
[Parameter]
public int? Id { get; set; }
BlogPost Post { get; set; } = new BlogPost();
List<Category>? Categories { get; set; }
List<Tag>? Tags { get; set; }
int selectedCategory = 0;
string? markDownAsHTML { get; set; }
```

We added a parameter for the ID of the blog post (if we want to edit one), a variable to hold the post we are editing, one that holds all the categories, and one that holds all the tags. We also added a variable that holds the currently selected category and one that holds the Markdown converted to HTML.

11. Now it is time to set up Markdig. Add the following code somewhere in the code section:

```
MarkdownPipeline pipeline;
protected override Task OnInitializedAsync()
{
    pipeline = new MarkdownPipelineBuilder()
            .UseEmojiAndSmiley()
            .Build();
    return base.OnInitializedAsync();
}
```

To configure Markdig, we need to create a pipeline. As I mentioned earlier in the chapter, this is the engine Microsoft uses for their docs site. It has many extensions available, including source code highlighting and emoticons.

To make it a little more fun, we added emoticons as well to the pipeline.

12. We also need to add code to load the data (blog post, categories, and tags). Add the following methods in the code section:

```
protected void UpdateHTML()
{
    markDownAsHTML =
        Markdig.Markdown.ToHtml(Post.Text, pipeline);
}
bool hasTag(MyBlog.Data.Models.Tag tag)
```

```
{
    return Post.Tags.Contains(tag);
}
protected override async Task OnParametersSetAsync()
{
    if (Id != null)
    {
        Post = await api.GetBlogPostAsync(Id.Value);
        if (Post.Category != null)
        {
            selectedCategory = Post.Category.Id;
        }
        UpdateHTML();
    }
    Categories = await api.GetCategoriesAsync();
    Tags = await api.GetTagsAsync();
    base.OnParametersSet();
}
```

13. Now run the site, navigate to /admin/blogposts, click on a blog post to edit
it, and test the new Markdown support. *Figure 6.4* shows the edit page with
Markdown support:

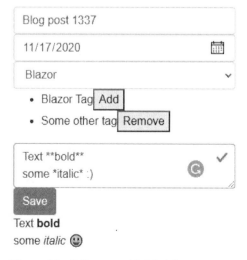

Figure 6.4 – Edit page with Markdown support

We have still got one more thing to do: we need to make sure that the blog post page shows a converted HTML version of the Markdown.

14. Open /Pages/Post.razor and add the following using statement at the top of the file:

```
@using Markdig;
```

15. Add the following code to the code section:

```
MarkdownPipeline pipeline;
protected override Task OnInitializedAsync()
{
    pipeline = new MarkdownPipelineBuilder()
            .UseEmojiAndSmiley()
            .Build();
    return base.OnInitializedAsync();
}
```

16. Replace the following row:

```
@((MarkupString)BlogPost.Text)
```

Replace it with this:

```
@((MarkupString)Markdig.Markdown.ToHtml(BlogPost.Text,
pipeline))
```

Great job! Now we have an admin interface up and running so that we can start writing blog posts.

Summary

In this chapter, we learned how to create forms. We made API calls to get and save data.

We built custom input controls and leveraged some of the new functionality in .NET 5 to get Bootstrap styling on our controls. Most business apps use forms, and by using data annotations, we can add logic close to the data (and even use annotations when we create the database, as we did in *Chapter 3, Introducing Entity Framework Core*).

The functionality that Blazor offers when it comes to validation and input controls will help us build amazing applications and will give our users a great experience. You may notice that right now the admin pages are wide open, so the next step is going to be securing our blog with login, but we will come back to that in *Chapter 8, Authentication and Authorization.*

In the next chapter, we will create an API so that we can get data in our Blazor WebAssembly project.

7
Creating an API

Blazor WebAssembly needs to be able to retrieve data and also change our data. For that to work, we need to have an API with which we can access the database. In this chapter, we will create a Web API.

When we are using Blazor Server, the API will be secured together with the page (if we add an `Authorize` attribute), so we get that for free. But with WebAssembly, everything will be executed in the browser, so we need something that WebAssembly can communicate with to update the database on the server.

To do this, we will cover need to cover three topics. In this chapter, we will cover the first two:

- Creating the service
- Creating the client

The third topic is *Calling the API*, but we won't cover that part in this chapter; instead, we will come back to it in *Chapter 9, Sharing Code and Resources*.

Technical requirements

Make sure you have read the previous chapters, or use the Ch6 folder as a starting point.

You can find the source code for this chapter's end result at `https://github.com/PacktPublishing/Web-Development-with-Blazor/tree/master/Chapter07`.

Creating the service

There are many ways to create a service, such as via REST or perhaps gRPC. In this book, we will cover REST.

For those who haven't worked with REST before, **REST** stands for **REpresentational State Transfer**. Simply put, it is a way for machines to talk to other machines using HTTP.

With REST, we use different HTTP verbs for different operations. It could look something like this:

URI	Verb	Action
/BlogPosts	Get	Gets a list of blog posts
/BlogPosts	Post	Creates a new blog post
/BlogPosts/{id}	Get	Gets a blog post with a specific ID
/BlogPost/{id}	Put	Replaces a blog post
/BlogPost/{id}	Patch	Updates a blog post
/BlogPost/{id}	Delete	Deletes a blog post

This is what we are going to implement for **tags**, **categories**, and **blog posts**.

Since the API takes care of whether the *post* should be created, we'll cheat a little bit and only implement *Put* (replace) because we don't know whether we are creating or updating the data.

The API will only be used by Blazor WebAssembly, so we will implement the API in the `MyBlogWebAssembly.Server` project.

Adding database access

Execute the following steps to provide database access:

1. In the `MyBlogWebAssembly.Server` project, open `Startup.cs`.

2. In the `Configure services` method, add the following lines (at the top of the method):

```
services.AddDbContextFactory<MyBlogDbContext>(opt => opt.
UseSqlite($"Data Source=../../MyBlog.db"));
services.AddScoped<IMyBlogApi, MyBlogApiServerSide>();
```

This is the same database configuration as with the `MyBlogServerSide` project.

We are even pointing to the same database, but since the folder structure is one level deeper for the Blazor WebAssembly project, we use `..\..\MyBlog.db` to reach the existing database.

3. Add a reference to the `MyBlog.Data` project by right-clicking **Dependencies** beneath the `MyBlogWebAssembly.Server` project and selecting **Add project reference**.

4. Check `MyBlog.Data` and click **Ok**.

5. Add the following namespaces:

```
using MyBlog.Data;
using MyBlog.Data.Interfaces;
using Microsoft.EntityFrameworkCore;
```

Now we have added access to the classes we have in the `MyBlog.Data` project.

We have configured it so that if we ask for an instance of `IMyBlogApi`, we will get an instance of the `MyBlogApiServerSide` class. This is because we are on the server side, so the API can have direct access to the database.

Now, let's create the API. In the `Controllers` folder, we already have an API to get weather forecast data.

Adding the API controller

Execute the following steps to create the API:

1. In the `MyBlogWebAssembly.Server` project, right-click on the `Controllers` folder and select **Add | Class**. Name the file `MyBlogApiController.cs`.

2. Add a `using` statement at the top of the file:

```
using Microsoft.AspNetCore.Mvc;
using MyBlog.Data.Interfaces;
using MyBlog.Data.Models;
using System.Collections.Generic;
using Microsoft.AspNetCore.Authorization;
```

3. Inherit from `ControllerBase` and add attributes. The class should look like this:

```
[ApiController]
[Route("[controller]")]
public class MyBlogApiController:ControllerBase
```

```
{

}
```

4. Now we need to access the data, and we will do that through the server-side API. Add the following code inside the class we just created:

```
internal readonly IMyBlogApi api;
public MyBlogApiController(IMyBlogApi api)
{
    this.api = api;
}
```

Now we can access the data through the `api` variable.

5. Next, we will add the code to get blog posts. Add the following code under the code we just added:

```
[HttpGet]
[Route("BlogPosts")]
public async Task<List<BlogPost>> GetBlogPostsAsync(int
numberofposts, int startindex)
{
    return await api.GetBlogPostsAsync(numberofposts,
        startindex);
}
```

We have created a method that returns the data directly from the database (the same API the Blazor Server project is using).

Go to the following URL: `https://localhost:5001/MyBlogApi/BlogPosts?numberofposts=10&startindex=0` (the port number might be something else). Make sure to start the `MyBlogWebAssembly.Server` project. We will get some JSON back with a list of our blog posts.

There are a couple of things worth noting. The method is called `GetBlogPostsAsync`. We choose to have the same name as the API, but the URL is not the same as the method name; it is specified by the `Route` attribute. We use the same method names as in `IMyBlogApi`; it is easier to follow the code when everything is named the same.

We also specify the `HttpGet` attribute, which will make sure the method only runs when we are using the *Get* verb.

We are off to a good start! Now we need to implement the rest of the API as well.

6. Let's add the function to get the blog post count:

```
[HttpGet]
[Route("BlogPostCount")]
public async Task<int> GetBlogPostCountAsync()
{
    return await api.GetBlogPostCountAsync();
}
```

We use the *Get* verb but with another route.

7. We also need to be able to get one blog post. Add the following method:

```
[HttpGet]
[Route("BlogPosts/{id}")]
public async Task<BlogPost> GetBlogPostAsync(int id)
{
    return await api.GetBlogPostAsync(id);
}
```

In this case, we are using the *Get* verb but with another URL containing the id for *Post* we want to get.

Next, we need an APIs that is protected, typically the one that updates or deletes things.

8. Let's add an API that saves a blog post. Add the following code under the code we just added:

```
[Authorize]
[HttpPut]
[Route("BlogPosts")]
public async Task<BlogPost> SaveBlogPostAsync([FromBody]
BlogPost item)
{
    return await api.SaveBlogPostAsync(item);
}
```

As I mentioned earlier in this chapter, we will only add one API for creating and updating blog posts, and we will use the *Put* verb (replace) to do that. We have added the `Authorize` attribute to the method, which will make sure that the user needs to be authenticated to be able to call the method.

9. Next up, we add a method for deleting blog posts. To do this, add the following code:

```
[Authorize]
[HttpDelete]
[Route("BlogPosts")]
public async Task DeleteBlogPostAsync([FromBody] BlogPost
item)
{
    await api.DeleteBlogPostAsync(item);
}
```

In this case, we use the *Delete* verb, and just as with saving we also add the `Authorize` attribute.

10. Next, we need to do this for `Categories` and `Tags` as well. Let's start with `Categories`. Add the following code to the `MyBlogApiController` class:

```
[HttpGet]
[Route("Categories")]
public async Task<List<Category>> GetCategoriesAsync()
{
    return await api.GetCategoriesAsync();
}
[HttpGet]
[Route("Categories/{id}")]
public async Task<Category> GetCategoryAsync(int id)
{
    return await api.GetCategoryAsync(id);
}
[Authorize]
[HttpPut]
[Route("Categories")]
public async Task<Category> SaveCategoryAsync([FromBody]
Category item)
```

```
{
    return await api.SaveCategoryAsync(item);
}
[Authorize]
[HttpDelete]
[Route("Categories")]
public async Task DeleteCategoryAsync([FromBody] Category
item)
{
    await api.DeleteCategoryAsync(item);
}
```

These are all the methods needed to handle **Categories**.

11. Next, let's do the same thing with **Tags**. Add the following code under the code we just added:

```
[HttpGet]
[Route("Tags")]
public async Task<List<Tag>> GetTagsAsync()
{
    return await api.GetTagsAsync();
}
[HttpGet]
[Route("Tags/{id}")]
public async Task<Tag> GetTagAsync(int id)
{
    return await api.GetTagAsync(id);
}
[Authorize]
[HttpPut]
[Route("Tags")]
public async Task<Tag> SaveTagAsync([FromBody] Tag item)
{
    return await api.SaveTagAsync(item);
}
[Authorize]
[HttpDelete]
```

```
[Route("Tags")]
public async Task DeleteTagAsync([FromBody] Tag item)
{
    await api.DeleteTagAsync(item);
}
```

Great! We have an API! Now it's time to write the client that will access that API.

Creating the client

To access the API, we need to create a client. There are many ways of doing this, but we will do it in the simplest way possible by writing the code ourselves.

The client will implement the same IMyBlogApi interface. This is so we have the exact same code regardless of which implementation we are using, direct database access with MyBlogApiServerSide or MyBlogApiClientSide, which we are going to create next:

1. Right-click on the **Dependencies** node under MyBlog.Data and select **Manage NuGet Packages**.

2. Search for Microsoft.AspNetCore.Components.WebAssembly. Authentication and click **Install**.

3. Also, search for Newtonsoft.Json and Microsoft.Extensions.Http and click **Install**.

4. We need some helper methods, so add a folder by right-clicking on MyBlog.Data, then **Add | Folder**, and name the folder Extensions.

5. Right-click on the new folder and select **Add | Class**. Name the class HttpClientExtensions.cs.

6. Add the following namespaces:
   ```
   using Newtonsoft.Json;
   using System.Net.Http;
   using System.Threading;
   ```

7. Replace the class with the following code:
   ```
   public static class HttpClientExtensions
   {
       public static Task<HttpResponseMessage>
           DeleteAsJsonAsync<T>(this HttpClient httpClient,
   ```

```
                string requestUri, T data)
            => httpClient.SendAsync(new
               HttpRequestMessage(HttpMethod.Delete,
                  requestUri) { Content = Serialize(data) });
        public static Task<HttpResponseMessage>
           DeleteAsJsonAsync<T>(this HttpClient httpClient,
              string requestUri, T data, CancellationToken
              cancellationToken)
            => httpClient.SendAsync(new
               HttpRequestMessage(HttpMethod.Delete,
                  requestUri) { Content = Serialize(data) },
                     cancellationToken);
        public static Task<HttpResponseMessage>
           DeleteAsJsonAsync<T>(this HttpClient httpClient,
              Uri requestUri, T data)
            => httpClient.SendAsync(new
               HttpRequestMessage(HttpMethod.Delete,
                  requestUri) { Content = Serialize(data) });
        public static Task<HttpResponseMessage>
           DeleteAsJsonAsync<T>(this HttpClient
              httpClient, Uri requestUri, T data,
              CancellationToken cancellationToken)
            => httpClient.SendAsync(new
               HttpRequestMessage(HttpMethod.Delete,
                  equestUri) { Content = Serialize(data) },
                     cancellationToken);
        private static HttpContent Serialize(object data)
           => new StringContent
             (JsonConvert.SerializeObject(data), Encoding.UTF8,
               "application/json");
    }
```

These are some extension methods that will help us call the API.

8. Right-click on the `MyBlog.Data` project and select **Add | Class**. Name the class `MyBlogApiClientSide.cs`.

9. Open the newly created file.

10. Add `IMyBlogApi` to the class and make it public like this:

```
public class MyBlogApiClientSide:IMyBlogApi
    {}
```

11. Some of the API calls are going to be public (do not require authentication), but HttpClient will be configured to always require a token (we will do that later in the chapter).

    So, we are going to need one authenticated HttpClient and one not authenticated HttpClient, depending on what API we are calling.

12. To be able to call the API, we need to inject HttpClient. Add the following code to the class:

```
private readonly IHttpClientFactory factory;
public MyBlogApiClientSide(IHttpClientFactory factory)
{
    this.factory = factory;
}
```

13. We also need to add the following namespaces:

```
using MyBlog.Data.Interfaces;
using System.Net.Http;
using MyBlog.Data.Models;
using System.Net.Http.Json;
using Microsoft.AspNetCore.Components.WebAssembly.
Authentication;
using MyBlog.Data.Extensions;
using Newtonsoft.Json;
```

14. Now it's time to implement calls to the API. Let's begin with the *Get* calls for blog posts. Add the following code:

```
public async Task<BlogPost> GetBlogPostAsync(int id)
{
    var httpclient = factory.CreateClient("Public");
    return await httpclient.GetFromJsonAsync<BlogPost>
        ($"MyBlogAPI/BlogPosts/{id}");
}
public async Task<int> GetBlogPostCountAsync()
{
    var httpclient = factory.CreateClient("Public");
    return await httpclient.GetFromJsonAsync<int>
        ("MyBlogAPI/BlogPostCount");
```

```
}
public async Task<List<BlogPost>> GetBlogPostsAsync(int
numberofposts, int startindex)
{
    var httpclient = factory.CreateClient("Public");
    return await
      httpclient.GetFromJsonAsync<List<BlogPost>>
       ($"MyBlogAPI/BlogPosts?numberofposts=
          {numberofposts}&startindex={startindex}");
}
```

We use the HttpClient we injected and then call GetFromJsonAsync, which will automatically download the JSON and convert it to the class that we supply into the generic method.

Now it gets a little trickier: we need to handle authentication Luckily, this is built into HttpClient so we only need to handle AccessTokenNotAvailable Exception. If a token is missing it will automatically try and renew it, but if there is a problem (for example, the user is not logged in) we can redirect to the login page.

We will come back to tokens and how authentication works in *Chapter 8, Authentication and Authorization.*

15. Next, we add the API calls that need authentication, such as saving or deleting a blog post.

Add the following code under the code we just added:

```
public async Task<BlogPost> SaveBlogPostAsync(BlogPost
item)
{
    try
    {
        var httpclient =
          factory.CreateClient("Authenticated");
        var response= await
          httpclient.PutAsJsonAsync<BlogPost>
            ("MyBlogAPI/BlogPosts",item);
        var json = await
          response.Content.ReadAsStringAsync();
        return
```

```
                    JsonConvert.DeserializeObject<BlogPost>(json);
        }
    catch (AccessTokenNotAvailableException exception)
    {
        exception.Redirect();
    }
    return null;
}
public async Task DeleteBlogPostAsync(BlogPost item)
{
    try
    {
        var httpclient =
            factory.CreateClient("Authenticated");
        await httpclient.DeleteAsJsonAsync<BlogPost>
            ("MyBlogAPI/BlogPosts", item);
    }
    catch (AccessTokenNotAvailableException exception)
    {
        exception.Redirect();
    }
}
```

If the call throws AccessTokenNotAvailableException, that means HttpClient couldn't get or renew a token automatically and the user needs to log in.

This state should probably never happen because we will make sure that when the user navigates to that page they will need to be logged in, but it's better to be safe than sorry.

We also use an HttpClient named Authenticated, which we need to configure, but we will come back to that in *Chapter 8, Authentication and Authorization.*

16. Now we need to do the same for **Categories**. Add the following code to the MyBlogApiClientSide class:

```
public async Task<List<Category>> GetCategoriesAsync()
{
```

```
        var httpclient = factory.CreateClient("Public");
        return await
          httpclient.GetFromJsonAsync<List<Category>>
            ($"MyBlogAPI/Categories");
    }
public async Task<Category> GetCategoryAsync(int id)
    {
        var httpclient = factory.CreateClient("Public");
        return await httpclient.GetFromJsonAsync<Category>
          ($"MyBlogAPI/Categories/{id}");
    }
public async Task DeleteCategoryAsync(Category item)
    {
        try
        {
            var httpclient =
              factory.CreateClient("Authenticated");
            await httpclient.DeleteAsJsonAsync<Category>
              ("MyBlogAPI/Categories", item);
        }
        catch (AccessTokenNotAvailableException exception)
        {
            exception.Redirect();
        }
    }
public async Task<Category> SaveCategoryAsync(Category
item)
    {
        try
        {
            var httpclient =
              factory.CreateClient("Authenticated");
            var response = await
              httpclient.PutAsJsonAsync<Category>
                ("MyBlogAPI/Categories", item);
            var json = await
              response.Content.ReadAsStringAsync();
            return
```

```
        JsonConvert.DeserializeObject<Category>(json);
    }
    catch (AccessTokenNotAvailableException exception)
    {
        exception.Redirect();
    }
    return null;
}
```

17. And next up, we will do the same for **Tags**. Add the following code just under the code we just added:

```
public async Task<Tag> GetTagAsync(int id)
{
    var httpclient = factory.CreateClient("Public");
    return await httpclient.GetFromJsonAsync<Tag>
        ($"MyBlogAPI/Tags/{id}");
}
public async Task<List<Tag>> GetTagsAsync()
{
    var httpclient = factory.CreateClient("Public");
    return await
        httpclient.GetFromJsonAsync<List<Tag>>
        ($"MyBlogAPI/Tags");
}
public async Task DeleteTagAsync(Tag item)
{
    try
    {
        var httpclient =
            factory.CreateClient("Authenticated");
        await httpclient.DeleteAsJsonAsync<Tag>
            ("MyBlogAPI/Tags", item);
    }
    catch (AccessTokenNotAvailableException exception)
    {
        exception.Redirect();
    }
```

```
        }
    public async Task<Tag> SaveTagAsync(Tag item)
    {
        try
        {
            var httpclient =
                factory.CreateClient("Authenticated");
            var response = await
                httpclient.PutAsJsonAsync<Tag>
                    ("MyBlogAPI/Tags", item);
            var json = await
                response.Content.ReadAsStringAsync();
            return
                JsonConvert.DeserializeObject<Tag>(json);
        }
        catch (AccessTokenNotAvailableException exception)
        {
            exception.Redirect();
        }
        return null;
    }
```

Great job! Our API client is now done!

Overall, the two steps are completed, only one left; as mentioned earlier in the chapter, we won't cover the last part in this chapter. Instead, we will come back to it in *Chapter 9, Sharing Code and Resources*.

Summary

In this chapter, we learned how to create an API and an API client, which is an important part of most applications. This way, we can get blog posts from our database and show them in our Blazor WebAssembly app.

In the next chapter, *Chapter 8, Authentication and Authorization*, we will add login functionality to our sites.

In the chapter after that, *Chapter 9, Sharing Code and Resources*, we will finally get both projects running on the same code, and that is where we will try out our API for the first time.

8
Authentication and Authorization

In this chapter, we will learn how to add authentication and authorization to our blog, because we don't want just anyone to be able to create or edit blog posts.

Covering authentication and authorization fully would itself take a whole book, so we will keep things simple here. The goal of this chapter is to get the built-in authentication and authorization functionalities working, building on the already existing functionality that's built in to ASP.NET. That means that there is not a lot of Blazor magic involved here; there are a lot of resources that already exist that we can take advantage of.

Almost every system today has some way to log in, whether it is an admin interface (like ours) or a member login portal. There are many different login providers, such as Google, Twitter, and Microsoft. We can use all of these providers since we will just be building on already existing architecture.

We will keep things simple and add our users to a database.

We will cover the following topics in this chapter:

- Implementing authentication
- Adding authorization

Technical requirements

Make sure you have followed the previous chapters, or use the `Chapter07` folder as a starting point.

You can find the source code for this chapter's end result at `https://github.com/PacktPublishing/Web-Development-with-Blazor/tree/master/Chapter08`.

Implementing authentication

There are a lot of built-in functionalities when it comes to authentication. The easiest way to achieve authentication is to just select an authentication option when you create a project, but we are here to learn how things work properly, so we will implement authentication ourselves.

We need to implement authentication separately for the Blazor Server project and the Blazor WebAssembly project because they work a bit differently.

But there are still things we can share between these two projects – first, let's add the necessary tables to our database.

Adding tables to the database

To be able to add authentication, we need to add the necessary tables to our database. This is something we can do using Entity Framework:

1. In the `MyBlog.Data` project, we need to add a couple of NuGet packages; right-click on **Dependencies** and select **Manage NuGet Packages**.

2. Search for `Microsoft.AspNetCore.Identity.EntityFrameworkCore` and click **Install**.

3. Search for `Microsoft.AspNetCore.Diagnostics.EntityFrameworkCore` and click **Install**.

4. We also need to add `IdentityServer`. Search for `Microsoft.AspNetCore.ApiAuthorization.IdentityServer` and click **Install**.

   If you only intend to use Blazor Server, you won't need this step, but since we want our solution to work on both Blazor Server and Blazor WebAssembly, we will make sure to add this `IdentityServer` now.

5. Open the `MyBlogDbContext.cs` file. Change the code so that `MyBlogDbContext` inherits from `ApiAuthorizationDbContext<AppUser>` and add a new constructor and overridden `OnModelCreating` as follows:

```
public class MyBlogDbContext :
ApiAuthorizationDbContext<AppUser>
{
        public MyBlogDbContext(DbContextOptions
            options) : base(options, new
                OperationalStoreOptionsMigrations())
        { }

    protected override void OnModelCreating(ModelBuilder
    builder)
        {
                base.OnModelCreating(builder);
        }
```

By adding this code, we are including the tables from the inherited classes as well.

6. In the `MyBlogDbContext.cs` file, we have a class called `MyBlogDbContextFactory`. Change the path to the database to `../MyBlog.db` as follows:

```
optionsBuilder.UseSqlite("Data Source = ../MyBlog.db");
```

This way, when we update the database, we will update it for all our projects (all our projects are using the same database file).

7. Also, add this class (use the same file since the projects are tightly coupled):

```
public class OperationalStoreOptionsMigrations :
IOptions<OperationalStoreOptions>
{
    public OperationalStoreOptions Value => new
        OperationalStoreOptions()
    {
        DeviceFlowCodes = new
            TableConfiguration("DeviceCodes"),
        EnableTokenCleanup = false,
```

```
            PersistedGrants = new
                TableConfiguration("PersistedGrants"),
            TokenCleanupBatchSize = 100,
            TokenCleanupInterval = 3600,
        };
    }
```

We use this class to configure `IdentityServer`, and we need this class because we are using the same data context for both the identity part (the usernames, passwords, and tokens) and our data (blog posts, tags, and categories).

To be able to create `DbContextFactory`, we need to have a constructor with only one parameter.

We could have created multiple database contexts, one for our data and one for the identity information, but what we've done will prove to be an easier solution as we move forward.

Add the following `using` statements:

```
using Microsoft.AspNetCore.Identity.EntityFrameworkCore;
using IdentityServer4.EntityFramework.Options;
using Microsoft.AspNetCore.ApiAuthorization.
IdentityServer;
using Microsoft.Extensions.Options;
```

8. Right-click on the `models` folder and select **Add | Class**. Name the class `AppUser.cs`.

9. Open the `AppUser` class and replace the content with the following:

```
using Microsoft.AspNetCore.Identity;
namespace MyBlog.Data.Models
{
    public class AppUser : IdentityUser
    {}
}
```

Now we need to create a migration, and just as we did before in *Chapter 3, Introducing Entity Framework Core*; we will do that using PowerShell.

10. Open PowerShell and navigate to the folder that you have the `MyBlog.Data` project in.

    This can also be done from within Developer PowerShell in Visual Studio.

11. Execute the following commands:

```
dotnet ef migrations add Identity
dotnet ef database update
```

    Just as a reminder, we are running the `dotnet` tool to create a migration with the name `Identity`.

    We also update the database so that it gets all the latest migrations, and we are ready to start using the new data context.

Next, we need to configure the Blazor Server project.

Configuring the Blazor Server project

We need to tell the Blazor Server project that we want it to use authentication. We do that by adding configurations in `Startup.cs`:

1. In the `MyBlogServerSide` project, right-click on the **Dependencies** node and select **Manage NuGet Packages**.

2. Search for `Microsoft.AspNetCore.Identity.UI` and click **Install**.

    This package contains a UI and extensions that will help us when it comes to user login.

    ASP.NET has support for a lot of different ways of authenticating, and so leveraging what already exists in terms of its authentication infrastructure makes a lot of sense.

3. Right-click on the `MyBlogServerSide` project, select **Add Folder**, and name the folder `Authentication`.

4. Right-click on the folder and select **Add | Class**, and name the class `RevalidatingIdentityAuthenticationStateProvider.cs`.

5. We don't need to talk about the content of this class since this is normally provided in a Blazor template. Simply copy the content from the GitHub repository found here: `https://github.com/PacktPublishing/Web-Development-with-Blazor/blob/master/Chapter08/MyBlog/MyBlogServerSide/Authentication/RevalidatingIdentityAuthenticationStateProvider.cs`.

This is one of the files that Microsoft will supply for us when we choose to add authentication when we create our project.

It will check whether the user credentials are still valid (after 30 minutes by default).

6. Open `Startup.cs` and add the following namespaces:

```
using MyBlog.Data.Models;
using Microsoft.AspNetCore.Components.Authorization;
using MyBlogServerSide.Authentication;
```

7. To not have to repeat ourselves, let's add the connection string as a setting instead.

Open `appsetting.json` and add the following just after the first curly brace:

```
"ConnectionStrings": {
    "MyBlogDB": "Data Source=../MyBlog.db"
},
```

8. Add this code at the bottom of the `ConfigureServices` method:

```
services.AddDbContext<MyBlogDbContext>(opt => opt.
UseSqlite(Configuration.GetConnectionString("MyBlogDB")));
services.AddDefaultIdentity<AppUser>(options => options.
SignIn.RequireConfirmedAccount = true)
        .AddEntityFrameworkStores<MyBlogDbContext>();
services.AddScoped<AuthenticationStateProvider,
RevalidatingIdentityAuthenticationStateProvider
<AppUser>>();
```

We configured the built-in identity provider so Blazor knows where to find the users and passwords.

We also need to add a configuration for `DbContext`. We will be using `DbContextFactory` for the rest of our application, but the `Identity` functionality needs `DbContext`, so we add a *duplicate* for the `Identity` functionality to work.

Make sure to change the connection string on `DBContextFactory` a few lines above the code we just added.

9. In the `Configure` method just beneath `app.UseRouting()`, add the following code:

```
app.UseAuthentication();
app.UseAuthorization();
```

10. Open the `App.Razor` file and replace the content with the following:

```
<CascadingAuthenticationState>
    <Router AppAssembly="@typeof(Program).Assembly"
        PreferExactMatches="@true">
        <Found Context="routeData">
            <AuthorizeRouteView RouteData="@routeData"
                DefaultLayout="@typeof(MainLayout)">
                <NotAuthorized>
                    <p>Not authorized</p>
                </NotAuthorized>
                <Authorizing>
                    <p>Checking</p>
                </Authorizing>
            </AuthorizeRouteView>
        </Found>
        <NotFound>
            <LayoutView Layout="@typeof(MainLayout)">
                <p>Sorry, there's nothing at this
                    address.</p>
            </LayoutView>
        </NotFound>
    </Router>
</CascadingAuthenticationState>
```

We added `CascadingAuthenticationState`, which will make sure that all the components have access to `AuthenticationState` (whether or not we are logged in).

We also added `AuthorizeRouteView`, which will check whether the page is authenticated or not.

If the user is not authenticated, we can show another message using the `NotAuthorized` template and another message while we check the authorization.

11. Right-click on the `components` folder and select **Add | Razor component**. Name the component `LoginDisplay.razor`.

12. Open the new component and replace the content with the following:

```
<AuthorizeView>
    <Authorized>
        <a href="Identity/Account/Manage">Hello,
            @context.User.Identity.Name!</a>
        <form method="post" action="/LogOut">
            <button type="submit" class="nav-link
                btn btn-link">Log out</button>
        </form>
    </Authorized>
    <NotAuthorized>
        <a href= "Identity/Account/Register"> Register
        </a>
        <a href="Identity/Account/Login">Log in</a>
    </NotAuthorized>
</AuthorizeView>
```

In this file, we use the built-in `AuthorizeView` component, which will make it possible to specify different views depending on whether or not the user is logged in.

If they are logged in, we want to show a log-out link, and if they are not logged in, we want to show a log-in or register link.

13. Open `_Imports.razor` and add the following `using` statement anywhere in the file:

```
@using MyBlogServerSide.Components
```

14. Open `Shared/MainLayout.razor` and add the component to the page just after the **About** link:

```
<LoginDisplay />
```

15. The identity UI needs a file called `_LoginPartial.cshtml` to work. Right-click on the `Pages` folder and select **Add | Folder**; name the folder `Shared`.

16. Right-click on the `Pages/Shared` folder and click **Add | New item**.

17. Click **Razor Page – Empty** and name the file `_LoginPartial.cshtml`.

18. Replace the content of the file with the following:

```
@using Microsoft.AspNetCore.Identity;
@using MyBlog.Data.Models;
@inject SignInManager<AppUser> SignInManager
@inject UserManager<AppUser> UserManager
@addTagHelper *, Microsoft.AspNetCore.Mvc.TagHelpers
<ul class="navbar-nav">
@if (SignInManager.IsSignedIn(User))
{
    <li class="nav-item">
        <a  class="nav-link text-dark"
          asp-area="Identity"
          asp-page="/Account/Manage/Index"
          title="Manage">
          Hello @User.Identity.Name!</a>
    </li>
    <li class="nav-item">
        <form class="form-inline" asp-area="Identity"
          asp-page="/Account/Logout"
          asp-route-returnUrl="/" method="post">
            <button  type="submit" class="nav-link
              btn btn-link text-dark">Logout</button>
        </form>
    </li>
}
else
{
    <li class="nav-item">
        <a class="nav-link text-dark"
          asp-area="Identity"
          asp-page="/Account/Register">Register</a>
    </li>
    <li class="nav-item">
```

```
                    <a class="nav-link text-dark"
                        asp-area="Identity"
                        asp-page="/Account/Login">Login</a>
            </li>
        }
    </ul>
```

The reason we have a file like that is that the login page comes from the `Microsoft.AspNetCore.Identity.UI` package, which supplies us with the functionality of logging in with Facebook, Google, Microsoft, Twitter, and other accounts.

We get all that functionality for free. We can customize the login page as well by scaffolding the views, but we won't go into that in this book.

More information on scaffolding can be found here: `https://docs.microsoft.com/en-us/aspnet/core/security/authentication/scaffold-identity?view=aspnetcore-5.0&tabs=visual-studio`.

19. Right-click on the `Pages` folder and select **Add | New item**.

20. Click **Razor Page – Empty** and name the file `Logout.cshtml`.

21. Replace the content of the file with the following:

```
@page
@using Microsoft.AspNetCore.Identity
@using MyBlog.Data.Models
@attribute [IgnoreAntiforgeryToken]
@inject SignInManager<AppUser> SignInManager
@functions {
    public async Task<IActionResult> OnPost()
    {
        if (SignInManager.IsSignedIn(User))
        {
            await SignInManager.SignOutAsync();
        }
        return Redirect("~/");
    }
}
```

22. Now we need something to secure. We need to edit the following four files and add the `@attribute [Authorize]` attribute to each file:

    `Pages/Admin/BlogPostEdit.razor`

    `Pages/Admin/BlogPostList.razor`

    `Pages/Admin/CategoryList.razor`

    `Pages/Admin/TagList.razor`

23. Change the startup project to `MyBlogServerSide` and run the project by pressing *F5*.

24. If you now navigate to `https://localhost:5001/admin/Tags` (the port number may differ), you will notice that you get a **Not authorized** message, as shown in *Figure 8.1*:

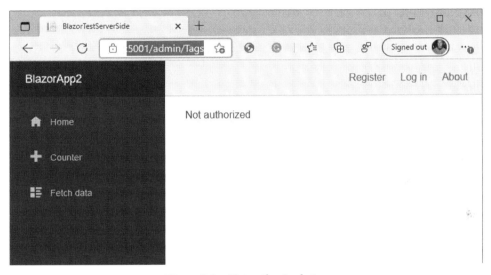

Figure 8.1 – Not authorized view

25. Click **Register** and log in with your credentials, and you will now have access to the `TagList` component.

Congratulations, you now have a site with login functionality running on the server side. Now we need to implement the same thing for Blazor WebAssembly.

Configuring the Blazor WebAssembly project

The `WebAssembly` project has some of the same functionalities; it is a tiny bit more complicated because it requires API authentication as well.

By default (if we choose to add authentication when we create the project), it will use `IdentityServer` to authenticate both the client and the API, which is what we are going to use as well.

`IdentityServer` is an open source project that will help us handle authentication for our site as well as our API.

Since we implemented `IdentityServer` in our `MyBlog.Data` project, we already have most of what we need in place.

Let's implement the rest.

First, we make some changes to the `MyBlogWebAssembly.Server` project.

Updating MyBlogWebAssembly.Server

Execute the following steps to update the `MyBlogWebAssembly.Server` project:

1. In the `MyBlogWebAssembly.Server` project, open `Startup.cs`.

2. Add the following namespaces:

```
using MyBlog.Data.Models;
using Microsoft.AspNetCore.Authentication;
```

3. Open `appsetting.json` and add the following just after the first curly brace:

```
"ConnectionStrings": {
  "MyBlogDB": "Data Source=../../MyBlog.db" },
```

4. In the `ConfigureServices` method, add the following at the bottom of the method (this needs to be after `AddDbContextFactory`):

```
services.AddDbContext<MyBlogDbContext>(opt => opt.
UseSqlite(Configuration.GetConnectionString("MyBlogDB")));
services.AddDefaultIdentity<AppUser>(options => options.
SignIn.RequireConfirmedAccount = false)
    .AddEntityFrameworkStores<MyBlogDbContext>();
services.AddIdentityServer()
```

```
        .AddApiAuthorization<AppUser, MyBlogDbContext>();
   services.AddAuthentication()
        .AddIdentityServerJwt();
```

We configure the database, pretty much the same thing we did for the Blazor Server project earlier in the chapter.

We also configure the `Identity` provider as well as `IdentityServer`.

We also added a JWT to the configuration. **JWT** stands for **JSON Web Token**, which is an internet standard for creating data with an optional signature/ encryption that holds JSON and can hold several claims.

The token is stored in the session storage in the browser. There are two tokens: one showing that we are logged in and one that we use for API access (this is handled by the framework for us).

This is what our API client (which we created at the beginning of this chapter) will send to the API to authenticate.

This will happen automatically for us.

5. In the `Configure` method, just above `app.UseEndpoints`, add the following code:

```
   app.UseIdentityServer();
   app.UseAuthentication();
   app.UseAuthorization();
```

These lines need to be between `app.UseRouting();` and `app.UseEndpoints`, otherwise you will get a warning that things might not work as you expect.

6. Now we need `_LoginPartial`, just as we did for the Blazor Server project. Right-click on the `Pages` folder and select **Add | Folder**; name the folder `Shared`.

7. Right-click on `Pages/Shared` and click **Add | Razor page**; name the page `_LoginPartial.cshtml`.

8. Add the following code to the file we just created:

```
   @using Microsoft.AspNetCore.Identity
   @using MyBlog.Data.Models
   @inject SignInManager<AppUser> SignInManager
   @inject UserManager<AppUser> UserManager
   @addTagHelper *, Microsoft.AspNetCore.Mvc.TagHelpers
```

```
@{
    var returnUrl = "/";
    if (Context.Request.Query.TryGetValue("returnUrl",
        out var existingUrl)) {
        returnUrl = existingUrl;
    }
}


<ul class="navbar-nav">
</ul>
```

9. Inside of the `<ul>` tag, add the following code:

```
@if (SignInManager.IsSignedIn(User))
{
    <li class="nav-item">
        <a   class="nav-link text-dark"
            asp-area="Identity"
            asp-page="/Account/Manage/Index"
            title="Manage">
            Hello @User.Identity.Name!</a>
    </li>
    <li class="nav-item">
        <form class="form-inline" asp-area="Identity"
          asp-page="/Account/Logout"
          asp-route-returnUrl="/" method="post">
            <button  type="submit" class="nav-link btn
              btn-link text-dark">Logout</button>
        </form>
    </li>
}
else
{
    <li class="nav-item">
        <a class="nav-link text-dark"
          asp-area="Identity"
          asp-page="/Account/Register"
          asp-route-returnUrl="@returnUrl">Register
        </a>
```

```
        </li>
        <li class="nav-item">
            <a class="nav-link text-dark"
               asp-area="Identity"
               asp-page="/Account/Login"
               asp-route-returnUrl="@returnUrl">Login</a>
        </li>
    }
```

Based on the user's current status, we show whether the user is logged in. If the user is logged in, we show a greeting and a **Log out** link.

10. We also need to create a controller for Open ID Connect.

    Right-click on the `Controllers` folder and select **Add | Class**; name the class `OidcConfigurationController.cs`.

11. Open the file we just created and replace the content with the following:

```
using Microsoft.AspNetCore.ApiAuthorization.
IdentityServer;
using Microsoft.AspNetCore.Mvc;
using Microsoft.Extensions.Logging;
namespace MyBlogWebAssembly.Server.Controllers
{
    public class OidcConfigurationController : Controller
    {
        private readonly
          ILogger<OidcConfigurationController> _logger;
        public OidcConfigurationController
            (IclientRequestParametersProvider
            clientRequestParametersProvider,
            ILogger<OidcConfigurationController>
            logger)
        {
```

```
              ClientRequestParametersProvider =
                clientRequestParametersProvider;
            _logger = logger;
        }
        public IclientRequestParametersProvider
          ClientRequestParametersProvider { get; }
        [HttpGet("_configuration/{clientId}")]
        public IactionResult
          GetClientRequestParameters([FromRoute] string
          clientId)
        {
            var parameters =
                ClientRequestParametersProvider.
                GetClientParameters(HttpContext, clientId);
            return Ok(parameters);
        }
      }
    }
```

This controller is responsible for sending the token to the client when the client requests it.

12. Open appsettings.json and add the following just above the last curly brace:

```
,
"IdentityServer": {
  "Clients": {
    "MyBlogWebAssembly.Client": {
      "Profile": "IdentityServerSPA"
    }
  }
}
```

This is the name of our client and needs to be specified; you must use the same client name in the API.

13. Open `appsettings.Development.json` and add the following:

```
,
"IdentityServer": {
  "Key": {
    "Type": "Development"
  }
}
```

The last two steps are to configure `IdentityServer`. We created a client called `MyBlogWebAssembly.Client` with the `IdentityServerSPA` profile. We also used a key type of `Development`, which created a fake certificate that we can use during development (but we need to replace it with a real certificate when deploying to a production server).

The server part is now done; now we need to make changes to the `MyBlogWebAssembly.Client` project.

Updating MyBlogWebAssembly.Client

Now we need to tell the client project that we want to tell the project to use authentication:

1. First, we need to add a couple of NuGet packages. Right-click on the `MyBlogWebAssembly.Client` project and click **Manage NuGet Packages**.

2. Search for `Microsoft.AspNetCore.Components.WebAssembly. Authentication` and click **Install**.

3. Search for `Microsoft.Extensions.Http` and click **Install**.

4. Open `Program.cs` and replace the line `builder.Services.AddScoped(sp => new HttpClient { BaseAddress = new Uri(builder. HostEnvironment.BaseAddress) });` with the following code block:

```
builder.Services.AddHttpClient("Authenticated", client
=> client.BaseAddress = new Uri(builder.HostEnvironment.
BaseAddress))
    .AddHttpMessageHandler<BaseAddressAuthorizationMessage
        Handler>();
builder.Services.AddHttpClient("Public", client =>
client.BaseAddress = new Uri(builder.HostEnvironment.
BaseAddress));
builder.Services.AddApiAuthorization();
```

We add two `HttpClient` dependency injections, one for calling authenticated APIs and one for calling any non-authenticated APIs.

The one for calling authenticated APIs will throw an exception if we call an API without a token (without being logged in); that's why we need to have a specific one for calling the APIs that do not require us to be logged in.

5. Add the following `using` statement:

```
using Microsoft.AspNetCore.Components.WebAssembly.
Authentication;
```

6. Now we need to add a couple of files. Right-click on the `Pages` folder, select **Add | Razor component**, and name the file `Authentication.razor`.

7. Replace the content of the file with the following:

```
@page "/authentication/{action}"
@using Microsoft.AspNetCore.Components.WebAssembly.
Authentication
<RemoteAuthenticatorView Action="@Action" />
@code{
    [Parameter] public string Action { get; set; }
}
```

The component will redirect and log in on the server.

This is where a lot of magic happens: based on the action, it will redirect you to the server and the built-in authentication UI.

`RemoteAuthenticatorView` has a lot of different templates that you can use to customize the component, such as `LogInFailed`, `CompletingLogOut`, and `LoggingIn`.

We use the server for authentication and the client will get a token back so that we know we are logged in and that we can get data from our APIs.

8. Right-click on the `Shared` folder, select **Add | Razor component**, and name the file `LoginDisplay.razor`.

9. Replace the content of the file with the following:

```
@using Microsoft.AspNetCore.Components.Authorization
@using Microsoft.AspNetCore.Components.WebAssembly.
Authentication
```

```
@inject NavigationManager Navigation
@inject SignOutSessionStateManager SignOutManager
<AuthorizeView>
    <Authorized>
        <a href="authentication/profile">Hello,
          @context.User.Identity.Name!</a>
        <button class="nav-link btn btn-link"
          @onclick="BeginSignOut">Log out</button>
    </Authorized>
    <NotAuthorized>
        <a href="authentication/register">Register</a>
        <a href="authentication/login">Log in</a>
    </NotAuthorized>
</AuthorizeView>
@code{
    private async Task BeginSignOut(MouseEventArgs args)
    {
        await SignOutManager.SetSignOutState();
        Navigation.NavigateTo("authentication/logout");
    }
}
```

This file differs a bit from the file we created for Blazor Server. It uses the `authentication` component we just created and makes calls back to the server.

It will log out the client and the server.

10. Right-click on the `Shared` folder, select **Add | Razor component**, and name the file `RedirectToLogin.razor`.

11. Replace the content of the file with the following:

```
@inject NavigationManager Navigation
@using Microsoft.AspNetCore.Components.WebAssembly.Authentication
@code {
    protected override void OnInitialized()
    {
```

```
                    Navigation.NavigateTo($"authentication/
                         login?returnUrl={Uri.EscapeDataString
                         (Navigation.Uri)}");
            }
    }
```

The component will redirect to the login page, again using the `authentication` component.

12. Open `_Imports.razor` and add this:

```
@using Microsoft.AspNetCore.Components.Authorization
@using Microsoft.AspNetCore.Components.WebAssembly.
Authentication
```

13. Now we need to activate authentication by opening `App.Razor` and replacing the content with the following code:

```
<CascadingAuthenticationState>
    <Router AppAssembly="@typeof(Program).Assembly"
        PreferExactMatches="@true">
        <Found Context="routeData">
            <AuthorizeRouteView RouteData="@routeData"
                DefaultLayout="@typeof(MainLayout)">
                <NotAuthorized>
                    @if (!context.User.Identity.
                        IsAuthenticated)
                    {
                        <RedirectToLogin />
                    }
                    else
                    {
                        <p>You are not authorized to
                            access this resource.</p>
                    }
                </NotAuthorized>
            </AuthorizeRouteView>
        </Found>
        <NotFound>
            <LayoutView Layout="@typeof(MainLayout)">
```

```
                    <p>Sorry, there's nothing at this
                    address.</p>
            </LayoutView>
        </NotFound>
    </Router>
</CascadingAuthenticationState>
```

14. Now we need to add a reference to the JavaScript file. Open wwwroot/index.html and just above the reference to blazor.webassembly.js, add the following:

```
<script src="_content/Microsoft.AspNetCore.Components.
WebAssembly.Authentication/AuthenticationService.js"></
script>
```

Now everything is in place, but we need something to call the API as well.

15. Open Pages/FetchData.razor and inject IhttpClientFactory after the @page directive:

```
@inject IHttpClientFactory factory
```

16. Change the content of the OnInitializedAsync method to this:

```
try
{
    var httpclient =
        factory.CreateClient("Authenticated");
            forecasts = await
                httpclient.GetFromJsonAsync
                <WeatherForecast[]>("WeatherForecast");
}
catch (AccessTokenNotAvailableException exception)
{
    exception.Redirect();
}
```

This will call the weather forecast service, and if the token is missing, it will redirect to the login page.

17. Add the following namespace:

```
@using Microsoft.AspNetCore.Components.WebAssembly.
Authentication
```

18. Now it's time to run the project. Make sure to set `MyBlogWebAssembly.Server` as a startup project and press *F5*.

19. Now navigate to the weather forecast service and you will be redirected to the login/registration page, where you can create an account or log in.

Great, now everything is in place for logging in to our site. Sometimes, we want to grant different users different rights, which is what the next section is all about.

Adding authorization

At this point, we know whether the user is authenticated or not, but does the user have access to a specific function? That is what authorization is all about. Luckily, the built-in functions support this as well, even though we have to write some code for it.

The server side has all the tables needed to add roles to our users. There are, however, no UIs available. For our application, we'll just add a role manually in the database, but first, we need to configure roles.

Adding roles from the server

Execute the following steps to add roles from the server:

1. In the `MyBlogWebAssembly.Server` project, open the `Startup.cs` file.

2. In the `ConfigureServices` method, add options to `.AddApiAuthorization` and remove the default claim mapping as follows:

```
.AddApiAuthorization<AppUser, MyBlogDbContext>(options =>
{
    options.IdentityResources["openid"].UserClaims.
    Add("name");
    options.ApiResources.Single().UserClaims.Add("name");
    options.IdentityResources["openid"].UserClaims.
    Add("role"); options.ApiResources.Single().
    UserClaims.Add("role");
});
```

```
JwtSecurityTokenHandler.DefaultInboundClaimFilter.
Remove("role");
```

This will include roles in the token so that we can use the token on the client.

3. Add roles to `Services.AddDefaultIdentity` so it now looks like this:

```
services.AddDefaultIdentity<AppUser>(options =>
        options.SignIn.RequireConfirmedAccount = false)
            .AddRoles<IdentityRole>()
                .AddEntityFrameworkStores<MyBlogDbContext>();
```

4. Add the namespace:

```
using Microsoft.AspNetCore.Identity;
using System.IdentityModel.Tokens.Jwt;
```

The server will now send the roles over to the client, but the client won't be listening; so, next up, we need to make changes to the client.

Adding roles to the client

For the client to pick up the roles, we need to parse them from the access token. Don't worry, it's not as complicated as it sounds:

1. Right-click in the `MyBlogWebAssembly.Client` project, then click **Add | New folder**; name the folder `Authentication`.

2. Right-click on the `Authentication` folder and select **Add | Class**, then name the class `RoleAccountClaimsPrincipalFactory.cs`.

3. Replace the content of the file with the code from GitHub here: `https://github.com/PacktPublishing/Web-Development-with-Blazor/blob/master/Chapter08/MyBlog/MyBlogWebAssembly/Client/Authentication/RoleAccountClaimsPrincipalFactory.cs`.

    What we are doing here is we are making sure that we get the JSON node where the roles can be found. Depending on how many nodes are returned, there can be a string or an array of strings. We check whether it is an array and if it is, we add every item to the user; if it is a string, we add just that single item to the user.

4. Now we need to add that to the dependency injection pipeline. Open `program.cs` and replace `builder.Services.AddApiAuthorization();` with the following:

```
builder.Services.AddApiAuthorization()
.AddAccountClaimsPrincipalFactory<RoleAccountClaims
PrincipalFactory>();
```

5. Add the following namespace:

```
using MyBlogWebAssembly.Client.Authentication;
```

Now that everything is in place for using roles, next we need to add a role to our database.

Adding a role to the database

To add data to our database, we can use a tool called DB Browser for SQLite:

1. Download DB Browser for SQLite from `https://sqlitebrowser.org/` (if you have some other application you'd rather use, feel free to use that instead).

2. Open `MyBlog.db` in DB Browser; there should be 15 tables there.

3. Click the **Browse data** tab and select the `AspNetRoles` table.

4. Now create a role – let's call it `Administrator`. Click on the **Insert new row into the current table** button (a document with a small +) and use the following values:

    Id: *Leave empty*

    Name: `Administrator`

    NormalizedName: `administrator`

    ConcurencyStamp: *Leave empty*

5. Change table to `AspNetUsers` and copy the ID of your user (a GUID).

6. Change table to `AspNetUserRoles` and click on the **Insert new row into the current table** button (a document with a small +), then paste in the ID of the user and the ID of the role.

Great! Now our user is an administrator. Let's test it real quick:

1. In the `MyBlogWebAssembly.Client` project, open `Pages/Index.razor` and add the following to the bottom of the component:

```
<AuthorizeView Roles="Administrator">
```

```
    <Authorized>
        You are an admin!
    </Authorized>
    <NotAuthorized>
        Not logged in or not administrator
    </NotAuthorized>
</AuthorizeView>
```

2. Open `_Imports.razor` and add this as a namespace:

```
@using MyBlogWebAssembly.Client.Pages
```

3. Open `Shared/MainLayout.razor` and add the component to the page just after the **About** link:

```
<LoginDisplay />
```

4. Set `MyblogWebAssembly.Server` as a startup project.

5. Now run the project (*Ctrl + F5*) and you will see the message **Not logged in or not administrator**, and when you log in, it will change to **You are an admin!**.

Awesome! We have authentication and authorization working!

Summary

In this chapter, we learned how to add authentication to our existing site. It is easier to add authentication at the point of creating a project, but now we have a better understanding of what is going on under the hood.

In the next chapter, we will share the components between our Blazor Server project and our Blazor WebAssembly project, making both projects look the same (and look great) as well as calling our web API for the first time.

9
Sharing Code and Resources

In this chapter, it's time to bring the projects together. It is possible to share code between Blazor Server and Blazor WebAssembly. This is also how we would create reusable components and share them in the community or just in the workplace.

Using this approach, it is no longer important to choose Server or WebAssembly. This way, you can use Blazor Server while you are porting your existing site and when you are done, just move the shared library to a new hosting model.

We will also add static content such as CSS.

In this chapter, we will cover the following topics:

- Cleaning up the project
- Setting up the API
- Moving the components
- Adding static files
- CSS isolation

Technical requirements

Make sure you have followed the previous chapters or use the `Chapter08` folder as a starting point.

You can find the source code for this chapter's end result at `https://github.com/PacktPublishing/Web-Development-with-Blazor/tree/master/Chapter09`.

> **Note**
>
> If you are jumping into this chapter using the code from GitHub, make sure to register the user with an email and follow the instructions for adding a user and adding the Administrator role to the database. You can find the instructions in *Chapter 8, Authentication and Authorization*.

Cleaning up the project

Throughout the book, we have generated a bunch of files, and if we used the repository at any point, we probably have a bunch more files. So, the first thing we need to do is to clean up the project a bit.

In the `MyBlogServerSide` project, delete the following files (if you don't have a particular file in the following list, don't worry, just go to the next one):

- `Pages/Alert` – folder
- `Pages/Events` – folder
- `Form`-folder
- `Pages/ComponentWithCascadingParameter.razor`
- `Pages/ComponentWithCascadingValue.razor`
- `Pages/CounterWithoutRazor.cs`
- `Pages/CounterWithParameter.razor`
- `Pages/DBTest.razor`
- `Pages/FetchDataWithCodeBehind.razor`
- `Pages/FetchDataWithInherits.razor`
- `Pages/Parameters.razor`
- `Pages/ParentCounter.razor`
- `Pages/SetFocus.razor`

Great! We now have a project that is a bit cleaner. The next step is to set up the Blazor WebAssembly project and make it use our new API.

Setting up the API

It is only Blazor WebAssembly that needs access to the Web API since it does not have direct database access. The most common architecture is probably to use a Web API for Blazor Server as well.

Let's hook up our `MyBlog.WebAssembly` project to our API and here is where dependency injection shines.

In our Blazor Server project, we have the `services.AddScoped<IMyBlogApi, MyBlogApiServerSide>();` configuration telling our app that when we ask for an instance of `IMyBlogApi`, Blazor should return an instance of the `MyBlogApiServerSide` class, which is a version of the API that has direct access to the database.

Our shared components only know the interface, and the instance that should be returned is configured per project.

In the Blazor WebAssembly project, we will instead return an instance of the Web API client we created in *Chapter 7, Creating an API*.

However, it doesn't make sense that the Blazor WebAssembly project references a library that has direct database access (like `MyBlog.Data` has). We would get an error message were we to try.

So, we need to move the files we can share into another library. Perform the following steps:

1. Right-click on the `MyBlog` solution and select **Add | New Project**.

2. Search for `Class Library (.NET Core)` and then click **Next**.

3. Name the project `MyBlog.Data.Shared` and keep the location as is and then click **Create**.

4. Select **target framework .NET 5.0 (Current)** and then click **Create**.

5. Right-click on the **Dependencies** node under the `MyBlogWebAssembly.Client` project.

    Click **Add project reference**, check the **MyBlog.Data.Shared** and **MyBlog.Shared** checkboxes, and then click **OK**.

6. Move the following files from the `MyBlog.Data` project to `MyBlog.Data.Shared`:

    `Extension` – folder

    `Interfaces` – folder

    `Models/BlogPost.cs`

    `Models/Category.cs`

    `Models/Tag.cs`

    `MyBlogApiClientSide.cs`

    These are the files that are the same regardless of the hosting model.

7. We need to add some NuGet Packages to get things working. Right-click in the **Dependencies** node under the `MyBlog.Data.Shared` project and select **Manage NuGet Packages**.

8. Search for `Newtonsoft.Json` and then click **Install**.

9. Search for `Microsoft.AspNetCore.Components.WebAssembly.Authentication` and then click **Install**.

10. Search for `Microsoft.Extensions.Http` and then click **Install**.

11. Now we need to reference the new project. Right-click on the **Dependencies** node under the `MyBlog.Data` project and click **Add project reference**.

12. Check **MyBlog.Data.Shared** and then click **OK**.

13. Right-click on the **Dependencies** node under the `MyBlog.Shared` project and then click **Add project reference**.

14. Check **MyBlog.Data.Shared** and then click **OK**.

Now we have moved the classes that are shareable to a new library. The next step is to move the files that we want to share between the projects.

Moving the components

We are going to move the components that we can share between the Blazor Server and Blazor WebAssembly projects. This is one of the amazing powers of Blazor; the only thing that differs between the two projects is the hosting model. The code can remain the same (for most cases).

In our case, we made sure to have different ways of accessing the data just to cover those possibilities as well, but we will come back to that in the next section.

First, we need to create a new project and move some files. To do this, perform the following steps:

1. Right-click on the `MyBlog` solution and select **Add | New project**.

2. Search for `Razor` and you should find a template called **Razor Class Library**. Select that template and click **Next**.

3. Name the project `MyBlog.Shared`, leave the location as is (it should be in the correct folder already), and then click **Next**.

4. Select **Target Framework .NET 5.0 (Current)** and make sure **Support pages and views** are unchecked. Then, click **Create**.

5. Add a reference to the `MyBlog.Data.Shared` project by right-clicking the **Dependencies** node under the `MyBlog.Shared` project and selecting **Add project reference**.

    Check the **MyBlog.Data.Shared** checkbox and then click **OK**.

6. Add a NuGet package by right-clicking **Dependencies** under the **MyBlog.Shared** node and selecting **Manage NuGet Packages**.

7. Search for `Markdig` and then click **Install**.

8. Tick the **Include pre-release** box (at the time of writing, NuGet is only available as pre-release).

    Search for `Microsoft.AspNetCore.Components.Web.Extensions` and then click **Install**.

    Untick the **Include pre-release** box.

9. Search for `Microsoft.AspNetCore.Components.WebAssembly.Authentication` and then click **Install**.

10. Now we need to add some namespaces. Open the `_Imports.razor` file and replace the content with the following:

```
@using System.Net.Http
@using Microsoft.AspNetCore.Authorization
@using Microsoft.AspNetCore.Components.Authorization
@using Microsoft.AspNetCore.Components.Forms
@using Microsoft.AspNetCore.Components.Routing
@using Microsoft.AspNetCore.Components.Web
@using Microsoft.AspNetCore.Components.Web.Virtualization
@using Microsoft.JSInterop
```

```
@using MyBlog.Shared
@using MyBlog.Shared.Components
@using MyBlog.Data.Models;
@using MyBlog.Data.Interfaces;
@using Microsoft.AspNetCore.Components.Web.Extensions.
Head
```

11. Right-click on the `MyBlog.Shared` project and then select **Add | New Folder**. Name the folder `Components`.

12. Now, move all the files except `LoginDisplay.razor` from the `Components` folder in the `MyBlogServerSide` project to the `Components` folder in the `MyBlog.Shared` project.

    The **Login** display differs a bit depending on the hosting platform, so we don't want to share that one.

13. Right-click on the `MyBlog.Shared` project and then select **Add | New Folder**. Name the folder `Pages`.

14. Move the `Admin` folder from the `Pages` folder in the `MyBlogServerSide` project to the `Pages` folder in the `MyBlog.Shared` project.

15. Move the `Index.razor` and `Post.razor` files from the `Pages` folder in the `MyBlogServerSide` project to the `Pages` folder in the `MyBlog.Shared` project.

16. Right-click on the `MyBlog.Shared` project and then select **Add | New Folder**. Name the folder `Shared`.

17. Move the `NavMenu.razor` file from the `Shared` folder in the `MyBlogServerSide` project to the `Shared` folder in the `MyBlog.Shared` project.

18. Add a reference to the `MyBlog.Shared` project by right-clicking the **Dependencies** node under the `MyBlogServerSide` project and selecting **Add project reference**.

    Check the **MyBlog.Shared** checkbox and then click **OK**.

Now we have moved all the files we want to share between the projects and configured the `MyBlogServerSide` project. Next, we will look at cleaning up the shared files.

Cleaning up the shared files

At this point, everything should build but we have moved files around, so let's make sure the moved files have matching namespaces:

1. In the `MyBlog.Shared` project, change the namespace to `MyBlog.Shared.Components` on the following files:

   `Components/BootstrapFieldCssClassProvider.cs`

   `Components/ CustomCssClassProvider.cs`

2. We also have a couple of files referring to that namespace. Remove `@using MyBlogServerSide.Components` from the following files:

   `Pages/Admin/BlogPostEdit.razor`

   `Pages/Admin/BlogPostList.razor`

   `Pages/Admin/CategoryList.razor`

   `Pages/Admin/TagList.razor`

3. Since we removed the namespace, we need to add the new one, but we can do that in `_Imports.razor`. In the `MyBlog.Shared` project, add the following namespaces to the `_Imports.razor` file:

   ```
   @using MyBlog.Shared
   @using MyBlog.Shared.Components
   ```

   Now we might ask ourselves, *Why didn't we do that from the outset?* Great question! The best practice is to avoid having `using` statements inside our razor components and always have them inside `_Imports.razor`.

   But to show that both options work just fine, we had them in the component, but then it was time to clean that *mess* up.

Fantastic! We have a couple of new projects and we have cleaned them up. Now, it is time to add the API.

Adding the API

We have ensured that we can access the API by splitting the data project up into two. Now it's time to add it to the Blazor WebAssembly project. Perform the following steps:

1. In the `MyBlogWebAssembly.Client` project, open `Program.cs` and add the following:

    ```
    builder.Services.AddScoped<IMyBlogApi,
    MyBlogApiClientSide>();
    ```

    When we ask the dependency injection for `IMyBlogApi`, we will get back an instance of `MyBlogApiClientSide`, which will call the API we host on the server side (instead of direct database calls).

2. Add the following namespaces at the top of the file:

    ```
    using MyBlog.Data;
    using MyBlog.Data.Interfaces;
    ```

3. Delete the `Pages/Index.razor` file (since we will be getting that one from our shared library instead).

4. The same goes for `Shared/NavMenu.razor`. Delete that file as well.

5. Open `App.Razor` and, in the `router` component, add the following as an additional property:

    ```
    AdditionalAssemblies="new[] { typeof(MyBlog.Shared.Pages.
    Index).Assembly}"
    ```

    This is telling the router to look for matches in the current project, but also in the `MyBlog.Shared` assembly.

    In this case, we ask for the nature of the index page and then get the assembly. This way, we get a little more control (the compiler will help us) as compared to just adding the assembly name as a string.

6. Add the following namespaces to `_Imports.razor`:

    ```
    @using MyBlog.Shared
    @using MyBlog.Shared.Shared
    ```

    We add these namespaces so that our code will be able to find our pages and our `NavMenu` component.

7. In the `MyBlogWebAssembly.Server` project, open the `Startup.cs` file and replace `services.AddControllersWithViews();` with the following code:

```
services.AddControllersWithViews().AddJsonOptions(options
=>
{
    options.JsonSerializerOptions.ReferenceHandler =
        System.Text.Json.Serialization.ReferenceHandler.
        Preserve;
    options.JsonSerializerOptions.PropertyNamingPolicy =
        null;
});
```

Since we are serializing Entity Framework objects, we can get a circular reference. This way, we make sure that it won't serialize all the levels. In the book, we kept it simple. In a real-world project, the API entities might not have circular references, so this step might not be necessary.

This is a great way to add JSON options to our project. These are the same settings we did in the API client in *Chapter 7, Creating an API*.

8. Set `MyBlogWebAssembly.Server` as the start up project by right-clicking the project and selecting **Set as Startup Project** and pressing *Ctrl + F5*.

9. You should now see blogposts getting listed and you should be able to navigate to a blog post by clicking the link.

Awesome! We now have the same Blazor components running in Blazor Server as well as Blazor WebAssembly.

But the layout still leaves a lot to be desired, and guess what?

That is what we will fix next.

Adding static files

Blazor can use static files, such as images, CSS, and JavaScript. If we put our files in the wwwroot folder, they will automatically be exposed to the internet and accessible from the root of our site. The nice thing about Blazor is that we can do the same with a library, it is super easy to distribute static files within a library.

At work, we share components between all of our Blazor projects, and the shared library can depend on other libraries as well. We need to add a link to the static file using the _content folder.

Take a look at this example:

```
<link rel="stylesheet" href="_content/MyBlog.Shared/
MyBlogStyle.min.css" />
```

The HTML `link` tag, `rel`, and `href` are ordinary HTML tags and attributes, but by adding the URL that starts with `_content`, this is telling us that the content we want to access is in another library. The name of the library (assembly name) is followed by, in this case, `MyBlog.Shared`, and then the file we want to access, which is stored in the `wwwroot` folder in our library.

Blazor is, in the end, just HTML, and HTML can be styled using CSS. As mentioned, the Blazor templates are using Bootstrap by default and we will continue to use that as well.

There is a great site with easy-to-use Bootstrap themes ready to be downloaded that can be found at `https://bootswatch.com/`.

I like the Darkly theme, so that's the one we'll use, but feel free to experiment with this later on.

CSS versus LESS versus SASS

CSS stands for **Cascading Style Sheets**, where you can style the output of your site. **LESS** stands for **Leaner Style Sheets** and extends CSS. **SASS** stands for **Syntactically Awesome Style Sheets** and works the same way as LESS.

We can use any one of these in our project. LESS and SASS make writing styles a bit easier in my opinion. Bootstrap uses SASS, so let's do the same and download Bootstrap to our project.

SASS transpiles to CSS and we can use nested tags. So, take a look at this CSS:

```
section { font-family: 'Comic Sans MS'; }
section h1, section .h1 {color: red; }
section h2, section .h2 { color: green; }
```

The preceding CSS can be written in SASS:

```
section{
    font-family:'Comic Sans MS';
    h1{color:red;}
    h2{color:green;}
}
```

SASS has less code to write and is easier to keep track of. There are other benefits as well, such as variables, loops, and much more besides. There are two flavors of SASS – SASS and SCSS. We are going to use SCSS, which is the most recent, and it has brackets, so it should feel a bit more familiar to a C# developer.

Since SASS is transpiled, we need something that can transpile the SASS to CSS. So, the first step is to install Web Essentials 2019.

Preparing CSS/SASS

When using SASS, I prefer to have everything, or at least as much as possible, in SASS. This means that we need to download the SASS files for Bootstrap and install an extension.

We will also bring in a new theme to our project:

1. In Visual Studio, click on the **Extensions** menu and select **Manage Extensions**.

2. Search for `Web essentials 2019`, select it from the search result, and then click **Download**.

3. You will be prompted to restart Visual Studio. Please do so (all instances if you have more than one open) to finish the installation.

    Web Essentials 2019 is a collection of many different extensions that are useful when developing web apps.

4. Next, we need to download the SASS files for Bootstrap. Open a web browser and navigate to `https://getbootstrap.com/docs/5.0/getting-started/download/`.

5. Click the **Download Source** button and extract the ZIP file.

6. In the `MyBlog.Shared` project, create a folder called `Bootstrap`.

7. Copy the `scss` folder from the ZIP file into the `Bootstrap` folder.

8. Next, we need to download a new theme. Navigate to `https://bootswatch.com/darkly/`.

9. In the top menu called **Darkly**, there are some links. Download `_bootswatch.scss` and `_variables.scss`.

10. In the `MyBlog.Shared` project, create three new folders so that the new structure looks like this: `Bootswatch/Dist/Darkly`.

11. Copy _bootswatch.scss and _variables.scss into the Darkly folder.

12. Since we have installed Web Essentials, we can now use one of the extensions.

13. We can now create a new SASS file by doing this:

    Select the wwwroot folder and press *Shift + F2*, which will show a small dialog where you can supply a filename. It will use the file extension to load the correct template. Name the file MyBlogStyle.scss.

14. In the new file, add the following:

    ```
    @import "../Bootswatch/Dist/Darkly/_variables";
    @import "../Bootstrap/scss/bootstrap";
    @import "../Bootswatch/Dist/Darkly/_bootswatch";
    ```

    This will import the Bootswatch variables, as well as the Bootstrap and Bootswatch files, and, when generated, it will take all the files and put them in a single file.

15. We get some styles with Blazor that we can move to our SCSS file. We want to keep the styles for the error message box from site.css.

    Add the following at the end of MyblogStyle.scss:

    ```
    .content {
        padding-top: 1.1rem;
    }
    .navbar-brand
    {
        margin-left:30px;
    }
    .bi
    {
        margin-right:5px;
    }


    #blazor-error-ui {
        background: lightyellow;
        bottom: 0;
        box-shadow: 0 -1px 2px rgba(0, 0, 0, 0.2);
        display: none;
        left: 0;
        padding: 0.6rem 1.25rem 0.7rem 1.25rem;
    ```

```
    position: fixed;
    width: 100%;
    z-index: 1000;
}
#blazor-error-ui .dismiss {
    cursor: pointer;
    position: absolute;
    right: 0.75rem;
    top: 0.5rem;
}
```

So, in this case, we are mixing SASS (Bootstrap and Bootswatch) with the CSS that came with the Blazor template.

16. Right-click on the `MyBlogStyle.scss` file and select **Web compiler | Compile file**.

    You will notice that it will create four new files. First, we have `MyBlogStyle.css` and `MyBlogStyle.min.css`, which is the generated CSS and a minified version of CSS. They are located under the `MyBlogStyle.css` node. We also get `compilerconfig.json` and `compilerconfig.json.defaults`, which are the settings for the web compiler.

Now we have all the prerequisites in place and CSS that we can add to our site.

Adding CSS to MyBlogServerSide

Now it's time to add the new style to our sites. Let's start with `MyBlogServerSide`:

1. Open `Pages/_Host.cshtml`.

2. Remove these rows:

    ```
    <link rel="stylesheet" href="css/bootstrap/bootstrap.min.css" />
    <link href="css/site.css" rel="stylesheet" />
    ```

3. Add a reference to our new stylesheet (containing both Bootstrap and the BootSwatch Darkly theme):

    ```
    <link rel="stylesheet" href="_content/MyBlog.Shared/MyBlogStyle.min.css" />
    ```

4. Open `App.Razor` and, in the `router` component, add the following as an additional property:

```
AdditionalAssemblies="new[] { typeof(MyBlog.Shared.Pages.
Index).Assembly}"
```

This is the same thing we did for our WebAssembly project earlier in the chapter.

5. In `_Imports.Razor`, add the following namespaces:

```
@using MyBlog.Shared
@using MyBlog.Shared.Shared
```

6. Set `MyBlogServerSide` as the start up project and run the project by pressing *Ctrl + F5*.

Great! Our Blazor Server project is now updated to use the new style.

Adding CSS to MyBlogWebAssembly.Client

Now let's do the same with the Blazor WebAssembly project:

1. In the `MyBlogWebAssembly.Client` project, open `wwwroot/index.html`:
2. Remove the following lines:

```
<link href="css/bootstrap/bootstrap.min.css"
rel="stylesheet" />
<link href="css/app.css" rel="stylesheet" />
```

3. Add the CSS:

```
<link rel="stylesheet" href="_content/MyBlog.Shared/
MyBlogStyle.min.css" />
```

4. Set `MyBlogwebAssembly.Server` as the start up project and run the project by pressing *Ctrl + F5*.

Now we have the same layout for both projects.

Making the admin interface more useable

Let's now clean it up some more. We have only started with the admin functionality, so let's make it more accessible. The menu on the left is no longer required, so let's change it so that the menu is only visible if you are an administrator.

We need to implement the change in both projects:

1. Open `MyBlogWebAssembly.Client/Shared/MainLayout.razor` and put `AutorizeView` around the `sidebar div` like this:

```
<AuthorizeView Roles="Administrator">
    <div class="sidebar">
        <NavMenu />
    </div>
</AuthorizeView>
```

2. Do the same thing with `MyBlogServerSide/Shared/MainLayout.razor`.

3. Set `MyBlogServerSide` as the start up project and run it by pressing *Ctrl + F5*.

4. Verify that the menu is only visible when you are logged in by logging in and out.

   Now we need to make the menu look better. Even though the counter is really fun to click on, it doesn't make much sense when it comes to our blog.

Since the `nav` menu is now shared, we can put it in one place and it will change for both Blazor Server and Blazor WebAssembly.

Making the menu more useful

We should replace the links with links to our admin pages instead and you may have noticed that the icons in the links have disappeared (since we removed the old CSS), but fear not, as Bootstrap has some icons we can use:

1. Open a web browser and navigate to `https://github.com/twbs/icons/releases/latest/`.

2. At the bottom of the page under the **Assets** header, there is a link to `bootstrap-icons-{versionnumber}.zip`. Download that file.

3. Once it's downloaded, extract the ZIP and copy `bootstrap-Icons-{versionnumber}` to the wwwroot folder in our `MyBlog.Shared` project.

   In the `MyBlogStyle.scss` add the following line:

```
@import "./bootstrap-icons-1.4.1/bootstrap-icons";
```

   In this case, it's the `1.4.1` version, and you can change that depending on the version number.

   Since SASS is fully CSS compatible, we can import the CSS like this and since there are files (font files) that the browser needs to access, we put it in the wwwroot folder.

4. We also need to make a small change at the top of the `wwwroot\bootstrap-icons-1.4.1\font\bootstrap-icons.css` file.

    The path to the files needs to be the correct one taking into account that the file is in a library.

    Change the top of the file (the only thing that changed is the path) `./fonts` to `/_content/MyBlog.Shared/bootstrap-icons-1.4.1/fonts`:

    ```
    @font-face {
    font-family: "bootstrap-icons";
    src: url("/_content/MyBlog.Shared/
    bootstrap-icons-1.4.1/fonts/bootstrap-icons.
    woff2?231ce25e89ab5804f9a6c427b8d325c9") format("woff2"),
    url("/_content/MyBlog.Shared/bootstrap-icons-1.4.1/fonts/
    bootstrap-icons.woff?231ce25e89ab5804f9a6c427b8d325c9")
    format("woff");
    }
    ```

5. Click on `MyBlog.Shared/wwwroot/bootstrap-icons-1.4.1/fonts/bootstrap-icons.woff` and make sure that **Copy to Output directory** is set to **Copy if newer**.

6. Click on `MyBlog.Shared/wwwroot/bootstrap-icons-1.4.1 /fonts/bootstrap-icons.woff2` and make sure that **Copy to Output directory** is set to **Copy if newer**.

7. In the `MyBlog.Shared` project, open the `Shared/Navmenu.razor` file.

    Edit the code so that it looks like this (keep the code block as is):

    ```
    <div class="top-row pl-4 navbar navbar-dark">
        <a class="navbar-brand" href="">MyBlog Admin</a>
        <button class="navbar-toggler"
          @onclick="ToggleNavMenu">
            <span class="navbar-toggler-icon"></span>
        </button>
    </div>

    <div class="@NavMenuCssClass" @onclick="ToggleNavMenu">
        <ul class="nav flex-column">
            <li class="nav-item px-3">
                <NavLink class="nav-link" href=""
                  Match="NavLinkMatch.All">
    ```

```
                    <span class="bi bi-house-door"
                          aria-hidden="true"></span> Home
            </NavLink>
        </li>
        <li class="nav-item px-3">
            <NavLink class="nav-link"
              href="Admin/Blogposts">
                <span class="bi bi-signpost-2"
                    aria-hidden="true"></span> Blog posts
            </NavLink>
        </li>
        <li class="nav-item px-3">
            <NavLink class="nav-link"
              href="Admin/Tags">
                <span class="bi bi-tags"
                    aria-hidden="true"></span> Tags
            </NavLink>
        </li>
        <li class="nav-item px-3">
            <NavLink class="nav-link"
              href="Admin/Categories">
                <span class="bi bi-collection"
                    aria-hidden="true"></span> Categories
            </NavLink>
        </li>
    </ul>
</div>
```

We changed the links and the icons in the file.

Making the blog look like a blog

The admin interface is done (at least for now) and we should focus on the front page of our blog. The front page should have the title of the blog post and some descriptions. For my blog, I have taken the first paragraph as a teaser, so this is something we might do here as well:

1. In the `MyBlog.Shared` project, open the `Pages/index.razor` file.
2. We no longer need fake blog posts, so let's remove the button from the top of the page, as well as the `<br/>` tag.

3. Remove the `AddSomePosts` method. Now, when we have an admin, we can create our posts.

4. To be able to get the first paragraph, we need to add the following method:

```
public string GetFirstParagraph(string html)
{
    var m = System.Text.RegularExpressions.
      Regex.Matches(html, @"<p>(.*?)</p>",System.Text.
        RegularExpressions.RegexOptions.Singleline);
    if (m.Count>0)
    {
        return m[0].Groups[1].Value;
    }
    else
    {
        return "";
    }
}
```

It uses a regular expression to find the content between the first `<p>` tag and the first `</p>` tag.

If no paragraph is found, it returns an empty string. We could take the first 100 letters or so, but that might cut words in half or make the rest of the posts look odd because we are missing a close tag.

In this case, we keep this part simple. It should be easy, so make sure there is a paragraph in our blog posts.

5. Inside the `Virtualize` component, change the content (`RenderFragment`) to the following:

```
<article>
    <h2>@p.Title</h2>
    @((MarkupString)GetFirstParagraph(Markdig.Markdown.
      ToHtml(p.Text, pipeline)))
    <br />
    <a href="/Post/@p.Id">Read more</a>
</article>
```

Also remove the `<ul>` tag.

For this code to work, we also need to add the code for `Markdig`.

6. Add a `using` statement for `Markdig` at the top of the file:

```
@using Markdig;
```

7. Add an `OnInitializedAsync` method that will handle the instantiation of the `Markdig` pipeline (this is the same code we have in the `post.razor` file):

```
MarkdownPipeline pipeline;
protected override Task OnInitializedAsync()
{
    pipeline = new MarkdownPipelineBuilder()
                .UseEmojiAndSmiley()
                .Build();
    return base.OnInitializedAsync();
}
```

8. Now, run the project using *Ctrl + F5* and take a look at our new front page.

Sharing problems

When sharing code, there are some things we need to think about. Things worked fine with Blazor Server (due to low latency from the database), but some problems will surface now and again when we go through an API:

1. In the `MyBlog.Shared` project, open `Pages/Admin/BlogPostEdit.razor`.

   There are two bugs in this file that worked when we ran this on Blazor Server. We are looping over the **Categories** and **Tags** lists; both are nullable.

   We should always check whether objects might be null before we loop over them. I kept this bug in there to show that what was working fine on Blazor Server might not work on Blazor WebAssembly.

   However, we should always perform null checks.

2. Add a null check around the `category` loop:

```
@if (Categories != null)
{
@foreach (var category in Categories)
    {
        <option value="@category.Id">@category.Name
        </option>
```

```
        }
    }
```

3. Add a null check around the `tag` loop:

```
@if (Tags != null)
    {
        @foreach (var tag in Tags)
        {
            <li>
                @tag.Name
                @if (Post.Tags.Any(t => t.Id ==
                tag.Id))
                {
                    <button type="button"
                    @onclick="@(() => {
                    Post.Tags.Remove
                    (Post.Tags.Single(t => t.Id
                    == tag.Id)); })">Remove
                    </button>
                }
                else
                {
                    <button type="button"
                    @onclick="@(() =>
                        { Post.Tags.Add(tag); })">
                    Add</button>
                }
            </li>
        }
    }
```

It's good to keep in mind to always check for nulls, but sometimes these things sneak past us. When sharing code, it is always good to go through the code one more time.

CSS isolation

In .NET 5, Microsoft added something called isolated CSS. This is something that many other frameworks have as well. The idea is to write CSS specifically for one component. The upsides, of course, are that the CSS that we create won't impact any of the other components.

The template for Blazor uses isolated CSS for `Shared/MainLayout.razor` and `NavMenu.Razor`. If you expand `Shared/MainLayout.razor` in the `MyBlogWebAssebly.Client` project, you'll see a file called `MainLayout.razor.css`.

You can also use SASS here by adding a file called `MainLayout.razor.scss`. The important thing is that the file we add should generate a file called `MainLayout.razor.css` in order for the compiler to pick it up.

This is a naming convention that will make sure to rewrite CSS and the HTML output.

CSS has the following naming convention:

```css
.main {
    flex: 1;
}
```

It will be rewritten as follows:

```css
.main[b-bf15h5967n] {
    flex: 1;
}
```

This means that the elements need to have an attribute called `b-bf15h5967n` (in this case) in order for the style to be applied.

The `div` tag that has the CSS tag within the `MainLayout` component will be outputted like this:

```html
<div class="main" b-bf15h5967n>
```

For all of this to happen, we also need to have a link to the CSS (which is provided by the template) and it looks like this:

```html
<link href="{Assemblyname}.styles.css" rel="stylesheet">
```

This now becomes useful for component libraries. We have one component that has isolated CSS in our shared library (`NavMenu`) and the CSS for the `NavMenu` component is included in the `{Assemblyname}.styles.css` file.

We don't have to do anything extra in order for our shared CSS to be included. If you are creating a library for anyone to use, I would think about using the isolated CSS approach, if your components need some kind of CSS to work properly.

This way, our users won't have to add a reference to our CSS and there is no risk of our CSS breaking something in the user's app (since it's isolated). I prefer to write CSS that works for the whole site rather than just for one component. I think it is easier to keep track of that way.

Many in the community use the same argument as a reason to use isolated CSS (easier to keep track of). I do like the fact that it lives closer to the component. We now have a working admin interface and a good-looking site (yeah, I know it's not perfect, but now we know how to deal with styles).

Summary

In this chapter, we have moved components into a shared library and used that library with both our Blazor Server and Blazor WebAssembly projects.

Using shared libraries like this is the way to create shared libraries (for others to use) and it is also a great way to structure our in-house projects (so that it is easy to change from Blazor Server to Blazor WebAssembly, or the other way around). If you have a site already, you can build your Blazor components in a shared library, as we did in the chapter.

By using components as part of your existing site (using Blazor Server), you can get started with Blazor bit by bit until you have converted the whole thing. When that is done, you can decide whether or not to keep using Blazor Server (as I mentioned, we use Blazor Server at work) or move to Blazor WebAssembly.

We also learned how we can use dependency injection to use different ways of accessing data depending on the platform. And last but not least, we talked about how to use SASS and CSS in our site, both *regular* CSS and isolated CSS.

In the next chapter, we will learn about the one thing we are trying to avoid (at least I am) as Blazor developers – JavaScript.

10
JavaScript Interop

In this chapter, we will take a look at JavaScript. In certain scenarios, we still need to use JavaScript or we want to use an existing library that relies on JavaScript. Blazor uses JavaScript to update the **Document Object Model** (**DOM**), download files, and access things such as local storage on the client.

So, there are, and always will be, cases when we need to communicate with JavaScript, or have JavaScript communicate with us. Don't worry. The Blazor community is an amazing one, so chances are someone has already built the interop that we need.

In this chapter, we will cover the following topics:

- Why do we need JavaScript?
- .NET to JavaScript
- JavaScript to .NET
- Implementing an existing JavaScript library

Technical requirements

Make sure that you have followed the previous chapters or use the Chapter09 folder as a starting point.

You can find the source code for this chapter's end result at https://github.com/PacktPublishing/Web-Development-with-Blazor/tree/master/Chapter10.

> **Note**
>
> If you are jumping into this chapter using the code from GitHub, make sure to register the user with an email and follow the instructions for adding a user and adding the Administrator role to the database. You can find the instructions in *Chapter 8, Authentication and Authorization.*

Why do we need JavaScript?

Many say that Blazor is the JavaScript killer, but the truth is that Blazor needs JavaScript in order to work. Some events only get triggered in JavaScript, and if we want to use those events, we need to make an interop.

I jokingly say that I have never written so much JavaScript as when I started developing with Blazor. Calm down… it's not that bad.

I have written a couple of libraries that require JavaScript in order to work. They are called `Blazm.Components` and `Blazm.Bluetooth`.

The first one is a grid component and uses JavaScript interop to trigger C# code (JavaScript to .NET) when the window is resized to remove columns if all of them can't fit inside the window.

When that is triggered, the C# code calls JavaScript to get the size of the columns based on the client width, something that only the web browser knows, and, based on that answer, it removes columns if needed.

The second one, `Blazm.Bluetooth` makes it possible to interact with Bluetooth devices using Web Bluetooth, which is a web standard accessible through, you guessed it, JavaScript.

It uses two-way communication; Bluetooth events can trigger C# code and C# code can iterate over devices and send data to them. They are both open source, so if you are interested in taking a look at a real-world project, you can check them out on my GitHub: `https://github.com/EngstromJimmy`.

I would argue that in most cases, we won't need to write JavaScript ourselves. The Blazor community is really big, so chances are that someone has already written what we need. But, we don't need to be afraid of using JavaScript either, next we will take a look at different ways to add JavaScript calls to our Blazor project.

.NET to JavaScript

Calling JavaScript from .NET is pretty simple. There are two ways of doing that:

- Global JavaScript
- JavaScript Isolation

We will go through both ways to see what the difference is.

Global JavaScript (the old way)

One way is to make the JavaScript method we want to call accessible globally through the JavaScript window, which is kind of a bad practice since it is accessible by all scripts and could replace the functionality in other scripts (if we were to accidentally use the same names).

What we can do is, for example, to use scopes, create an object in the global space, and put our variables and methods on that object so that we lower the risk a bit at least.

Using a scope could look something like this:

```
window.myscope = {};

window.myscope.methodName = () => { ... }
```

We create an object with the name `myscope`. Then we declare a method on that object called `methodName`. In this example, there is no code in the method; this is only to demonstrate how it could be done.

Then, to call the method from C#, we would call it using `JSRuntime` like this:

```
@inject IJSRuntime jsRuntime
await jsRuntime.InvokeVoidAsync("myscope.methodName ");
```

There are two different methods we can use to call JavaScript:

- `InvokeVoidAsync`, which calls JavaScript, but doesn't expect a return value
- `InvokeAsync<T>`, which calls JavaScript and expects a return value of type `T`

We can also send in parameters to our JavaScript method if we would like. We also need to refer to JavaScript, and JavaScript must be stored in the `wwwroot` folder.

The other way is JavaScript Isolation, which uses the methods described here, but with modules.

JavaScript Isolation

In .NET 5, we got a new way to add JavaScript using JavaScript Isolation, which is a much nicer way to call JavaScript. It doesn't use global methods and it doesn't require us to refer to the JavaScript file.

This is awesome for both component vendors and end users because JavaScript will be loaded when we need it. It will only be loaded once (Blazor handles that for us) and we don't need to add a reference to the JavaScript file, which makes it easier to start and use a library.

So, let's implement that instead.

Isolated JavaScripts need to be stored in the `wwwroot` folder as well. We can't have the JavaScript file nicely tucked in under the component node, at least not with the built-in functionality.

After discussing this with Mads Kristensen (Program Manager for Visual Studio and the author of the Web Essentials Extension), he suggested that perhaps we could use another functionality in Visual Studio to make it work.

Let's do just that!

In our project, we can delete categories and components. Let's implement a simple JavaScript call to reveal a prompt to make sure that the user wants to delete the category or tag:

1. In the `MyBlog.Shared` project, select the `Components/ItemList.razor` file, create a new file by pressing *Shift + F2*, and name the file `ItemList.razor.js`.

2. Open the new file and add the following code:

```
export function showConfirm(message) {
    return confirm(message);
}
```

JavaScript Isolation uses the standard ES modules and can be loaded on-demand. The methods it exposes are only accessible through that object and not globally, as with the *old* way.

3. Open `ItemList.razor` and inject `IJSRuntime` at the top of the file:

```
@inject IJSRuntime jsRuntime
```

4. In the code section, let's add a method that will call JavaScript:

```
IJSObjectReference jsmodule;
private async Task<bool> ShouldDelete()
{
    jsmodule = await jsRuntime.
    InvokeAsync<IJSObjectReference>("import", "/_content/
    MyBlog.Shared/ItemList.razor.js");
    return await jsmodule.InvokeAsync<bool>
       ("showConfirm", "Are you sure?");
}
```

IJSObjectReference is a reference to the specific script that we will import further down. It has access to the exported methods in our JavaScript, nothing else.

We run the Import command and send the filename as a parameter. This will run the JavaScript command, let mymodule = import("/_content/MyBlog. Shared/ItemList.razor.js"), and return the module.

Now we can use that module to access our showConfirm method and send in the argument "Are you sure?".

5. Change the **Delete** button we have in the component to the following:

```
<td><button class="btn btn-danger" @onclick="@(async
()=>{ if (await ShouldDelete()) { await DeleteEvent.
InvokeAsync(item); } })">Delete</button></td>
```

Instead of just calling our Delete event callback, we first call our new method. Let JavaScript confirm that you really want to delete it, and if yes, then run the Delete event callback.

But there is one more thing we need to do, and we have two options here. We could move ItemList.razor.js to the wwwroot folder (and keep it there). Or we can let Visual Studio do it and keep the file close to the component.

I prefer the second option.

In a Blazor project, we can right-click on the project file and select **Manage Client- Side libraries**, which will create libman.json, but since this is a library, we need to create it manually.

6. Click on MyBlog.Shared, press *Shift + F2*, and name the file libman.json.

7. Replace the content in the file with the following code:

```
{
  "version": "1.0",
  "defaultProvider": "filesystem",
  "libraries": [
    {
      "library": "Components",
      "files": [
        "*.js"
      ],
      "destination": "wwwroot/"
    }
  ]
}
```

The libman.json file is the configuration file for Library Manager and it will copy all the files with the .js extension to wwwroot.

8. To make the script run, we build the project by right-clicking the MyBlog.Shared project and selecting **Edit Project file**.

9. Add the following code somewhere in the file:

```
<ItemGroup>
  <PackageReference
    Include="Microsoft.Web.LibraryManager.Build"
      Version="2.1.76" />
</ItemGroup>
```

There are some *gotchas* with this method. The script will run only if we make changes to files that needs to be compiled. So we may find ourselves in a situation where we made a change but the change didn't seem to go through.

Make sure that the script ran. You can just save the libman.json file to make it run.

This workaround is pretty nice since we can keep the JavaScript file, Razor, CSS, and code together in the same place. This method is not entirely hassle-free. In some cases, we'll need to delete the JavaScript file manually from the wwwroot folder.

The alternative is to put the file in the wwwroot folder to start with.

JavaScript to .NET

What about the other way around? I would argue that calling .NET code from JavaScript isn't a very common scenario, and if we find ourselves in that scenario, we might want to think about what we are doing.

I think that as Blazor developers, we should avoid using JavaScript as far as possible. There are, of course, times where JavaScript is the only option, and as I mentioned earlier, Blazm uses communication both ways.

There are three ways of doing a callback from JavaScript to .NET code:

- Static .NET method call
- Instance method call
- Component instance method call

Let's take a closer look at them.

Static .NET method call

To call a .NET function from JavaScript, we can make the function static and we also need to add the `JSInvokable` attribute to the method.

We can add a function such as this in the `code` section of a Razor component, or inside a class:

```
[JSInvokable]
public static Task<int[]> ReturnArrayAsync()
{
    return Task.FromResult(new int[] { 1, 2, 3 });
}
```

In the JavaScript file, we can call that function using the following code:

```
DotNet.invokeMethodAsync('BlazorWebAssemblySample',
'ReturnArrayAsync')
        .then(data => {
            data.push(4);
                console.log(data);
        });
```

The `DotNet` object comes from the `Blazor.js` or `blazor.server.js` file.

`BlazorWebAssemblySample` is the name of the assembly, and `ReturnArrayAsync` is the name of the static .NET function.

It is also possible to specify the name of the function in the `JSInvokeable` attribute if we don't want it to be the same as the method name like this:

```
[JSInvokable("DifferentMethodName")]
```

In this sample, JavaScript makes a call back to .NET code, which returns an `int` array.

It is returned as a promise in the JavaScript file that we are waiting for, and then (using the `then` operator) we continue with the execution, adding a 4 to the array and then outputting the values in the console.

Instance method call

This method is a little bit tricky; we need to pass an instance of the .NET object to be able to call it (this is the method that `Blazm.Bluetooth` is using).

First, we need a class that will handle the method call:

```
using Microsoft.JSInterop;

public class HelloHelper
{
    public HelloHelper(string name)
    {
        Name = name;
    }

    public string Name { get; set; }

    [JSInvokable]
    public string SayHello() => $"Hello, {Name}!";
}
```

This is a class that takes a string (a name) in the constructor and a method called `SayHello` that returns a string containing "`Hello,`" and the name we supplied when we created the instance.

So, what we need to do is to create an instance of that class, supply a name, and create `DotNetObjectReference<T>`, which will give JavaScript access to the instance.

But first, we need JavaScript that can call the .NET function:

```javascript
export function sayHello (hellohelperref) {
    return hellohelperref.invokeMethodAsync('SayHello')
      .then(r => console.log(r));
}
```

In this case, we are using the export syntax and we export a function called `sayHello`, which takes an instance of `DotNetObjectReference` called `dotnetHelper`.

In that instance, we invoke the `SayHello` method, which is the `SayHello` method on the .NET object. In this case, it will be a reference to an instance of the `HelloHelper` class.

We also need to call the JavaScript method and we can do that from a class or, in this case, from a component:

```razor
@page "/interop"
@inject IJSRuntime jsRuntime
@implements IDisposable
<button type="button" class="btn btn-primary" @onclick="async
()=> { await TriggerNetInstanceMethod(); }">
    Trigger .NET instance method HelloHelper.SayHello
</button>
@code {
    private DotNetObjectReference<HelloHelper> objRef;

    IJSObjectReference jsmodule;
    public async ValueTask<string>
      TriggerNetInstanceMethod()
    {
        objRef = DotNetObjectReference.Create(new
          HelloHelper("Bruce Wayne"));
        jsmodule = await jsRuntime.
          InvokeAsync<IJSObjectReference>("import", "/_content/
            MyBlog.Shared/Interop.razor.js");
```

```
            return await
            jsmodule.InvokeAsync<string>("sayHello", objRef);
    }


    public void Dispose()
    {
        objRef?.Dispose();
    }
}
```

Let's go through the class. We inject `IJSRuntime` because we need one to call the JavaScript function. To avoid any memory leaks, we also have to make sure to implement `IDiposable` and, toward the bottom of the file, we make sure to dispose of the `DotNetObjectReference` instance.

We create a private variable of the `DotNetObjectReference<HelloHelper>` type, which is going to contain our reference to our `HelloHelper` instance. We create `IJSObjectReference` so that we may load our JavaScript function.

Then we create an instance of `DotNetObjectReference.Create(new HelloHelper("Bruce Wayne"))` of our reference to a new instance of the `HelloHelper` class, which we supply with the name "Bruce Wayne".

Now we have `objref`, which we will send to the JavaScript method, but first, we load the JavaScript module and then we call `JavaScriptMethod` and pass in the reference to our `HelloHelper` instance. Now, the JavaScript `sayHello` method will run `hellohelperref.invokeMethodAsync('SayHello')`, which will make a call to `SayHelloHelper` and get back a string with "Hello, Bruce Wayne".

There are two more ways that we can use to call .NET functions from JavaScript. We can call a method on a component instance where we can have an action triggered. It is, however, not a recommended approach for Blazor Server. We can also call a method on a component instance by using a `helper` class.

Since calling .NET from JavaScript is pretty rare, we won't go into examples of the two. Instead, we'll dive into things to think about when implementing an existing JavaScript library.

Implementing an existing JavaScript library

The best approach, in my opinion, is to avoid porting JavaScript libraries. Blazor needs to keep the DOM and the render tree in sync, and having JavaScript manipulate the DOM can jeopardize that.

Most component vendors, such as Telerik, Synfusion, Radzen, and, of course, Blazm, have native components, which means that they don't just wrap a JavaScript library but are written specifically for Blazor in C#. Even though the components use JavaScript in some capacity, the goal is to keep that to a minimum.

So, if you are a library maintainer, my recommendation would be to write a native Blazor version of the library, keep JavaScript to a minimum, and, most importantly, do not make Blazor developers have to write JavaScript to use your components.

Some components will not be able to use JavaScript implementations since they need to manipulate the DOM.

Blazor is pretty smart when it comes to syncing the DOM and render tree, but try to avoid manipulating the DOM. If we need to use JavaScript for something, make sure to put a tag outside the manipulation area. Blazor will then keep track of that tag and will not think about what is inside the tag.

Since we started with Blazor at my workplace very early, many of the vendors were not fully done with their Blazor components yet. We needed a graph component fast. In our previous website (before Blazor), we used a component called **Highcharts**.

Highcharts is not a free component, but it's free to use for non-commercial projects. When building our wrapper, we had a couple of things that we wanted to make sure of. We wanted the component to work in a similar way to the existing one and we wanted it to be as simple to use as possible.

Let's walk through what we did.

First, we added a reference to the Highcharts JavaScript:

```
<script src="https://code.highcharts.com/highcharts.js"></
script>
```

And then we added a JavaScript file as follows:

```
export function loadHighcharts(id, json) {
var obj = looseJsonParse(json);
    Highcharts.chart(id, obj);
```

```
    };

    export function looseJsonParse(obj) {
        return Function('"use strict";return (' + obj + ')')();
    }
```

The `loadHighchart` method takes `id` of the `div` tag, which should be converted to a chart and the JSON for configuration.

There is also a method that converts the JSON to a JSON object so that it can be passed into the `chart` method.

The Highchart Razor component looks like this:

```
@inject Microsoft.JSInterop.IJSRuntime jsruntime

<div>
    <div id="@id.ToString()"></div>
</div>

@code
{
    [Parameter] public string Json { get; set; }
    private string id { get; set; } = "Highchart" +
        Guid.NewGuid().ToString();


    protected override void OnParametersSet()
    {
        StateHasChanged();
        base.OnParametersSet();
    }
    IJSObjectReference jsmodule;
    protected async override Task OnAfterRenderAsync(bool
        firstRender)
    {
        if (!string.IsNullOrEmpty(Json))
        {
            jsmodule = await jsruntime.
```

```
                  InvokeAsync<IJSObjectReference>("import", "/_
                      content/MyBlog.Shared/HighChart.razor.js");
            await jsmodule.InvokeAsync<string>
                ("loadHighcharts", new object[] { id, Json });
        }


        await base.OnAfterRenderAsync(firstRender);
    }
}
```

The important thing to notice here is that we have two nested `div` tags, one on the outside that we want Blazor to track, and one on the inside that Highchart will add things to.

There is a JSON parameter where we pass in the JSON for the configuration and then we call our JavaScript function. We run our JavaScript interop in the `OnAfterRenderAsync` method because otherwise, it would throw an exception, as you may recall from *Chapter 4, Understanding Basic Blazor Components*.

Now, the only thing left is to use the component, and that looks like this:

```
@page "/HighChartTest"
<HighChart Json="@chartjson">

</HighChart>

@code {
    string chartjson = @" {
    chart: { type: 'pie' },
    series: [{
        data: [{
            name: 'Does not look like Pacman',
            color:'black',
            y: 20,
        }, {
            name: 'Looks like Pacman',
            color:'yellow',
            y: 80
        }]
    }]
```

```
}";
}
```

This test code will show a pie chart that looks like *Figure 10.1*:

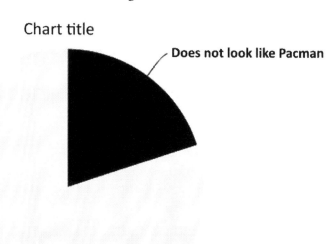

Figure 10.1 – Chart example

We have now gone through how we got a JavaScript library to work with Blazor, so this is an option if there is something we need.

As mentioned, the components' vendors are investing in Blazor, so chances are that they have what we need, so we might not need to invest time in creating our own component library.

Summary

In this chapter, we learned about calling JavaScript from .NET as well as calling .NET from JavaScript. In most cases, we won't need to do JavaScript calls, and chances are that the Blazor community or component vendors have solved the problem for us.

We also looked at how we can port an existing library if we need to.

In the next chapter, we will take a look at state management.

11
Managing State

In this chapter, we will take a look at managing state. Most applications manage state in some form.

A state is simply information that is persisted in some way. It can be data stored in a database, session states, or even something stored in a URL.

The user state is stored in memory either in the web browser or at the server. It contains the component hierarchy and the most recent rendered UI (Render Tree). It also contains the values or fields and properties in the component instances as well as the data stored in service instances in dependency injection.

If we make JavaScript calls, the values we set are also stored in memory. Blazor Server relies on the circuit (SignalR connection) to hold the user state, and Blazor WebAssembly relies on the browser's memory. If we reload the page, the circuit and the memory will be lost. Managing state is not about handling connections or connection issues, but rather how can we keep the data even if we reload the web browser.

Saving state between page navigations or sessions improves the user experience and could be the difference between a sale or not. Imagine reloading the page and all our items in the shopping cart were gone; chances are you won't shop there again.

Now imagine coming back to a page a week or month later and all those things are still there.

In this chapter, we will cover the following topics:

- Storing data on the server side

- Storing data in the URL

- Implementing browser storage

- Using an in-memory state container service

Some of these things we have already talked about and even implemented. Let's take this opportunity to recap the things we have already talked about as well as introduce some new techniques.

Technical requirements

Make sure you have followed the previous chapters or use the `Chapter10` folder as a starting point.

You can find the source code for this chapter's end result at `https://github.com/PacktPublishing/Web-Development-with-Blazor/tree/master/Chapter11`.

> **Note**
>
> If you are jumping into this chapter using the code from GitHub, make sure to register the user with an email and follow the instructions for adding a user and adding the Administrator role to the database. You can find the instructions in *Chapter 8, Authentication and Authorization*.

Storing data on the server side

There are many different ways in which to store data on the server side. The only thing to remember is that Blazor WebAssembly will always need an API. Blazor Server doesn't need an API since we can access the server-side resourcesdirectly.

I have had discussions with many developers when it comes to APIs or direct access and it all boils down to what you intend to do with the application. If you are building a Blazor Server application and have no interest in moving to Blazor WebAssembly, I would probably go for direct access, as we have done in the `MyBlog` project.

I would not do direct database queries in the components though. I would keep it in an API, just not a Web API. As we have seen, exposing those API functions in an API, as we did in *Chapter 7, Creating an API*, and *Chapter 9, Sharing Code and Resources*, is not a lot of steps. We can always start with direct sever access and move to an API if we want to.

When it comes to ways of storing data, we can save data in Blob storage, key-value storage, a relational database (like we did), or table storage.

There is no end to the possibilities. If .NET can communicate with the technology, we will be able to use it.

Storing data in the URL

At first glance, this option might sound horrific, but it's not. Data, in this case, can be the blog post ID or the page number if we are using paging. Typically, the things you want to save in the URL are things you want to be able to link to later on, such as blog posts in our case.

To read a parameter from the URL, we use the following syntax:

```
@page "/post/{BlogPostId:int}"
```

The URL is post followed by Id of the post.

To find that particular route, BlogPostId must be an integer, otherwise the route won't be found.

We also need a public parameter with the same name:

```
    [Parameter]
    public int BlogPostId{ get; set; }
```

If we store data in the URL, we need to make sure to use the OnParametersSet or OnParametersSetAsync methods, otherwise the data won't get reloaded if we change the parameter. If the parameter changes, Blazor won't run OnInitializedAsync again.

This is why our post.razor component loads the things that change based on the parameter in the URL in OnParametersSet, and load the things that are not affected by the parameter in OnInitializedAsync.

We can use optional parameters by specifying them as nullable like this:

```
@page "/post/{BlogPostId:int?}"
```

Route constraints

When we specify what type the parameter should be, this is called a **route constraint**. We add a constraint so the match will only happen if the parameter value can be converted into the type we specified.

The following constraints are available:

- `bool`
- `datetime`
- `decimal`
- `float`
- `guid`
- `int`
- `long`

The URL elements will be converted to a `CLR` object. Therefore, it's important to use an invariant culture when adding them to a URL.

Using a query string

So far we have only talked about routes that are specified in the `page` directive, but we can also read data from the query string.

`NavigationManager` gives us access to the URI, so by using this code, we can access the query string parameters:

```
@inject NavigationManager Navigation
@code{
var query = new Uri(Navigation.Uri).Query;
}
```

We won't dig deeper into this, but now we know that it is possible to access query string parameters if we need to.

Scenarios that are not that common

Some scenarios might not be as common to use, but I didn't want to leave them out of the book completely since I have used them in some of my implementations. I want to mention them in case you might run into the same requirements as I did.

By default, Blazor will assume that a URL that contains a dot is a file and will try and serve the user a file (and will probably not find one if we are trying to match a route).

By adding the following in `Startup.cs` to the Blazor WebAssembly server project (a server-hosted WebAssembly project), the server will redirect the request to the `index.html` file:

```
endpoints.MapFallbackToFile("/example/{param?}", "index.html");
```

If the URL is *example/some.thing*, it will redirect the request to the Blazor WebAssembly entry point and the Blazor routes will take care of it. Without it, the server would just say **file not found**.

The routing, including a dot in the URL, will work, and to do the same, we would need to add the following to `Startup.cs` in our Blazor Server project:

```
endpoints.MapFallbackToPage("/example/{param?}", "/_Host");
```

We are doing the same thing here, but instead of redirecting to `index.html`, we are redirecting to `_Host`, which is the entry point for Blazor Server. The other scenario that is not that common is to handle routes that will catch everything.

Simply put, we are catching a URL that has multiple folder boundaries, but we are catching them as one parameter:

```
@page "/catch-all/{*pageRoute}"
@code {
    [Parameter]
    public string PageRoute{ get; set; }
}
```

The preceding code will catch `"/catch-all/OMG/Racoons/are/awesome"` and the `pageRoute` parameter will contain `"OMG/Racoons/are/awesome"`.

I used both techniques when I created my own blog in order to be able to keep the old URLs and make them work even though everything else (including the URLs) had been rewritten.

Having data in the URL is not really storing the data we always have to make sure to include it in the URL. If we want to store data that we don't need to include every time in the URL, we can use the browser storage instead.

Implementing browser storage

The browser has a bunch of different ways of storing data in the web browser. They are handled differently depending on what type we use. **Local storage** is scoped to the user's browser window. If the user reloads the page or even closes the web browser, the data will still be saved.

The data is also shared across tabs. **Session storage** is scoped to the **Browser** tab, if you reload the tab, the data will be saved, but if you close the tab, the data will be lost. `SessionsStorage` is, in a way, safer to use because we avoid risks with bugs that may occur due to multiple tabs manipulating the same values in storage.

To be able to access the browser storage, we need to use JavaScript. Luckily, we won't need to write the code ourselves.

In .NET 5, Microsoft introduced **Protected browser storage**, which uses data protection in ASP.NET core and is not available in WebAssembly. We can, however, use an open source library called `Blazored.LocalStorage`, which can be used by both Blazor Server and Blazor WebAssembly.

But, we are here to learn new things, right?

So let's implement an interface so that we can use both versions in our app depending on which hosting model we are using.

Creating an interface

First, we need an interface that can read and write to storage:

1. In the **MyBlog.Shared** project, right-click on the project name and select **Add|New Folder**. Name the folder `Interfaces`.

2. Select the new folder and create a new class by pressing *Shift+ F2*, and name the file `IBrowserStorage.cs`.

3. Replace the content in the file with the following code:

```
using System.Threading.Tasks;
namespace MyBlog.Shared.Interfaces
{
    public interface IBrowserStorage
    {
        Task<T>GetAsync<T>(string key);
        Task SetAsync(string key,object value);
```

```
    Task DeleteAsync(string key);
  }
}
```

Now we have an interface containing get, set, and delete methods.

Implementing Blazor Server

For Blazor Server, we will use protected browser storage:

1. Right-click on the **MyBlogServerSide** project and select **Add|New folder**. Name the folder Services.

2. Select the folder and press *Shift+ F2*. Name the file MyBlogProtectedBrowserStorage.cs.

    (I realize the naming is overkill, but it will be easier to tell them apart because we will soon create another one.)

3. Open the new file and add the following using statements:

    ```
    using Microsoft.AspNetCore.Components.Server.
    ProtectedBrowserStorage;
    using MyBlog.Shared.Interfaces;
    using System.Threading.Tasks;
    ```

4. Replace the class with this one:

    ```
    public class MyBlogProtectedBrowserStorage :
      IBrowserStorage
    {
      ProtectedSessionStorage Storage { get; set; }
      public MyBlogProtectedBrowserStorage
        (ProtectedSessionStorage storage)
      {
        Storage = storage;
      }
      public async Task DeleteAsync(string key)
      {
        await Storage.DeleteAsync(key);
      }
      public async Task<T?> GetAsync<T>(string key)
    ```

```
    {
        var value = await Storage.GetAsync<T>(key);
        if (value.Success)
        {
            return value.Value;
        }
        else
        {
            return default(T);
        }
    }
    public async Task SetAsync(string key, object value)
    {
        await Storage.SetAsync(key,value);
    }
}
```

The `MyBlogProtectedBrowserStorage` class implements the `IBrowserStorage` interface for protected browser storage. We inject a `ProtectedSessionStorage` instance and implement the `set`, `get`, and `delete` methods.

5. In `Startup.cs`, add the following namespaces:

```
using MyBlog.Shared.Interfaces;
using MyBlogServerSide.Services;
```

6. Add the following at the bottom of the `ConfigureServices` method:

```
services.AddScoped<IBrowserStorage,MyBlogProtectedBrowser
    Storage>();
```

7. Protected browser storage will use JavaScript to get the information, and as you may recall from *Chapter 10, JavaScript Interop*, we can only do those calls from `OnAfterRenderAsync` or `OnAfterRender`, but there is another way.

    The reason for JavaScript not working in places other than the `OnAfterRender` methods is the pre-rendering feature of Blazor Server.

8. Open `Pages/_host.chtml` and change the `render` mode from `<component type="typeof(App)" render-mode="ServerPrerendered" />` to `<component type="typeof(App)" render-mode="Server" />`.

   This will make it possible for us to call JavaScript outside of the `OnAfterRender` methods.

We are configuring Blazor to return an instance of `MyBlogProtectedBrowserStorage` when we inject `IBrowserStorage`.

This is the same as we did with the API. We inject different implementations depending on the platform.

Implementing WebAssembly

For Blazor WebAssembly, we will use `Blazored.SessionStorage`:

1. Right-click on the **Dependencies** node under the **MyBlogWebAssembly.Client** project and select **Manage Nuget Package**.

2. Search for `Blazored.SessionStorage` and click **Install**.

3. Right-click on the **MyBlogWebAssembly.Client** project and select **Add|New Folder**. Name the folder `Services`.

4. Select the new folder and press *Shift+ F2*. Name the file `MyBlogBrowserStorage.cs`.

5. Open the new file and replace the content with the following code:

```csharp
using MyBlog.Shared.Interfaces;
using System.Threading.Tasks;
using Blazored.SessionStorage;
namespace MyBlogWebAssembly.Client.Services
{
    public class MyBlogBrowserStorage :
        IBrowserStorage
    {
        ISessionStorageService Storage { get; set; }
        public MyBlogBrowserStorage
            (ISessionStorageService storage)
        {
            Storage = storage;
```

```
        }

        public async  Task DeleteAsync(string key)
        {
            await Storage.RemoveItemAsync(key);
        }

        public async Task<T> GetAsync<T>(string key)
        {
            return await Storage.GetItemAsync<T>(key);
        }

        public async Task SetAsync(string key, object
            value)
        {
            await Storage.SetItemAsync(key,value);
        }
    }
}
```

The implementation of `ProtectedBrowserStorage` and `Blazored.SessionStorage` are pretty close to one another. The names of the methods are different, but the parameters are the same.

6. In the `Program.cs` file, add the following namespaces:

```
using Blazored.SessionStorage;
using MyBlog.Shared.Interfaces;
using MyBlogWebAssembly.Client.Services;
```

7. Add the following code just above `await builder.Build().RunAsync();`:

```
builder.Services.AddBlazoredSessionStorage( options =>
    {
        options.JsonSerializerOptions.ReferenceHandler =
        System.Text.Json.Serialization.ReferenceHandler.
        Preserve;
        options.JsonSerializerOptions.
        PropertyNamingPolicy = null;
```

```
            });
builder.Services.AddScoped<IBrowserStorage,
MyBlogBrowserStorage>();
```

The `AddBlazoredSessionStorage` extension method hooks up everything so that we can start using the browser session storage. We also supply it with some configurations to be able to serialize our data objects.

Then we add our configuration for `IBrowserStorage`, just as we did with the server, but in this case, we return `MyBlogBrowserStorage` when we ask the dependency injection for `IBrowserStorage`.

Implementing the shared

We also need to implement some code that calls the services we just created:

1. In the **MyBlog.Shared** project, open `Pages/Admin/BlogPostEdit.razor`. We are going to make a couple of changes to the file.

2. Inject `IBrowserStorage`:

```
@inject MyBlog.Shared.Interfaces.IBrowserStorage storage
```

3. In the `OnParameterSetAsync` method, we load `post` if `Id` is not `null`.

   Add an `else` clause to the `if` statement:

```
else
{
    var saved = await storage.GetAsync<BlogPost>
        ("EditCurrentPost");
    if (saved != null)
    {
        Post = saved;
    }
}
```

When we load a file and `Id` is null, this means we are editing a new file and then we can check whether we have a file saved in browser storage.

This implementation can only have one file in the draft and only saves new posts. If we were to edit an existing post, it will not save those changes. This part would break if we didn't change the `render` mode to `Server` for Blazor Server.

Here is more information on handling protected browser storage with prerender: https://docs.microsoft.com/en-us/aspnet/core/blazor/state-management?view=aspnetcore-5.0&pivots=server#handle-prerendering.

4. We need our `UpdateHTML` method to become async. Change the method to look like this:

```
protected async Task UpdateHTMLAsync()
{
    if (Post.Text != null)
    {
        markDownAsHTML = Markdig.Markdown.ToHtml
            (Post.Text, pipeline);
        if (Post.Id == 0)
        {
            await storage.SetAsync("EditCurrentPost",
                Post);
        }
    }
}
```

If `Id` on the blog post is `0` (zero), we will store the post in the browser storage. Make sure to change all the references from `UpdateHTML` to `UpdateHTMLAsync`.

5. In the `MyBlog.Data.Shared` project in the `Models/BlogPost.cs` file, instantiate the `Tags` collection like this:

```
public ICollection<Tag> Tags { get; set; } = new
Collection<Tag>();
```

We are done. Now it's time to test the implementation:

1. Right-click on **MyBlogServerSide**, select **Set as Startup Project**, and run the project by pressing *Ctrl+ F5*.

2. Log in to the site (so we can access the admin tools).

3. Click **Blog posts** followed by **New blog post**.

4. Type anything in the boxes, and as soon as we type something in the text area, it will save the post to storage.

5. Click **Blog posts** (so we navigate away from our blog post).

6. Click **New blog post** and all the information will still be there.

7. Press *F12* to see the browser developer tools. Click **Application | Session storage | https://localhost:5000**.

    You should see one post with the key `EditCurrentPost`, and the value of that post should be an encrypted string, as seen in *Figure 11.1*:

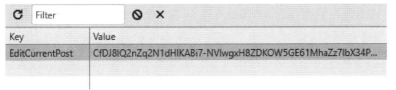

Figure 11.1 – The encrypted protected browser storage

Let's test the Blazor WebAssembly next:

1. Right-click on **MyBlogWebAssembly.Server**, select **Set as Startup Project**, and run the project by pressing *Ctrl+ F5*.

2. Log in to the site (so we can access the admin tools).

3. Click **Blog posts** and then **New blog post**.

4. Type anything in the boxes, and as soon as we type something in the text area, it will save the post to storage.

5. Click **Blog posts** (so we navigate away from our blog post).

6. Click **New blog post** and all the information should still be there.

7. Press *F12* to see the browser developer tools. Click **Application | Session storage | https://localhost:5000**.

    You should see one post with the key `EditCurrentPost`, and the value of that post should be a JSON string, as seen in *Figure 11.2*.

    If we were to change the data in the storage, it would also change in the application, so keep in mind that this is plain text, and the end user can manipulate the data:

Figure 11.2 – Browser storage that is unprotected

Now we have implemented protected browser storage for Blazor Server and session storage for Blazor WebAssembly.

We only have one way left to go through, so let's make it the most fun.

Using an in-memory state container service

When it comes to in-memory state containers, we simply use dependency injection to keep the instance of the service in memory for the predetermined time (scoped, singleton, transient).

In *Chapter 4*, *Understanding Basic Blazor Components*, we discussed how the scope of dependency injections differs from Blazor Server and Blazor WebAssembly. The big difference for us in this section is the fact that BlazorWebAssembly runs inside the web browser and doesn't have a connection to the server or other users.

To show how in-memory state works, we will do something that might seem like a bit of overkill for a blog, but it will be kinda cool to see. When we edit our blog post, we will make sure to update all the web browsers connected to our blog in real time (I did say overkill).

We will have to implement that a bit differently depending on hosting. Let's start with Blazor Server.

Implementing real-time updates on Blazor Server

The implementation for Blazor Server can also be used for Blazor WebAssembly, but since WebAssembly is running in our browser, it would only notify the users connected to the site, which would be just you. But it might be good to know that the same way works in Blazor Server as well as Blazor WebAssembly:

1. In the `MyBlog.Shared` project, select the `Interfaces` folder and press *Shift + F2*. Name the file `IBlogNotificationService.cs`.

2. Add the following code:

```
using MyBlog.Data.Models;
using System;
using System.Threading.Tasks;
namespace MyBlog.Shared.Interfaces
{
    public interface IBlogNotificationService
    {
        Action<BlogPost>BlogPostChanged{ get; set; }
        Task SendNotification(BlogPost post);
    }
}
```

We have an action that we can subscribe to when the blog post is updated and a method we can call when we update a post.

3. In the `MyBlogServerSide` project, select the `Services` folder and press *Shift+ F2*. Name the file `BlazorServerBlogNotificationService.cs`.

It might seem unnecessary to give the class a name that includes `BlazorServer`, but it makes sure we can easily tell the classes apart.

Replace the content with the following code:

```
using MyBlog.Data.Models;
using MyBlog.Shared.Interfaces;
using System;
using System.Threading.Tasks;
namespace MyBlogServerSide.Services
```

```
{
    public class BlazorServerBlogNotificationService :
        IBlogNotificationService
    {
        public Action<BlogPost>BlogPostChanged{ get;
            set; }
        public Task SendNotification(BlogPost post)
        {
            BlogPostChanged?.Invoke(post);
            return Task.CompletedTask;
        }
    }
}
```

The code is pretty simple here. If we call `SendNotification`, it will check whether anyone is listening for the `BlogPostChanged` action and whether to trigger the action.

4. In `Startup.cs` at the end of `ConfigureServices`, add the dependency injection:

```
services.AddSingleton<IBlogNotificationService,
    BlazorServerBlogNotificationService>();
```

Whenever we ask for an instance of the type `IBlogNotificationService`, we will get back an instance of `BlazorServerBlogNotificationService`.

We add this dependency injection as a **Singleton**. I can't stress this enough. When using Blazor Server, this will be the same instance for *ALL* users, so we must be careful when we use Singleton.

In this case, we want the service to notify all the visitors of our blog that the blog post has changed.

5. In the `MyBlog.Shared` project, open `Post.razor`.

6. Add the following code at the top (or close to the top) of the page:

```
@using MyBlog.Shared.Interfaces
@inject IBlogNotificationService notificationService
@implements IDisposable
```

We add dependency injection for `IBlogNotificationService` and we also need to implement `IDisposable` to avoid any memory leaks.

At the top of the `OnInitializedAsync` method, add the following:

```
notificationService.BlogPostChanged += PostChanged;
```

We added a listener to the event so we know when we should update the information.

7. We also need the `PostChanged` method, so add this code:

```
private async void PostChanged(BlogPost post)
{
    if (BlogPost.Id == post.Id)
    {
        BlogPost = post;
        await InvokeAsync(()=>this.StateHasChanged());
    }
}
```

If the parameter has the same ID as the post we are currently viewing, then replace the content with the post in the event and call `StateHasChanged`.

Since this is happening on another thread, we need to call `StateHasChanged` using `InvokeAsync` so that it runs on the UI thread.

The last thing in this component is to stop listening to the updates by implementing the `Dispose` method. Add the following:

```
void IDisposable.Dispose()
{
    notificationService.BlogPostChanged -= PostChanged;
}
```

We simply remove the event listener.

8. Open the `Pages/Admin/BlogPostEdit.Razor` file.

9. When we make changes to our blog post, we need to send a notification as well. At the top of the file, add the following:

```
@using MyBlog.Shared.Interfaces
@inject IBlogNotificationService notificationService
```

We add a namespace and inject our notification service.

10. In the `UpdateHTMLAsync` method, add the following just under the `Post.Text!=null` if statement:

```
await notificationService.SendNotification(Post);
```

Every time we change something, it will now send a notification that the blog post changed. I do realize that it would make more sense to do this when we save a post, but it makes for a much cooler demo.

11. Right-click on `MyBlogServerSide`, select **Set as Startup Project**, and run the project by pressing *Ctrl+ F5*.

12. Copy the URL and open another web browser. We should now have two web browser windows open showing us the blog.

    In the first window, open a blog post (doesn't matter which one), and in the second window, log in and edit the same blog post.

13. When we change the text of the blog post in the second window, the change should be reflected in real time in the first window.

I am constantly amazed how a feature that would be a bit tricky to implement without using Blazor only required 13 steps, and if we didn't prepare for the next step, it would take even fewer steps.

Next, we will implement the same feature for Blazor WebAssembly, but Blazor WebAssembly runs inside the user's web browser. There is no real-time communication built in, as with Blazor Server.

Implementing real-time updates on Blazor WebAssembly

We already have a lot of the things in place. We only need to add a real-time messaging system and since SignalR is both easy to implement and is awesome, let's use that.

The first time I used SignalR, my first thought was, wait, it can't be that easy. I have forgotten something or something is missing.

Let's see whether that still holds true today:

1. Right-click on the **MyBlogWebAssembly.Server** project, select **Add new folder**, and name the folder `Hubs`.

2. Select the `Hubs` folder and press *Shift+ F2*. Name the file `BlogNotificationHub.cs`.

3. Replace the code with the following:

```
using System.Threading.Tasks;
using Microsoft.AspNetCore.SignalR;
using MyBlog.Data.Models;
namespace MyBlogWebAssembly.Server.Hubs
{
    public class BlogNotificationHub : Hub
    {
        public async Task SendNotification(BlogPost post)
        {
            await Clients.All.SendAsync
                ("BlogPostChanged", post);
        }
    }
}
```

The class inherits from the Hub class. There is a method called
SendNotification. Keep that name in mind; we will come back to that.

We call Clients.All.SendAsync, which means we will send a message called
BlogPostChanged with the content of a blog post.

The name BlogPostChanged is also important, so keep that in mind as well.

4. In the Startup.cs file at the top of the ConfigureService method, add
the following:

```
services.AddSignalR().AddJsonProtocol(options => {
options.PayloadSerializerOptions.ReferenceHandler =
ReferenceHandler.Preserve;
options.PayloadSerializerOptions.PropertyNamingPolicy =
null;
});
```

This adds SignalR and configures the JSON serialization to handle the entity
framework.

5. At the bottom of the method, add the following:

```
services.AddResponseCompression(opts =>
{
opts.MimeTypes = ResponseCompressionDefaults.MimeTypes.
```

```
Concat(
new[] { "application/octet-stream" });
});
```

6. Add the following namespace:

```
using MyBlogWebAssembly.Server.Hubs;
```

7. In app.UseEndpoints, just above endpoints.
   MapFallbackToFile("index.html");, add the following:

```
endpoints.MapHub<BlogNotificationHub>("/
BlogNotificationHub");
```

Here we configure what URL BlogNotificationHub should use. In this case, we are using the same URL as the name of the hub.

The URL here is also important. We will use that in just a bit.

8. In the MyBlogWebAssembly.Client project, right-click on the **Dependencies** node and select **Manage NuGet Packages**.

9. Search for Microsoft.AspNetCore.SignalR.Client and click **Install**. Select the Services folder and press *Shift+ F2*. Name the file BlazorWebAssemblyBlogNotificationService.cs.

In this file, we will implement the SignalR communication.

10. Add the following namespaces:

```
using Microsoft.AspNetCore.Components;
using Microsoft.AspNetCore.SignalR.Client;
using Microsoft.Extensions.DependencyInjection;
using MyBlog.Data.Models;
using MyBlog.Shared.Interfaces;
using System;
using System.Threading.Tasks;
```

11. Add this class:

```
public class
   BlazorWebAssemblyBlogNotificationService:
     IBlogNotificationService, IAsyncDisposable
{
    NavigationManager _navigationManager;
```

```csharp
public BlazorWebAssemblyBlogNotificationService
  (NavigationManager navigationManager)
{
    _navigationManager = navigationManager;

    _hubConnection = new
      HubConnectionBuilder().AddJsonProtocol
        (options => {
            options.PayloadSerializerOptions.
            ReferenceHandler = System.Text.Json.
            Serialization.ReferenceHandler.Preserve;
            options.PayloadSerializerOptions.
            PropertyNamingPolicy = null;
        })
      .WithUrl(navigationManager.ToAbsoluteUri
        ("/BlogNotificationHub"))
      .Build();

    _hubConnection.On<BlogPost>
      ("BlogPostChanged", (post) =>
    {
        BlogPostChanged?.Invoke(post);
    });

    _hubConnection.StartAsync();
}

private HubConnection _hubConnection;

public Action<BlogPost> BlogPostChanged
  { get;set; }
public async Task SendNotification(BlogPost post)
{
    await _hubConnection.SendAsync
      ("SendNotification", post);
}

public async ValueTask DisposeAsync()
```

```
        {
            await _hubConnection.DisposeAsync();
        }
    }
```

A lot is happening here. The class is implementing
`IBlogNotificationService` and `IAsyncDisposable`.

In the constructor, we use dependency injection to get `NavigationManager`, so
we can figure out the URL to the server.

Then we configure the connection to the hub. As with the server, we need to
configure the JSON serialization to handle the entity framework. Then we specify
the URL to the hub; this should be the same as we specified in *step 7*.

Now we can configure the hub connection to listen for events, in this case, we listen
for the `BlogPostChanged` event, the same name we specified in *step 3*. When
someone sends the event, the method we specify will run.

The method in this case simply triggers the event we have in
`IBlogNotificationService`. Then we start the connection. Since the
constructor can't be async, we won't await the `StartAsync` method.

`IBlogNotificationService` also implements the `SendNotification`
method, and we simply trigger the event with the same name on the hub, which will
result in the hub sending the `BlogPostChanged` event to all connected clients.

The last thing we do is to make sure that we dispose of the hub connection.

12. In the `Program.cs` file, we need to configure dependency injection. Just above
`await builder.Build().RunAsync();`, add the following:

```
builder.Services.AddSingleton<IBlogNotificationService,
BlazorWebAssemblyBlogNotificationService>();
```

13. Add the following namespace:

```
MyBlogWebAssembly.Client.Services;
```

14. Now it's time to carry out testing and we do that in the same way as for the Blazor
Server project.

    Right-click on **MyBlogWebAssembly.Server**, select **Set as Startup Project**, and run
    the project by pressing *Ctrl+F5*.

15. Copy the URL and open another web browser. We should now have two web browser windows open showing us the blog.

    In the first window, open a blog post (it doesn't matter which one), and in the second window, log in and edit the same blog post.

16. When we change the text of the blog post in the second window, the change should be reflected in real time in the first window.

In 16 steps, we have implemented real-time communication between server and client, a Blazor WebAssembly client with .NET code running inside the web browser.

And no JavaScript!

Summary

In this chapter, we learned how we can handle state in our application and how we can use local storage to store data, both encrypted and not. We looked at different ways of doing that and we also made sure to include SignalR to be able to use real-time communication with the server.

Almost all applications need to save data in some form. Perhaps it can be settings or preferences. The things we covered in the chapter are the most common ones, but we should also know that there are many open source projects we can use to persist state. We could save the information using IndexDB.

In the next chapter, we will take a look at debugging. Hopefully, you won't have needed to read that chapter beforehand.

Section 3: Debug, Test, and Deploy

In this section, you will see how to debug your application both using client-side and server-side Blazor. We'll cover how to add tests and what to think about when it comes to deploying your application.

This section includes the following chapters:

- *Chapter 12, Debugging*
- *Chapter 13, Testing*
- *Chapter 14, Deploying to Production*
- *Chapter 15, Where to Go from Here*

12
Debugging

In this chapter, we will take a look at debugging. The debugging experience of Blazor is a good one, and hopefully, you haven't got stuck anywhere and had to jump to this chapter.

Debugging code is a really good way to solve bugs, understand the workflow, or simply look at specific values. Blazor has three different ways to debug code, and we will take a look at each one of those.

In this chapter we will cover the following:

- Making things break
- Debugging Blazor Server
- Debugging Blazor WebAssembly
- Debugging Blazor WebAssembly in the browser
- Hot reload (almost the real thing)

To debug something, we should first make something break!

Technical requirements

Make sure you have followed the previous chapters or use the Chapter11 folder as a starting point.

You can find the source code for this chapter's end result at `https://github.com/PacktPublishing/Web-Development-with-Blazor/tree/master/Chapter12`.

> **Note**
>
> If you are jumping into this chapter using the code from GitHub, make sure to register the user with an email and follow the instructions for adding a user and adding the Administrator role to the database. You can find the instructions in *Chapter 8, Authentication and Authorization*.

Making things break

Edsger W. Dijkstra once said,

> *"If debugging is the process of removing software bugs, then programming must be the process of putting them in."*

This is definitely true in this section because we will add a page that will throw an exception:

1. In the `MyBlog.Shared` project, select the `Pages` folder, and press *Shift + F2*. Name the new file `ThrowException.razor`.

2. Replace the contents of the file with the following code block:

   ```
   @page "/ThrowException"
   <button @onclick="@(() => {throw new Exception("Something
   is broken"); })">Throw an exception</button>
   ```

   This page simply shows a button and when you press the button, it will throw an exception.

   Great! We have our application's Ivan Drago (he wants to break you, but we might just beat him with some fancy debugging).

The next step is to take a look at Blazor Server debugging.

Debugging Blazor Server

If you have debugged any type of .NET application in the past, you will feel right at home. If you haven't, don't worry – we will go through it. Debugging Blazor Server is just as we might expect and is the best debugging experience of the three different types we will cover.

I usually keep my Razor pages in a shared library and while building my project, I use Blazor Server for two reasons – first, it's a bit faster to run the project, and second, the debugging experience is better.

Let's give it a try!

1. Right-click on **MyBlogServerSide** and click **Set As Startup project**.

2. Press *F5* to start the project (this time with debugging).

3. Using the web browser, navigate to `https://localhost:5001/throwexception` (the port number may vary).

4. Press *F12* to show the web browser developer tools.

5. In the developer tools, click **Console**.

6. Click the **Throw exception** button on our page.

    At this point, Visual Studio should request focus and it should show the exception as shown in *Figure 12.1*:

Figure 12.1 – Exception in Visual Studio

7. Press *F5* to continue and switch back to the web browser. We should now be able to see the exception message in the developer tools as shown in *Figure 12.2*:

```
[2021-02-20T19:53:28.737Z] Error: System.Exception: Something is broken   blazor.server.js:19
    at MyBlog.Shared.Pages.ThrowException.<>c.<BuildRenderTree>b__0_0() in
C:\Code\B16009\Ch12\MyBlog\MyBlog.Shared\Pages\ThrowException.razor:line 3
    at Microsoft.AspNetCore.Components.EventCallbackWorkItem.InvokeAsync[T](MulticastDelegate
delegate, T arg)
    at
Microsoft.AspNetCore.Components.ComponentBase.Microsoft.AspNetCore.Components.IHandleEvent.Ha
ndleEventAsync(EventCallbackWorkItem callback, Object arg)
    at Microsoft.AspNetCore.Components.RenderTree.Renderer.DispatchEventAsync(UInt64
eventHandlerId, EventFieldInfo fieldInfo, EventArgs eventArgs)
```

Figure 12.2 – Exception in the web browser

As we can see in *Figure 12.1* and *Figure 12.2*, we get the exception both in Visual Studio while debugging and also in the developer tools.

This makes it quite easy to find the problem if there is an exception in an app in production (perish the thought) – that feature has saved us many times.

Now let's try a breakpoint:

1. In Visual Studio, open `MyBlog.Shared/Pages/Index.razor`.

2. Anywhere in the `LoadPosts` method, set a breakpoint by clicking the leftmost border (making a red dot appear). We can also add a breakpoint by pressing *F9*.

3. Go back to the web browser and navigate to `https://localhost:5001/` (the port number may vary).

Visual Studio should now hit the breakpoint and by hovering over variables, we should be able to see the current values.

Both breakpoints and exception debugging work as we might expect. Next, we will take a look at debugging Blazor WebAssembly.

Debugging Blazor WebAssembly

Blazor WebAssembly can of course be debugged as well, but there are some things we need to think about. Since we have our exception page in our shared library, we can go straight into debugging.

But let's start with breakpoints:

1. Right-click on **MyBlogWebAssembly.Server** and select **Set as Startup Project**.

2. Press *F5* to debug the project.

Here we can notice the first difference – assuming we still have the breakpoint we set in the *Debugging Blazor Server* section (in the `LoadPosts` method), the breakpoint did not get hit.

Breakpoints won't get hit on the initial page load in Blazor WebAssembly. We need to navigate to another page and back to the index page again for it to hit.

We can't just change the URL, as we could in Blazor Server, simply because that will reload the app again and not trigger the breakpoint because it was an *initial page load*.

Debugging Blazor WebAssembly is made possible by the following line of code in the `launchsetting.json` file:

```
"inspectUri": "{wsProtocol}://{url.hostname}:{url.port}/_
framework/debug/ws-proxy?browser={browserInspectUri}"
```

But it is supplied for us when we create the project, so we don't need to add that manually.

We can also put breakpoints in our `MyBlogWebAssembly.Server` server project if we want to and they will get hit just as we would expect.

Now let's see what happens with our exception:

1. In the web browser, navigate to `https://localhost:5001/`
    `throwexception`.

2. Click the **Throw exception** button.

3. The unhandled exception won't get hit in Visual Studio. We get the exception in the developer tools in the web browser as shown in *Figure 12.3*:

```
❌ ▶ crit:                                        blazor.webassembly.js:1
   Microsoft.AspNetCore.Components.WebAssembly.Rendering.WebAssemblyRende
   rer[100]
         Unhandled exception rendering component: Something is broken
   System.Exception: Something is broken
      at MyBlog.Shared.Pages.ThrowException.<>c.<BuildRenderTree>b__0_0()
   in
   C:\Code\B16009\Ch12\MyBlog\MyBlog.Shared\Pages\ThrowException.razor:li
   ne 3
      at
   Microsoft.AspNetCore.Components.EventCallbackWorkItem.InvokeAsync[Obje
   ct](MulticastDelegate delegate, Object arg)
      at
   Microsoft.AspNetCore.Components.EventCallbackWorkItem.InvokeAsync(Obje
   ct arg)
      at
   Microsoft.AspNetCore.Components.ComponentBase.Microsoft.AspNetCore.Com
   ponents.IHandleEvent.HandleEventAsync(EventCallbackWorkItem callback,
   Object arg)
      at Microsoft.AspNetCore.Components.EventCallback.InvokeAsync(Object
   arg)
      at
   Microsoft.AspNetCore.Components.RenderTree.Renderer.DispatchEventAsync
   (UInt64 eventHandlerId, EventFieldInfo fieldInfo, EventArgs eventArgs)
```

Figure 12.3 – WebAssembly error

The debugging experience in Blazor WebAssembly is simply not as polished as with Blazor Server but it is polished enough to be able to get the job done.

We have one method left to explore – debugging in the web browser.

Debugging Blazor WebAssembly in the web browser

The first debugging experience for Blazor WebAssembly was the ability to debug right in the web browser:

1. In Visual Studio, start the project by pressing *Ctrl + F5* (run without debugging).

2. In the web browser, press *Shift + Alt + D*.

    We will get an error message with instructions on how to start the web browser in debug mode.

    I am running Edge, so the way to start Edge would be something like this:

    ```
    msedge --remote-debugging-port=9222 --user-data-dir="C:\
    Users\Jimmy\AppData\Local\Temp\blazor-edge-debug"
    --no-first-run https://localhost:5001/
    ```

    Copy the command.

3. Press *Win + R* and paste the command.

4. A new instance of Chrome or Edge will open. In this new instance, press *Shift + Alt + D*.

5. We should now see a source tab containing C# code from our project. From here, we can put breakpoints that will be hit, and we can hover over variables.

The debug UI can be seen in *Figure 12.4:*

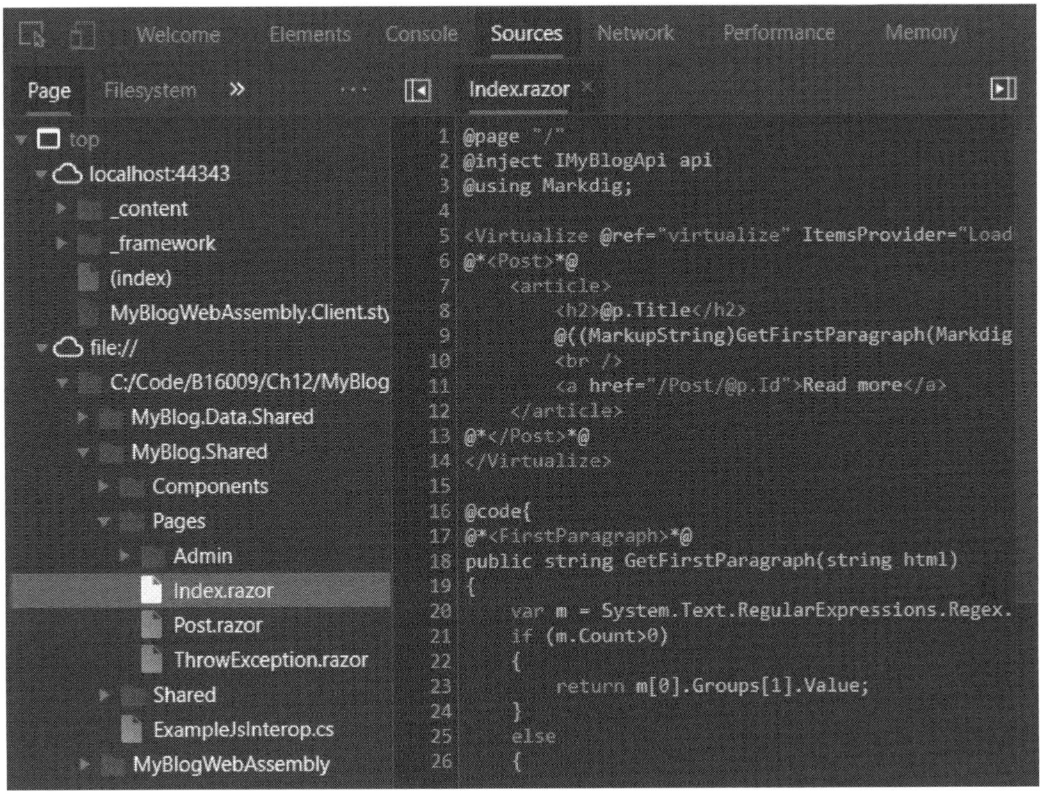

```
1  @page "/"
2  @inject IMyBlogApi api
3  @using Markdig;
4
5  <Virtualize @ref="virtualize" ItemsProvider="Load
6  @*<Post>*@
7      <article>
8          <h2>@p.Title</h2>
9          @((MarkupString)GetFirstParagraph(Markdig
10         <br />
11         <a href="/Post/@p.Id">Read more</a>
12     </article>
13 @*</Post>*@
14 </Virtualize>
15
16 @code{
17 @*<FirstParagraph>*@
18 public string GetFirstParagraph(string html)
19 {
20     var m = System.Text.RegularExpressions.Regex.
21     if (m.Count>0)
22     {
23         return m[0].Groups[1].Value;
24     }
25     else
26     {
```

Figure 12.4 – Screenshot of the in-browser debug

Debugging C# code in the browser is pretty amazing, but since we have been debugging directly in Visual Studio, I personally don't see much use for this kind of debugging.

Next, we will take a look at something that might not fall under debugging but is really useful while developing Blazor apps.

Hot reload (almost the real thing)

With .NET 5, we got the ability to reload our Blazor site when we make changes to a code file. Users have asked for hot reload and Microsoft is aiming to release hot reload in the .NET 6 timeframe.

To set this up, do the following:

1. In Visual Studio, select the **Tools** menu and then **Options**.

2. Select **Projects and Solutions** and then **ASP.NET Core**.

3. In the right box under the **General** heading, change the value of the **Auto build and refresh** option to **Auto build and refresh browser after saving the changes**.

4. Right-click on **MyBlogServerSide** and select **Set as Startup project**.

5. Now run the project by pressing *Ctrl + F5* (it only works without debugging).

6. In the web browser, bring up the counter page by adding `/counter` to the URL.

7. Make a change to the `Pages/Counter.razor` file and click **Save**.

   Our web browser should now reload, and the change will be shown.

This also works from the command line by running the following command:

```
dotnet watch run
```

There are a couple of limitations to this method though:

- It doesn't work with Blazor WebAssembly running an ASP.NET server backend (as we have in our project). For this to work, we need to manually reload the browser.

- The state of the application will restart.

- Changes in a shared project won't be reflected.

So, for our setup, this feature isn't very beneficial, but it is really good if our project doesn't fall into any of the previously mentioned limitations.

Summary

In this chapter, we looked at different ways to debug our Blazor application. There will always be moments where we need to step through the code, either to find a bug or to see what is happening. When these moments are upon us, Visual Studio delivers world-class functionality to help us achieve our goals.

The nice thing is that debugging Blazor applications, whether it's Blazor Server or Blazor WebAssembly, will work as you would expect from a Microsoft product. We get C# errors that are (in most cases) easy to understand and to solve.

In the next chapter, we will take a look at testing our Blazor components.

13
Testing

In this chapter, we will take a look at testing. Writing tests for our projects will help us develop things rapidly.

We can run the tests and make sure we haven't broken anything with the latest change, and also we don't have to invest our own time in testing the components since it is all done by the tests. Testing will increase the quality of the product since we know that things that worked earlier still function as they should.

But writing tests for UI elements isn't always as easy; the most common way is to spin up the site and use tools that click on buttons and then read the output to determine whether things work or not. The upside of this method is that we can test our site on different browsers and devices. The downside is that it usually takes a lot of time to do these tests. We need to spin up the web, start a web browser, verify the test, close the web browser, and repeat for the next test.

We can use this method in Blazor as well (as with any ASP.NET site) but with Blazor, we have other opportunities when it comes to testing.

Steve Sanderson created an embryo of a test framework for Blazor that Microsoft MVP Egil Hansen picked up and continued the development of.

Egil's framework is called **bUnit** and has become an industry standard in the Blazor community for testing Blazor components.

This chapter covers the following topics:

- What is bUnit?

- Setting up a test project

- Mocking the API

- Writing tests

Technical requirements

Make sure you have followed the previous chapters or use the `Chapter12` folder as a starting point.

You can find the source code for this chapter's end result at `https://github.com/PacktPublishing/Web-Development-with-Blazor/tree/master/Chapter13`.

> **Note**
>
> If you are jumping into this chapter using the code from GitHub, make sure to register the user with an email and follow the instructions for adding a user and adding the Administrator role to the database. You can find the instructions in *Chapter 8, Authentication and Authorization*.

What is bUnit?

As mentioned in the introduction, some tests spin up web browsers to test the pages/components, but bUnit takes another approach.

bUnit is made specifically for Blazor. It can define and set up tests using C# or Razor syntax. It can mock JavaScript interop as well as Blazor's authentication and authorization. To make our components more testable, sometimes we need to think about these things from the beginning or make minor changes to our code.

bUnit doesn't rely on a web browser but renders the output internally and exposes it to us so that we may test against predefined outputs.

It's time we get our hands dirty, so let's create a test project.

Setting up a test project

To be able to do tests, we need a test project:

1. To install the bUnit templates, open PowerShell and run the following command:

    ```
    dotnet new --install bunit.template
    ```

2. Make sure to check which is the current latest version of the templates on the bUnit web page: `https://bunit.egilhansen.com/`.

3. In Visual Studio, right-click **MyBlogSolution** and choose **Add | New Project**.

4. Search for bUnit and select **bUnit Test Project** in the results, and then click **Next**. Sometimes it takes time to find a template. We can also change the project type dropdown to **bUnit** to find the template. We might need to reboot Visual Studio to find it.

5. Name the project `MyBlog.Shared.Tests`, leave the location as is, and click **Next**.

6. Select **.NET 5** in the dropdown.

Great! We now have a test project.

Before we go into mocking the API, let's take a look at the different methods available to us so we can get a feel for how bUnit works.

In `MyBlog.Shared.Tests`, we should have the following three files:

*   `_Imports.razor` contains the namespaces that we want all of our Razor files to have access to.

*   `Counter.razor` is a copy of the same `Counter` components that we get by default in the Blazor template.

*   `CounterCSharpTest.cs` contains tests written in C#.

Let's start with the `CounterCSharpTest.cs` file, which contains two tests: one that checks that the counter starts at `0` and one that clicks the button and verifies the counter is now `1`. These two simple tests make sense for testing the `Counter` component.

The `CounterStartsAtZero` test looks like this:

```
[Fact]
public void CounterStartsAtZero()
{
```

```
// Arrange
var cut = RenderComponent<Counter>();
// Assert that content of the paragraph shows counter
// at zero
cut.Find("p").MarkupMatches("<p>Current count: 0</p>");
}
```

Let's break this down. The Fact attribute tells the test runner that this is a *normal* test that takes no parameters. We can also use the Theory attribute to tell the test runner that the test method needs parameter values, but for this use case, we don't need parameters.

First, we arrange the test. Simply put, we set up everything we need to do the test. Egil uses cut as the name of the component, which stands for **component under testing**.

We run the RenderComponent method and pass in the component type, which is the Counter component in this case. Next, we assert whether the component outputs the correct thing or not. We use the Find method to find the first paragraph tag and then verify that the HTML looks like <p>Current count: 0</p>.

The second test is a bit more advanced and it looks like this:

```
[Fact]
public void ClickingButtonIncrementsCounter()
{
    // Arrange
    var cut = RenderComponent<Counter>();
    // Act - click button to increment counter
    cut.Find("button").Click();
    // Assert that the counter was incremented
    cut.Find("p").MarkupMatches("<p>Current count: 1</p>");
}
```

Just as with the previous test, we start with arranging by rendering our Counter component. The next step is acting where we click the button. We look for the button and then click the button in our counter component. There is only one button so in this case, it's safe to look for the button this way.

Then it's time to assert again, and there we check the markup in the same way as the previous test but we look for 1 instead of 0.

Now let's run the tests and see whether they pass:

1. In Visual Studio, bring up **Test Explorer** by searching for it using *Ctrl + Q*. We can also find it in **View | Test Explorer**.

2. Press **Run all test** in the view. Test Explorer should look like *Figure 13.1*:

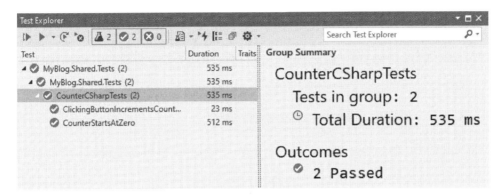

Figure 13.1 – Visual Studio Test Explorer

Wonderful, now we have our first test running and hopefully passing.

Next, we will take a look at mocking the API.

Mocking the API

There are different ways to test our application. Testing the API is outside the scope of this book but we still need to test the components and the components are dependent on the API. We could spin up the API and test against the API, but in this case, we are only interested in testing the Blazor component.

We can then mock the API or create a fake copy of the API that doesn't read from the database but reads from a predefined dataset. This way, we always know what the output should be.

Luckily, the interface we created for our API is just what we need to create a mock API.

We won't implement 100% of the tests for the project so we don't have to mock all the methods. Please feel free at the end of the chapter to implement tests for all the methods as an exercise.

There are two ways we can implement the mock API. We could spin up an in-memory database, but to keep things simple, we will choose the other option and generate posts when we ask for them:

1. Under `MyBlog.Shared.Tests`, right-click on the **Dependencies** node and select **Add Project References**.

2. Check **MyBlog.Shared** and click **Ok**. Now our test project has access to all the classes in our shared project as well as all the classes the shared project is referring to, such as **Interfaces** in the `MyBlog.Data.Shared` project.

3. Select the **MyBlog.Shared.Tests** project. Press *Shift + F2* to create a new file and name the file `MyBlogApiMock.cs`.

4. Add the following namespaces:

```
using MyBlog.Data.Interfaces;
using MyBlog.Data.Models;
```

5. Implement the `IMyBlogApi` interface; the class should look like this:

```
public class MyBlogApiMock :IMyBlogApi
{
}
```

Now we will implement each of the methods so we can get data.

6. For `BlogPost`, add the following code in the class:

```
public async Task<BlogPost>GetBlogPostAsync(int id)
{
BlogPost post=new()
    {
        Id = id,
        Text = $"This is a blog post no {id}",
        Title = $"Blogpost {id}",
        PublishDate = DateTime.Now,
        Category = await GetCategoryAsync(1),
    };
    post.Tags.Add(await GetTagAsync(1));
    post.Tags.Add(await GetTagAsync(2));
    return post;
}
```

```
public Task<int>GetBlogPostCountAsync()
{
    return Task.FromResult(10);
}
public async Task<List<BlogPost>>GetBlogPostsAsync(int
numberofposts, int startindex)
{
    List<BlogPost> list = new();
    for (int a = 0; a <numberofposts; a++)
    {
        list.Add(await GetBlogPostAsync(startindex +
            a));
    }
    return list;
}
```

When we get a blog post, we simply create one and fill it with predefined information that we can later use in our tests. The same thing goes for getting a list of blog posts.

We also say that we have a total of 10 blog posts in the database.

For categories, add the following code:

```
public async Task<List<Category>>GetCategoriesAsync()
{
    List<Category> list = new();
    for (int a = 0; a < 10; a++)
    {
        list.Add(await GetCategoryAsync(a));
    }
    return list;
}
public Task<Category>GetCategoryAsync(int id)
{
    return Task.FromResult(new Category() { Id = id,
        Name = $"Category {id}" });
}
```

Here we do the same thing: we create categories named `Category` followed by a number.

7. The same thing goes for tags; add the following code:

```
public Task<Tag>GetTagAsync(int id)
{
    return Task.FromResult(new Tag() { Id = id, Name =
        $"Tag {id}" });
}
public async Task<List<Tag>>GetTagsAsync()
{
    List<Tag> list = new();
    for (int a = 0; a < 10; a++)
    {
        list.Add(await GetTagAsync(a));
    }
    return list;
}
```

We will not add tests for other methods in the API. We do need to add them to the mock class to fulfill the interface. Add the following methods:

```
public Task<BlogPost>SaveBlogPostAsync(BlogPost item)
{
    return Task.FromResult(item);
}
public Task<Category>SaveCategoryAsync(Category item)
{
    return Task.FromResult(item);
}
public Task<Tag>SaveTagAsync(Tag item)
{
    return Task.FromResult(item);
}
public Task DeleteBlogPostAsync(BlogPost item)
{
    return Task.CompletedTask;
}
```

```
public Task DeleteCategoryAsync(Category item)
{
    return Task.CompletedTask;
}
public Task DeleteTagAsync(Tag item)
{
    return Task.CompletedTask;
}
```

We now have a mock API that does the same thing over and over again so we can make reliable tests.

Writing tests

Time to write some tests. As I mentioned earlier in the chapter, we won't create tests for the entire site; we will leave that to you to finish later if you want to. This is just to get a feel for how to write tests:

1. Right-click and select **MyBlog.Shared.Tests**, then select **Add | New folder**. Name the folder Pages.

    This is just so we can keep a bit of a structure (the same folder structure as the project we are testing).

2. Select the Pages folder. Press *Shift + F2* to create a new Razor component and name the file IndexTest.cs. Just remember not to name it the same as the component we are testing; otherwise, it will be hard to make sure we are testing the right one.

3. Open IndexTest.cs and add the bUnit namespace:

    ```
    using Bunit;
    using Microsoft.Extensions.DependencyInjection;
    using MyBlog.Data.Interfaces;
    using Xunit;
    ```

4. Inherit from TestContext by adding the following code:

    ```
    public class IndexTest: TestContext
    {
    }
    ```

5. Now we will add the test. Add the following code:

```
[Fact(DisplayName ="Shows 10 blog posts")]
public void Shows10Blogposts()
{
        var cut = RenderComponent
          <MyBlog.Shared.Pages.Index>();
        Assert.Equal(10,cut.FindAll("article").Count());
}
```

We give our test a display name so we understand what it does. The test is pretty simplistic; we know we have 10 blog posts coming from the mock API. We also know that each blog post is rendered within an `article` tag. We find all `article` tags and make sure we have 10 of them in total.

Since we are using injection, we need to configure the dependency injection and this is something we can do in the constructor.

6. We need to add the `IndexTest` method:

```
public IndexTest()
{
        Services.AddScoped<IMyBlogApi, MyBlogApiMock>();
}
```

This method will run when the class is created and here we declare that if the components ask for an instance of `IMyBlogApi`, it will return an instance of our mock API.

This works the same way as with Blazor Server, where we return an API that talks directly to the database, and with Blazor WebAssembly, where we return an instance of the API that talks to a web API.

In this case, it will return our mock API that returns data that is easy to test with. Now we need to write the actual test.

7. In Visual Studio, bring up Test Explorer by searching for it using *Ctrl + Q*. We can also find it in **View | Test Explorer**.

Run our tests to see whether we get a green light, as shown in *Figure 13.2*:

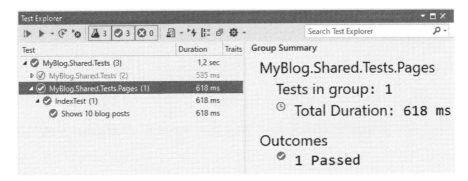

Figure 13.2 – Test Explorer with IndexTest

Now we have a test that tests the first post and the tenth post. It's an OK assumption to make that the posts in between are rendered as expected, given the test data we have, but it is, of course, possible to take the testing even further.

bUnit is a great framework for testing and the fact that it is written specifically for Blazor so that it takes advantage of Blazor's powers makes it amazing to work with.

Now we have a simplistic test testing our blog, but bUnit has support for more advanced features as well, such as authentication, for example.

Authentication

Using bUnit, we can test authentication and authorization.

It is, however, not the components themselves that are doing the authentication. It's `AuthorizeRouteView` that we added to `app.razor` in *Chapter 8, Authentication and Authorization*, so testing that in individual components won't make a difference.

But we can use `AuthorizeView`, for example, in our components like this:

```
<AuthorizeView>
    <Authorized>
        <strong>Authorized</strong>
    </Authorized>
    <NotAuthorized>
        <strong>Not Authorized</strong>
```

```
        </NotAuthorized>
    </AuthorizeView>
```

We can use the `AddTestAuthorization` method to authorize our tests like this:

```
[Fact(DisplayName = "Shows not authorized")]
public void ShowsNotAuthorized()
{
    var authContext = this.AddTestAuthorization();
    var cut = RenderComponent
        <MyBlog.Shared.Pages.AuthorizedOrNot>();
    var content = cut.Find("strong").TextContent;
    Assert.Equal("Not Authorized", content);
}
```

This method adds `TestAuthorization` but is not authorized. The page will then display the text **"Not Authorized"**. To test when the user is authorized, we just set the user as authorized:

```
[Fact(DisplayName = "Shows authorized")]
public void ShowsAuthorized()
{
    var authContext = this.AddTestAuthorization();
    authContext.SetAuthorized("Testuser",
        AuthorizationState.Authorized);

    var cut = RenderComponent
        <MyBlog.Shared.Pages.AuthorizedOrNot>();
    var content = cut.Find("strong").TextContent;
    Assert.Equal("Authorized", content);
}
```

We can add claims, roles, and much more. The user we utilize for testing has no correlation with the users or roles in the database; the authorization is mocked by bUnit.

Authentication and authorization could be tricky to test, but using bUnit, it is really simple. Something a bit harder to do is testing JavaScript, but bUnit has great support for that as well.

Testing JavaScript

Testing JavaScript is not supported by bUnit, which is understandable. We can, however, test the interop ourselves.

In this book, we have used the new .NET 5 syntax for our JavaScript. In our `MyBlog.Shared\Components\ItemList.razor` component, we make a JavaScript interop to confirm the deletion of an item.

The JavaScript call looks like this:

```
jsmodule = await jsRuntime.InvokeAsync<IJSObjectReference>
("import", "/_content/MyBlog.Shared/ItemList.razor.js");
return await jsmodule.InvokeAsync<bool>("showConfirm", "Are you
sure?");
```

We make sure that we load the JavaScript module and then execute the `showConfirm` method.

JavaScript testing in bUnit can be done in two different modes – `strict` and `loose`. The default value is `strict`, which means we need to specify every module and every method.

If we choose `loose`, all methods will just return the default value. For a Boolean, it would return `false`, for example.

To test the preceding JavaScript call, we can add the following code:

```
var moduleInterop = fixture.JSInterop.SetupModule
    ("/_content/MyBlog.Shared/ItemList.razor.js");
var showconfirm = moduleInterop.Setup<bool>
    ("showConfirm", "Are you sure?").SetResult(true);
```

We set up a module with the same path to the JavaScript as before, then we specify the method and any `in` parameters.

Lastly, we specify what the result should be. In this case, we return `true`, which would be the result of the JavaScript if we want to delete the item.

Great job! We now have tests in our project. Even though we aren't covering all the components, we should have all the building blocks to complete the tests.

Summary

In this chapter, we looked at testing our application. We looked at how we can mock an API to make reliable tests. We also covered how to test JavaScript interop as well as authentication.

Tests can speed up our development and, most importantly, the quality of what we build. With bUnit combined with dependency injection, it is easy to build tests that can help us test our components.

Since we can test every component by itself, we don't have to log in, navigate to a specific place in our site, and then test the entire page as many other testing frameworks would have us do.

Now we have our site, containing reusable components, authentication, APIs, both Blazor Server and WebAssembly, authentication, shared code, JavaScript interop, state management, and tests. We only have one more thing to do: ship it!

In the next chapter, *Chapter 14, Deploying to Production*, it's time to ship.

14
Deploy to Production

In this chapter, we will take a look at the different options we have when deploying our Blazor application to production. Since there are many different options, going through them all would be a book all by itself.

We won't go into detail but rather cover the different things we need to think about so that we can deploy to any provider.

In the end, deploying is what we need to do to make use of what we build.

In this chapter, we will cover the following:

- Continuous delivery options
- Deploying the database
- Hosting options

Technical requirements

This chapter is about general deployment so we won't need any code.

Continuous delivery options

When deploying anything to production, we should think about making sure to remove uncertain factors. For example, if we are deploying from our own machine, how do we know that it's the latest version? How do we know that our teammates didn't recently solve a problem and we don't have the fix in our branch? To be honest, how do we even know that the version in source control is the same in production? Or if the version in production even exists in source control?

This is where **Continuous Integration** and **Continuous Delivery/Deployment (CI/CD)** come into the picture. We simply make sure that something else makes the deployment to production. Deployment is a book in itself so we won't go that deep into the subject.

GitHub Actions and Azure DevOps (or Azure Pipelines) are two ways from Microsoft to do CI/CD. There are many more, such as Jenkins, TeamCity, and GitLab – the list is long. If the CI/CD system we are currently using supports deploying ASP.NET, it is going to be able to handle Blazor because, in the end, Blazor is just an ASP.NET site.

If we have tests (which we should have), we should also make sure to set up tests as part of our CI/CD pipeline. The nice thing is that we don't need to add any specific hardware to test our components; it is going to work if our CI/CS pipeline can run unit tests (nUnit, xUnit).

In our setup at work, we build and run all tests when we do a pull request. If the build and tests pass, someone else in the team does a code review and approves the change. If the team member approves the change, it will then trigger a release and the release deploys the site to our test environment. Our testers run through the test protocols and approve the changes.

When the sprint is over, the tester will run through the complete test protocol and approve the site. We then trigger another release that will deploy the site to production.

Since Blazor is ASP.NET, nothing is stopping us from going even further with the automated testing of our site.

Deploying the database

When it comes to deploying our database, Entity Framework does a lot for us. We could let Entity Framework apply the migrations if needed, but I am a bit of a control freak.

Entity Framework creates code for both applying and removing the change, so it should be pretty safe to let it do its thing. There is another option, and that is letting Entity Framework generate SQL scripts that we can apply ourselves.

By adding the `script` flag, we will get a SQL script we can run against our database:

```
dotnet ef migrations script 20180904195021_InitialCreate
```

There are many different databases we can use, such as Microsoft SQL, MySQL, and, as we used in this book, SQLite.

We could also go for a non-relational type of database. Blazor supports it all, so whatever is right for the project is what we should use.

Hosting options

When it comes to hosting Blazor, there are many options. Any cloud service that can host ASP.NET Core sites should be able to run Blazor without any problems.

There are some things we need to think about, so let's go through the options one by one.

Hosting Blazor Server

If the cloud provider has an option to enable/disable WebSockets, we want to enable them since that's the protocol used by SignalR. Depending on the load, we might want to use a service such as Azure SignalR Service, which will take care of all the connections and enable our application to handle more users.

In some cases, the cloud provider may support .NET Core 3.x but not support .NET 5 out of the box. But don't worry; by making sure to publish our application with the deployment mode as self-contained, we make sure the deployment also adds any files necessary to run the project (this might not be true for all hosting providers).

This is also a good thing to do to make sure that we are running on the exact framework version we expect.

Hosting Blazor WebAssembly

If we are using a .NET Core backend (like we do for the blog), we are hosting a .NET Core website, so the same rules apply as with hosting Blazor Server. For our blog, we also added SignalR, so we need WebSockets enabled as well.

There are some other considerations when it comes to hosting Blazor WebAssembly, such as these:

- We may need a .NET Core backend.
- The data we are getting may be static or hosted somewhere else.

In either of these cases, we can host our application in Azure Static Websites or even GitHub Pages.

Our blog uses Identity Server (which is also the default implementation for Blazor WebAssembly authentication), which runs with a developer certificate when we run it during development. If we want to deploy a site using Identity Server into production, we also need to create a certificate.

We are not going to get into how to do that or how to set it up in this book, but it is worth mentioning it so we know what to look for.

Hosting on IIS

We can also host our application on **Internet Information Server (IIS)**. Install the hosting bundle and it will also make sure to include the ASP.NET Core IIS module if installed on a machine with IIS.

Make sure to enable the WebSocket protocol on the server.

We currently run our sites on IIS and use Azure DevOps to deploy our sites. Since we are using Blazor Server, the downtime is very evident. As soon as the web loses the SignalR connection, the site will show a reconnect message.

For the sites we are using, it is about 8 to 10 seconds of downtime when deploying a new version, which is pretty quick.

Summary

In this chapter, we talked about why we should use CI/CD since it makes a huge difference to ensure the quality of the application. We looked at some of the things we need to do to run our Blazor app on any cloud provider supporting .NET 5.

Deploying is perhaps the most important step when it comes to an application. Without deploying our application, it's just code. With the things we mentioned in this chapter, such as CI/CD, hosting, and deployment, we are now ready to deploy the code.

In the next chapter, we will take a look at where we go from here.

15
Where to Go from Here

The book is coming to an end and I want to leave you with some of the things we have encountered from running Blazor in production ever since Blazor was in preview. We will also talk about where to go from here.

In this chapter, we will cover the following topics:

- Learnings from running Blazor in production
- Next steps

Technical requirements

In this chapter, we are not using the code that we have written throughout the book.

Learnings from running Blazor in production

Ever since Blazor was in preview, we have been running Blazor Server in production. In most cases, everything has run without issues. Occasionally, we encounter a few problems and I will share those learnings with you in this section.

We will look at the following:

- Solving memory problems
- Solving concurrency problems
- Solving errors
- Old browsers

These are some of the things we ran into, and we have solved them all in a way that works for us.

Solving memory problems

Our latest upgrade did add a lot of users and with that, a bigger load on the server. The server manages memory quite well, but with this release, the backend system was a bit slow, so users ended up pressing *F5* to reload the page. What happens then is that the circuit disconnects and a new circuit gets created. The old circuit waits for the user to perhaps connect to the server again for 3 minutes (by default).

The user now has a new circuit and will never connect to the old one again, but for 3 minutes, the user's state will still take up memory. For most applications, this is probably not a problem, but we are loading a lot of data into memory; the data, the render tree, and all the things surrounding that will be kept in memory.

So, what can we learn from that? Blazor is a single-page application. Reloading the page is like restarting an app, which means we should always make sure to add a possibility to update the data from within the page (if that makes sense for the application). We could also make sure to update the data as it changes, as we did in *Chapter 11, Managing State*.

In our case, we ended up adding more memory to the server and then made sure there were reload buttons in the UI that refresh the data without reloading the whole page. The ultimate goal is to add real-time updates that continuously update the UI when the data changes.

If adding more memory to the server isn't an option, we can try to change the garbage collection from Server to Desktop. The .NET garbage collection has two modes:

- **Workstation** mode is optimized for running on a workstation that typically doesn't have a lot of memory. It runs the garbage collection multiple times per second.
- **Server** mode is optimized for servers where there is usually lots of memory and it prioritizes speed, which means it will only run the garbage collector every 2 seconds.

The mode of the garbage collector can be set in the project file or the `runtimeconfig.json` file by changing the `ServerGarbageCollection` node:

```
<PropertyGroup>
<ServerGarbageCollection>true</ServerGarbageCollection>
</PropertyGroup>
```

Adding more memory is probably a better idea though.

Something else we have noticed is the importance of disposing of our database contexts. In this book, we have used `IDbContextFactory` to create an instance of the data context, and after we are done disposing of it, by using the `Using` keyword.

By using this method, it will only be available for a short time and then disposed of, freeing up memory fast.

Solving concurrency problems

We often ran into problems where the data context was already in use and couldn't access the database from two different threads.

This is something that is solved by using `IDbContextFactory` and disposing of the data context when we are finished using it.

In a non-Blazor site, having multiple components to load at the same time is never a problem (because the web is doing one thing at a time), so the fact that Blazor can do multiple things at the same time is something we need to think about when we design our architecture.

Solving errors

Blazor usually gives us an error that is easy to understand, but in some rare cases, we do run into problems that are hard to figure out. We can add detailed errors to our circuit (for Blazor Server) by adding the following option in `Startup.cs`:

```
services.AddServerSideBlazor().AddCircuitOptions(options => {
options.DetailedErrors = true; });
```

By doing so, we will get more detailed errors. I don't recommend using detailed errors in a production scenario, however. With that said, we have the setting turned on for an internal app in production because the internal users are briefed on it and understand how to handle it. It makes it easier for us to help our users and the error message is only visible in the developer tools of the web browser, and not in the face of the user.

Old browsers

Some of our customers were running old browsers on old systems, and even though Blazor supports all major browsers, that support doesn't include really old browsers. We ended up helping those customers upgrade to Edge or Chrome simply because we didn't think they should be browsing the web using browsers that no longer receive security patches.

Even our TV at home can run Blazor WebAssembly, so old browsers are probably not a big problem, but it can be worth thinking about when it comes to browser support. What browsers do we need/want to support?

Next steps

At this point, we know the difference between Blazor Server and Blazor WebAssembly. We know how to create reusable components, make APIs, manage state, and much more. But where do we go from here; what are the next steps?

The community

The Blazor community is not as big as other frameworks, but it is growing fast. Many people share content with the community in the form of blogs or videos. YouTube and PluralSight have a lot of tutorials and courses. Twitch has a growing amount of Blazor content, but it is not always easy to find in the vast catalog of content.

There are a couple of resources worth mentioning:

- **My blog**: My blog has a lot of Blazor content and more to come (`http://engstromjimmy.se/`).

- **Blazm**: The Blazm component library that we have written can be found here (`http://blazm.net/`).

- **Coding after Work**: We have many episodes of our podcast and our stream covering Blazor.

   Coding after Work Podcast: `http://codingafterwork.com/`.

   Twitch: `https://www.twitch.tv/CodingAfterWork`.

- **Awesome-Blazor**: A huge list of Blazor-related links and resources can be found here (`https://github.com/AdrienTorris/awesome-blazor`).

- **Jeff Fritz**: Jeff Fritz shares Blazor knowledge (among other things) on Twitch. He also maintains a Blazor library that helps Web Forms developers to adopt Blazor.

  Twitch: `https://www.twitch.tv/csharpfritz`

  GitHub: `https://github.com/FritzAndFriends/BlazorWebFormsComponents`

The components

Most third-party component vendors such as Progress Telerik, DevExpress, Syncfusion, Radzen, ComponentOne, and many more have invested in Blazor. Some cost money, some are free. There are also a lot of open source component libraries that we can use.

This question comes up a lot: *I am new to Blazor. What third-party vendor should I use?* My recommendation is to try to figure out what we need before investing in a library (money and/or time).

Many vendors can do all the things we need but, in some cases, it will be a bit more effort to make it work. We started to work on a grid component ourselves and, after a while, we decided to make it open source.

This is how Blazm was born. We had a few special requirements (not anything fancy), but it required us to have to write a lot of code over and over again to make it work in a third-party vendor component.

We learned so much from writing our component, and it is really easy to do. My recommendation is not to always write your own components. It is much better to focus on the actual business problem we are trying to solve.

For us, building a pretty advanced grid component taught us so much about the inner working of Blazor.

Think about what you need and try out the different vendors to see what works best for you, and perhaps it might be better to build the component yourself, at least in the beginning, to learn more about Blazor.

Summary

In this chapter, we looked at some of the things we have encountered during the time we have been running Blazor in production. We also talked about where to go from here.

Throughout the book, we have learned how Blazor works and how to create basic and advanced components. We implemented security with both authentication and authorization. We created and consumed an API connected to a database.

We made JavaScript calls and real-time updates. We debugged our application and tested our code, and last but not least, we looked at deploying to production.

We are now ready to take all this knowledge to the next adventure, the next app. I hope you have had as much fun reading this book as I have had writing it. Being part of the Blazor community is so much fun and we learn new things every day.

Thank you for reading this book, and please stay in touch. I would love to learn more about the things you build!

Welcome to the Blazor community!

`Packt.com`

Subscribe to our online digital library for full access to over 7,000 books and videos, as well as industry leading tools to help you plan your personal development and advance your career. For more information, please visit our website.

Why subscribe?

- Spend less time learning and more time coding with practical eBooks and Videos from over 4,000 industry professionals

- Improve your learning with Skill Plans built especially for you

- Get a free eBook or video every month

- Fully searchable for easy access to vital information

- Copy and paste, print, and bookmark content

Did you know that Packt offers eBook versions of every book published, with PDF and ePub files available? You can upgrade to the eBook version at `packt.com` and as a print book customer, you are entitled to a discount on the eBook copy. Get in touch with us at `customercare@packtpub.com` for more details.

At `www.packt.com`, you can also read a collection of free technical articles, sign up for a range of free newsletters, and receive exclusive discounts and offers on Packt books and eBooks.

Other Books You May Enjoy

If you enjoyed this book, you may be interested in these other books by Packt:

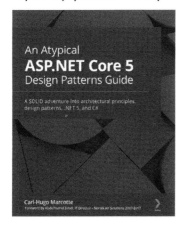

An Atypical ASP.NET Core 5 Design Patterns Guide

Carl-Hugo Marcotte

ISBN: 978-1-78934-609-1

- Apply the SOLID principles for building flexible and maintainable software
- Get to grips with .NET 5 dependency injection
- Work with GoF design patterns such as strategy, decorator, and composite
- Explore the MVC patterns for designing web APIs and web applications using Razor
- Discover layering techniques and tenets of clean architecture
- Become familiar with CQRS and vertical slice architecture as an alternative to layering
- Understand microservices, what they are, and what they are not
- Build ASP.NET UI from server-side to client-side Blazor

Customizing ASP.NET Core 5.0

Jürgen Gutsch

ISBN: 978-1-80107-786-6

- Explore various application configurations and providers in ASP.NET Core 5

- Understand dependency injection in .NET and learn how to add third-party DI containers

- Discover the concept of middleware and write your own middleware for ASP.NET Core apps

- Create various API output formats in your API-driven projects

- Get familiar with different hosting models for your ASP.NET Core app

- Develop custom routing endpoints and add third-party endpoints

- Configure WebHostBuilder effectively for your web applications

Packt is searching for authors like you

If you're interested in becoming an author for Packt, please visit `authors.packtpub.com` and apply today. We have worked with thousands of developers and tech professionals, just like you, to help them share their insight with the global tech community. You can make a general application, apply for a specific hot topic that we are recruiting an author for, or submit your own idea.

Hi!

I am Jimmy Engström, author of *Web Development with Blazor*. Thank you so much for picking up this book! I really hope you enjoyed reading this book and found it useful for increasing your productivity and efficiency with Blazor.

It would really help me (and other potential readers!) if you could leave a review on Amazon sharing your thoughts on *Web Development with Blazor*.

https://www.amazon.in/review/create-review/
error?asin=1-800-20872-3&

Your review will help me to understand what's worked well in this book, and what could be improved upon for future editions, so it really is appreciated.

And please feel free to reach out if you have any questions!

Best Wishes,

Index

Printed in Great Britain
by Amazon

64841642R00176